# ENERGY EFFICIENT OFFICE REFURBISHMENT

**EDITOR:**
Simon Burton

**CASE STUDY EDITOR:**
Marco Sala

Published by James & James (Science Publishers) Ltd,
35–37 William Road, London NW1 3ER, UK

© 2001 ECD Energy and Environment Ltd

A catalogue record for this book is available from the British Library

ISBN 1 902916 01 8

Printed in the UK by Hobbs The Printers

This manual has been produced as part of OFFICE, a project co-funded by the
European Commission DGXII, examining the passive and low energy
refurbishment of existing office buildings in Europe.

Written by OFFICE team members

Edited by Simon Burton
Case Studies edited by Marco Sala

Cover photograph: The south façade of the LESO building, with anidolic daylighting devices
Architects: D. Demetriades and D. Papadaniel, Lausanne, Switzerland
Photographer: F. Bertin, Grandvaux, Switzerland.

Disclaimer: Neither the European Commission nor ECD Energy and
Environment Ltd take any reponsibility for the use which might be made of the
information contained within.

# Contents

# Contributors

## EDITORS

Simon Burton
ECD Energy and Environment Ltd,
11–15 Emerald Street,
London, WC1N 3QL, UK.

## CASE STUDY EDITORS

Marco Sala, Paula Gallo
Department of Architectural Technology,
University of Florence,
via S.Niccolò 89/a
50125 Firenze, Italy.

## OFFICE PROJECT MANAGERS

Mat Santamouris, Elena Dascalaki
Group Building Environmental Studies,
Section Applied Physics,
Physics Department,
Building PHYS-5,
University Campus,
157-84, Athens, Greece.

## CONTRIBUTORS

Mat Santamouris, Elena Dascalaki
Group Building Environmental Studies,
Section Applied Physics,
Physics Department, Building PHYS-5,
University Campus,
157–84, Athens, Greece.

Simon Burton, Zac Grant
ECD Energy and Environment,
11–15 Emerald Street,
London, WC1N 3QL, UK.

Marco Sala, Paula Gallo
Department of Architectural Technology,
University of Florence, via S. Niccolò
89/a 50125 Firenze, Italy.

Alexander Tombazis, Nikos Vratsanos
MELETITIKI – Alexandros N. Tombazis and
Associates Architects, Ltd.
27 Monemvasias str.,
15125, Polydroso, Athens, Greece.

Niels-Ulrik Kofoed, Christina Henriksen
Esbensen, Vesterbrogade 124B,
DK1620 Copenhagen V, Denmark.

Gerard Guarraccino, Veronique Richalet
LASH/ENTPE, Rue M. Audin,
69518 Vaulx en Velin Cedex, France.

Lennart Jagemar
Department of Building Services Engineering,
Chalmers University of Technology,
S-412 96 Gothenburg, Sweden.

Siri-Hunnes Blakstad, Anne-Gunnarshaug Lien
SINTEF Civil and Building Engineering,
N-7465, Trondheim, Norway.

Anne-Grete Hestnes
Department of Building Technology,
NTNU, N-7491 Trondheim, Norway.

Claude-Alain Roulet
Swiss Federal Institute of Technology,
LESO, CH-1015, Lausanne EPFL, Switzerland

Ingo Lutkemeyer
IBUS-CASPAR-THEYSS-STRASSE 14A,
14193 Berlin, Germany.

# Part I

# — The Handbook —

# — 1 —

# Introduction

## 1.1 EUROPEAN OFFICE BUILDINGS

Office buildings provide the working environment for a large and increasing proportion of the European workforce. There is considerable diversity in the type and location of buildings used as offices throughout Europe, with new buildings being constructed and existing buildings renovated (Chapter 2). The principal requirement of office buildings is to provide comfortable, healthy and productive conditions for the workers, however costs, both capital and running, play an increasingly important part in decision-making for design, fitting out, etc. With increasing international concern about energy use and its environmental consequences, another dimension is becoming increasingly important, that of energy consumption in offices and the consequent production of carbon dioxide, and other ways in which offices can affect the local and global environments.

Energy is commonly used in offices for many activities, including heating, ventilation, cooling, lighting, equipment and catering. However, electrical and fossil fuel energy consumption can be reduced by the use of natural or solar energy for functions such as lighting, heating and passive ventilation, and can even be the host for the generation of electricity via photovoltaic arrays or for active solar water heating. Thus the design of an office building will have a large effect on its consumption of energy in use (Chapter 2). The size of the office sector compared with other users of energy, make this a highly significant area in which to take action to reduce global energy consumption.

## 1.2 OFFICE REFURBISHMENT

Existing offices undergo refurbishment from time to time, to upgrade the internal (and external) environment, to provide more modern accommodation and to attract new owners or tenants, refurbishment providing an alternative to demolition and construction of a new building. From a wide environmental perspective, refurbishment can be seen as a better option than demolition and rebuilding, although the basic building structure and the design and quality of the refurbishment will affect the overall environmental balance between refurbishment and demolition. Many factors must be taken into account, including demolition effects, construction energy including embodied energy of materials, subsequent energy use during the lifetime of the building, the quality of the internal environment produced, etc. On the other hand, refurbishment may simply be cheaper than demolition, may avoid planning restrictions on new developments and may make general economic sense.

Refurbishment of buildings is also undertaken to maintain historic buildings in active use and preserve historic areas, increasingly considered an important part of European heritage.

Apart from major refurbishment when an office approaches the end of its life, partial upgrading is used at intervals to improve conditions and/or performance, of which energy use may be an important component.

Any refurbishment provides the opportunity to improve the energy and environmental performance of offices and this can be achieved in a number of ways (Chapter 3).

## 1.3 ENERGY AND COMFORT IN OFFICES

Energy use and internal environmental quality must be considered together in offices. Energy use is frequently seen as a prerequisite for the required comfort conditions for occupants, but a design using passive techniques and natural forces can produce a good internal environment at very low energy cost. The European IAQ study[1] showed that there is no correlation between overall energy use and comfort.

Figure 1.1. The foyer of the refurbished offices of the Department of Trade and Industry (DTI), London

New buildings are frequently thought to provide more prestigious and efficient offices than older buildings. This need not be true if a refurbishment scheme is designed to provide the internal conditions expected in modern offices. In fact, in many cases refurbishment may provide generally higher standards than typical in new constructions, due to more generous space standards or use of higher quality materials. It is the quality of design, linked with the knowledge of how buildings operate, that will determine the final quality and energy consumption of an office, rather than whether it is a new or old building.

There are basically two different approaches to achieving good internal conditions in an office – using natural forces as far as possible, or relying on mechanical equipment. Natural methods include daylighting, insulation, solar gain, opening windows, solar shading, and cooling using thermal mass (Chapter 3). On the other hand, modern offices in many countries are built to rely on artificial lighting, heating, cooling and ventilation using mechanical equipment and sophisticated automatic control systems, and this trend also affects refurbishment. The energy consumption of offices with sophisticated mechanical systems is always many times higher than that of climate respecting buildings which minimize such equipment by the use of natural forces. In practice, many buildings rely on a mixture of natural forces and mechanical systems and, with careful design, a 'mixed system' can give the best internal conditions with low energy use.

However it must be remembered that 'comfort' can be defined in a number of ways and has different meanings to different people. Whilst an air-conditioned office can provide temperatures within a closely defined range (typically 19 to 22°C), a naturally ventilated office will have much higher temperatures in summer, though the effects of an open window and moving fresh air can make these equally or more acceptable. Similarly, an artificially lit office with tinted windows to reduce glare and solar gain will provide a consistent light level, but the changing light levels and clear views from a daylit office may provide a more pleasant and stimulating environment. Some research has demonstrated the importance to a person's perceived level of comfort, of individual control over the local environment, a concept becoming known as 'adaptive opportunities'.

## 1.4 OTHER ENVIRONMENTAL ISSUES IN OFFICES

The global environmental effects of energy consumption are not the only important environmental issues connected with new and refurbished offices. Environmental effects can be identified at global, local and indoor levels and design of both new buildings and refurbishment projects can reduce their negative impact. Particularly important in refurbishment are indoor air quality, daylighting and views from windows, glare, noise and humidity. At the 'local' level issues include the risk of Legionnaire's disease from wet cooling towers, water conservation, cycling facilities and access to public transport. At the 'global' level, emissions of $NO_x$ from boilers contributing to acid rain, the avoidance of ozone depleting substances and providing space for recycling of waste materials should be borne in mind.

## 1.5 BACKGROUND TO THE HANDBOOK

This book has been produced as part of the output from a European multi-country project, 'Passive retrofitting of office buildings to improve their energy performance and indoor working conditions', supported by a JOULE grant from the European Commission DGXII. Other reports and working documents are available. During the project, ten existing offices were chosen to represent as far as possible the diversity of office buildings found in Europe. These are described in Chapter 2. Monitoring of energy use and internal conditions was carried out over a one-year period and the data were analysed to validate computer modelling of each building.

Various retrofitting measures and packages of measures appropriate to each building were modelled to analyse the effects on energy consumption and internal comfort. The emphasis was on passive measures but packages also included improvements to mechanical services as necessary and appropriate. The design and costs of the various measures were explored to assess the practical applications and the most cost-effective measures.

The results of these analyses have been used to put together design guidance for architects and engineers on passive retrofit strategies and technologies. Chapter 3 discusses how the designer should approach refurbishment to minimize energy use whilst providing good internal conditions for occupants, and emphasizes the 'passive' opportunities. Each issue, such as heating, lighting, ventilation, etc., is dealt with separately and explanations of the theory behind the recommendations are given as appropriate.

In order to assess the changes in energy consumption and comfort produced by the refurbishment packages and to be able to compare different buildings (in different countries) an 'overall rating methodology' has been developed (Chapter 6).

In Part II of the book, each of the ten buildings studied has been described, together with all the retrofit packages and effects, in the form of individual case studies.

The work of this project has built on much previous work in this field, carried out in various participating countries. Particularly important are the PASSCOOL project, the European IAQ study, Energy Comfort 2000 (THERMIE) and 'Rehabilitation of old office buildings to improve their energy efficiency' (SAVE).

### REFERENCES

1   Bluyssen P, Fernandes E de O, Fanger PO, *et al*, (1995), *European Audit Project to Optimise Indoor Air Quality and Energy Consumption on Office Buildings*, final report edited by TNO, Delft, 1995. Information on this project can also be found in Proceedings of Healthy Buildings '96 conference, Milan, 1995.

# — 2 —

# Office buildings in Europe

## 2.1 OFFICE BUILDING TYPOLOGIES

### 2.1.1 The historical evolution

*MEDIEVAL TIMES*

The origins of the office building in Europe can be traced back to two main building types of medieval times. In the merchant's shop or the artisan's workshop, the owner, before going to rest upstairs in his house, retired to his writing desk in the corner to estimate his gains (or losses). This corner later evolved into a specially appointed 'room' within the shop. Then there were the palaces of the noble class, where special rooms were appointed to clerks, accountants, notaries, etc.

The growing awareness of the middle class resulted in special 'office' buildings supporting the administrative and legislative authorities, such as town halls, merchants' loggias (clubs) and courts. Still, the predominant use of these buildings was for social gatherings rather than actual office use.

*SEVENTEENTH AND EIGHTEENTH CENTURIES*

In the seventeenth and eighteenth centuries, the number of 'office' buildings increased following the founding of many new institutions such as banks, public services and universities. Still, these buildings were built more to serve the monumental expression of the institution they housed, rather than its real bureaucratic needs and functions.

*INDUSTRIAL REVOLUTION UNTIL EARLY TWENTIETH CENTURY*

The growth of the tertiary section that accompanied the industrial revolution resulted in the need for a new building type, especially in the more advanced countries such as England and Germany, and this also became a speculative venture. However, the building type that emerged was little different from the domestic type, as it kept its main characteristics:

- cellular organization of 'rooms' along a linear corridor, either single or double-sided;
- module of inner partitioning determined by the technical constraints of the time (ability to span using stone vault or wooden beam) leading to similar solutions to those used in the residential sector. Even advances such as the I-beam or, much later, the concrete frame did little to change the scale of the module;
- dependence on natural light and ventilation leading to building depths, dimensions of light shafts and enclosed courtyards similar to the domestic examples;
- overall dimensions dictated by the usual urban plots, as defined by property laws based on residential use;
- morphology and organization of the façade derived from the residential vocabulary.

The opposite seems to have been the case in the USA, where the progress in construction methods generated by the prefabricated building industry (steel structures, glass panes) and the invention of the elevator, permitted the construction of taller buildings utilizing cost- and time-efficient façade techniques (glazed or metallic infills – advance of the curtain wall) and, most important of all, large, 'open-plan' floor spaces similar to the factory or loft image. The theoretical justification of this new building typology came in the early 1930s when the economist Taylor promoted the industrialization of the office, both as an economic and a physical entity.[1]

'Taylorism' had some impact in countries of Northern Europe, but in general Europe was reluctant to adopt the 'factory techniques' in the office sector. Even more than that reluctance, the juxtaposition of office and residential areas within Europe's historic cities, discouraged the advance of new office building techniques from the USA, such as the notable 'Chicago window' or the 'New York City loft cast-iron façade'.

Thus, despite the growth of the speculative influence, the evolution of the European office building was slow up until the Second World War. Only in the late 1950s did Europe, with Germany pioneering, enter a new era in the design of office buildings, particularly adopting the open-plan solution.

Two factors helped this change. The first was the adoption of more efficient artificial means for lighting (the incandescent lamp being replaced by the fluorescent tube) and new heating, cooling and ventilation methods (water radiators and openable windows giving way to air-conditioning), encouraging the enlargement of the floor plan.

The second factor was expansion beyond the historic city boundaries and the creation of the 'new towns' where the tertiary sector was zoned away from the residential sector. The suburban expansion, helped by the improvements in commuting (trains, 'metro', peripheral highways), removed the size constraint from office buildings which now could achieve the optimum footprint (mostly 'square' solutions with large depths). Once again there was a difference between countries of the north, where this kind of expansion was promoted, and countries of the south where the lack of central regional planning discouraged suburban growth and where rationalized office development did not prevail over the traditional roots of historic buildings.

In parallel with the open-plan office, the more classical type continued to evolve during the 1960s, incorporating the technology of light partitions in place of masonry or brickwork internal walls.

## 2.1.2 Vicissitudes of open-plan offices

By the 1960s it was already clear that the logic of the open-plan office could lead to a dull uniformity, to the loss of individual identity and the alienation of the employee from the working environment.

Europe pioneered reactions to these disadvantages of the open-plan office. For example:

- a tree-like office organization, with a variety of intermediate spaces – the 'thresholds' – between the more private and more public spaces. There was a great effort to create and enhance spaces within the office building which were not strictly professional but dedicated to common use (atria, cafeterias, meeting places, standing and viewing points, etc.);
- the 'combi' office, a mainly Scandinavian contribution,

where the personal workspaces are in constant and flexible contact with a large common space;
- refining theories and techniques for rehabilitating historic urban centres in order to introduce offices with modern facilities into older shells. Mediterranean countries have had a leading role in this type of project.

A parallel development has been the re-evaluation of passive means of lighting, heating and cooling of buildings. The need for energy saving and the prestige of the 'green image', even among developers and companies, is leading gradually to solutions other than the fully air-conditioned, sealed box.

All trends have combined since the 1980s with the vastly improving building and infrastructure technology. Advances in materials such as glass and metal, sophisticated building management systems, integrated heating, ventilation and air-conditioning (HVAC) systems, 'intelligent façades', etc., have determined many of the design decisions. For example, false floors, along with false ceilings, are now a common feature used to accommodate the necessary service and information networks.

## 2.1.3 Future development

Office building design is today a far more complex procedure than it used to be, and it will certainly become more complicated in the near future. Several aspects, in addition to the age-old cost-efficiency and functional parameters, must now be taken into consideration:

- qualitative principles of design
- studies of social problems
- environmental consciousness ('green image')
- flexibility and integration of networks
- flexibility towards environmental and communicative changes
- environmental control.

As far as the physical design is concerned certain evolving typologies can be identified:

THE MICRO-CITY OFFICE BUILDING
The decline of the blue-collar population and increase in the white-collar one, the continuous merging of companies and the globalization of the office market, all lead to bigger office complexes. In order to break up these 'mega buildings', one

solution is to adopt city fabric forms within the buildings, such as atria, squares ('piazzas'), internal primary and secondary 'streets', landscaped gardens, water elements, etc. These forms are also very useful from a bioclimatic point of view, as they act as a buffer zone between the inside and outside of the building and create a pleasant microclimate.

### THE OUTDATED BUILDING

The existing stock of office buildings in Europe is to a large extent obsolete, particularly the stock built during the 1960s which, because of poor construction and poor craftsmanship, is rapidly deteriorating and urgently needs retrofitting. In addition, there is a tremendous stock of older buildings that have become redundant, such as dock facilities, lofts, railway yards and factories within cities, which constitute a cheap and fashionable opportunity for transformation into office space.

### THE HYBRID BUILDING

After decades of homogeneity in terms of land planning, the 'traditional' idea of a hybrid building that combines commercial and residential use, is returning in many European cities. As historic centres are rehabilitated and cleaned to remove the effects of pollution, there is some evidence that this type of building is becoming more popular.

### THE COMPUTER-BASED OFFICE BUILDING

This is at present more of a concept than an actual building type, though the implications for design are so great that it may evolve to a completely new building type.

The advance of computing technologies has two major effects on the office building industry. First, operation of the installed equipment depends more and more on a central building management scheme (BMS) that controls HVAC, the lighting system, the solar protection devices and many other parameters, so as to optimize the building's thermal behaviour according to pre-programmed specifications and constraints. Second, offices and homes are becoming more and more interconnected by the global computer network, creating the flexible office environment, including such possibilities as 'hot-desking' and parallel working environments (for example, office and home), and instant communication without personal contact.

## 2.1.4 Typology of the case studies selected in the 'Office' project

Apart from the British building which dates from 1920, all selected case studies belong to the last decades of the twentieth century, as the largest stock of office buildings belongs to this era and now requires retrofitting.

The fact that seven of the ten examples are buildings with a heavyweight structure, skin-oriented and cellular, confirms previous discussion that Europe, at least until recently, mostly employed the more traditional model of the narrow plan building, with daylit rooms off a central corridor. None of the selected cases belongs to the hermetically sealed box type, although the City West building (Bern, Switzerland) is close to this model.

To classify the offices studied in this project, and to provide guidance on classification of future offices to be retrofitted, we considered four different aspects.

First, in spacial terms, we propose a classification of four types of office buildings among the selected cases:

### TYPE I: DOMESTIC TYPE
CASE STUDY EXAMPLES
- Casa di Risparmio, Italy
- Central and West Houses, UK
- LESO, Switzerland

This refers to relatively small buildings with a central vertical core and rooms directly connected to the core and to the external envelope, on the domestic model. Buildings of this type are inevitably skin-oriented.

### TYPE II: SPINAL TYPE
CASE STUDY EXAMPLES
- Le Recamier, France
- Danfoss HQ, Denmark
- Postbank Berlin, Germany
- Sentralbygg 1, Norway

This common type consists of a linear floor plan with a central corridor giving access to cellular offices on the outside of the building. The structure is usually heavyweight and there is a tendency to higher buildings in this category. For reasons of security and access, there are at least two vertical cores. Frequently these buildings are free standing and may be articulated in order to conform to the traditional city block layout, as in the French example.

### TYPE III: 'DEEP PLAN' TYPE
CASE STUDY EXAMPLES
- AGET, Greece
- City West, Switzerland

There are two examples of this type, each with a slightly different arrangement. The first, AGET, is a true 'deep plan' building with inner office space not related to the skin, while the second is a more 'spinal' building wrapped around a central core.

TYPE IV: COMPLEX TYPE
CASE STUDY EXAMPLE
• Krokslatt, Sweden

This could be considered a variation of Type II (spinal type) as it consists of three linear blocks, but is considered as a separate type as the three wings form two enclosed atria, which act as an intermediate zone between inside and out.

In addition to the spacial classification, three other aspects need to be considered: the thermal mass of the structure; the importance of the skin in determining the internal conditions; and the surroundings of the building.

A lightweight building (e.g. steel frame with exterior sandwich elements) has little potential for storing heat or 'coolth', so its internal temperature will follow external temperature swings relatively closely. A heavyweight office building on the other hand has the potential to utilize its thermal mass to reduce temperature swings and to pre-cool the building at night when necessary.

Skin-dependence is an important parameter for the passive retrofitting potential of office buildings. It involves daylight, natural ventilation and heat flow and depends on: the depth and interior layout of the building; the size, location and orientation of openings; the thermal and solar properties of the openings; and the construction of walls, roofs and floors with ground coupling.

The surroundings of the building will also affect the retrofitting potential. A tight urban site surrounded by high buildings and considerable air pollution might significantly reduce the daylighting and natural ventilation potential of an office building being considered for retrofitting.

## 2.2 OFFICE ENERGY CONSUMPTION

Office buildings have one of the highest levels of energy consumption when compared with energy consumption in other building sectors. The annual energy consumption in office buildings varies between 100 and 1000 kWh per square metre, depending on geographic location, use and type of office equipment, operational schedules, type of envelope, use of HVAC systems, type of lighting, etc.

Most energy consumption in office buildings is for heating, cooling, ventilation and lighting purposes, but a significant portion may be used by office equipment. Results of extended surveys of energy use in office buildings are available from some projects and for some European countries. Limited information is also available from national statistics on the breakdown and the total energy consumption of different office building types in Europe.

### 2.2.1 Information from projects and surveys

THE 'INDOOR AIR QUALITY' (IAQ) RESEARCH PROJECT OF THE EUROPEAN COMMISSION[2]
The comparison of data on energy consumption in office buildings across Europe is generally limited to typical buildings classifications, where detailed data are available from monitoring exercises. Such information is provided in the IAQ research project, where 50 typical buildings from around Europe were selected and monitored. As can be seen in Figure 2.1, there are significant differences in the mean annual energy consumption for office buildings in the countries included in the study, with mean energy consumption for individual countries ranging from 170 kWh/m² in Greece to 438 kWh/m² in the UK.

'ENERGY EFFICIENT HVAC SYSTEMS IN OFFICE BUILDINGS' PROJECT[3]
This project collected comparisons of annual energy use for heating and total electrical energy use (including lighting, equipment, catering and HVAC systems) from monitored demonstration office buildings from projects in Denmark, Finland, Greece, Norway, Sweden, Switzerland, the UK and the USA. All the buildings included were constructed during the 1980s, thus reflecting contemporary design practice and

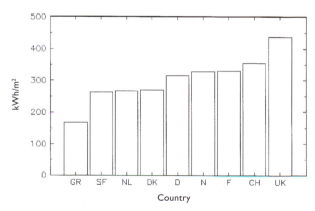

Figure 2.1. Mean annual energy consumption of the office buildings monitored in the European IAQ Survey project[2]

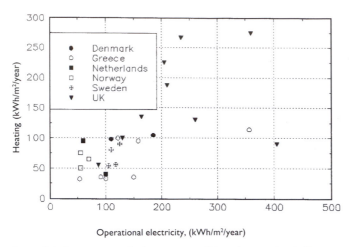

Figure 2.2. Energy use in the large, air-conditioned or mechanically ventilated offices[3]

equipment. The data were divided according to the size of the building (total floor area greater or less than 4650 m²) and into four categories depending on the type of HVAC system (air-conditioned, mechanically ventilated, mixed mode or naturally ventilated).

### LARGE, AIR-CONDITIONED OR MECHANICALLY VENTILATED BUILDINGS

Several conclusions can be drawn from the data for large, air-conditioned or mechanically ventilated buildings (Figure 2.2). Nearly all use of thermal energy was related to the HVAC system. The UK offices with computer suites had a very high use of electrical energy, regardless of the HVAC type. Four of the UK air-conditioned offices also used considerably more thermal energy than the other projects, even compared with locations in the colder Norwegian and Swedish climates.

### LARGE, NATURALLY VENTILATED OR MIXED MODE BUILDINGS

The large, naturally ventilated or mixed mode offices, showed different characteristics. Total electricity use was typically lower than the average for air-conditioned offices, although several air-conditioned buildings used no more electricity than the naturally ventilated ones; the energy for heating used by naturally ventilated or mixed mode offices was up to twice that used in air-conditioned and mechanically ventilated offices, with similar total electricity use. Somewhat striking is the high thermal energy use in Greek buildings despite the Mediterranean climate, with levels similar to offices in much colder climates of Northern Europe; however, Greek offices did not appear to use more electricity for HVAC systems during the summer season than Swedish or UK offices.

There was a wide spread of annual electrical energy use by HVAC systems for fairly similar overall electricity use. The share of the electrical energy use by HVAC systems was 15–50% of the annual operational electricity use. Of course, for large naturally ventilated offices, the HVAC electricity use is low by definition. For the UK mixed mode offices, the annual HVAC electricity use was 10–30 kWh/m², while it was less than 10 kWh/m² for the large, naturally ventilated Danish offices.

### SMALL BUILDINGS

None of the small offices had any computer suites and it is in this category that the majority of the naturally ventilated offices were found, almost all of them in the UK. Different patterns of energy use were observed in small buildings compared with the large buildings. The small offices do not use much over 100 kWh/m²/year in operational electricity, regardless of the HVAC system type and for the small, air-conditioned offices the annual HVAC electricity use is similar to the larger offices that have the same annual operational electricity use.

Naturally ventilated or mixed mode buildings show a wide spread of annual operational electricity and particularly of annual heating use. The annual thermal energy consumption is typically somewhat larger than for air-conditioned offices (due to the absence of heat recovery). Total annual electricity use is much lower for naturally ventilated offices than for air-conditioned ones.

### THE 'OFFICE' CASE STUDY BUILDINGS

The monitored energy consumption and related characteristics of the OFFICE case study buildings are summarized in Table 2.1.

The annual total energy consumption varied between 94 and 716 kWh/m². The energy consumption depended on the specific characteristics of each building (quality of the envelope, efficiency of the heating, cooling and lighting system, type of energy management, office equipment, etc.), and no trends were found regarding climatic zones or building typology. The same conclusions were true for the specific use of energy for heating and of electricity use.

## 2.2.2 National statistics on offices and their energy use in selected countries

All the survey results and analyses in the previous section demonstrate that the variation in energy consumption of offices is very great. This is due to the large number of variables

Table 2.1. Energy characteristics of the ten selected buildings in the OFFICE project

| Building | Thermal energy (kWh/m²) | Type of fuel | Electricity (kWh/m²) | Total energy consumption (kWh/m²) | Country | Heated / cooled area (m²) | Dependent on | Struc- ture | Module |
|---|---|---|---|---|---|---|---|---|---|
| Le Recamier | None | – | 94.1 | 94.1 | France | 4371 / 800 | Skin | Heavy | Cellular |
| Aget Heraklis | 154.1 | Diesel | 562.2 | 716.3 | Greece | 6403 / 6403 | Core | Heavy | Open plan |
| Sentralbygg 1 | 170 | District heat | 130 | 300 | Norway | 6400 / 0 | Skin | Heavy | Cellular |
| Danfoss HQ | 95.4 | Natural gas | 99.9 | 195.3 | Denmark | 13400 / 7000 | Skin | Heavy | Cellular |
| Postbank Berlin | 132 | District heat | 121 | 253 | Germany | 20200 / 11930 | Skin | Light | Cellular + open plan |
| Central and West Houses | 313.6 | Natural gas | 116.9 | 430.4 | UK | 1530 / 0 | Skin | Heavy | Cellular |
| LESO | 89.6 | Electricity in rooms and heat pump on lake water for district heated part | 65.2 | 154.7 | Switzerland | 670 / 0 | Skin | Heavy | Cellular |
| City West | 213.5 | District heating | 107.8 | 321.3 | Switzerland | 11683 / 25015 | Skin | Heavy | Cellular |
| Casa di Risparmio | 78.5 | Natural gas | 106 | 185 | Italy | 1900 / 1787 | Core | Heavy | Open plan |
| Krokslatt | 50 | District heating | 107.5 | 157.5 | Sweden | 29889 / 29889 | Skin | Heavy | Cellular |

affecting energy consumption. Standard values for these variables cannot be identified easily, making direct comparisons between buildings very difficult, if not impossible. In addition, very few countries have prepared national statistical data on office buildings, and where they have, classifications tend to be completely different. However, it is worthwhile to consider an analysis of data from those countries where more detailed information is available.

*OFFICE BUILDING STOCK*

Data on the existing office stock are available for some countries – the UK, France, Greece, Sweden and Norway – although they are not always expressed in the same way. Table 2.2 summarizes the available data.

*TOTAL ENERGY CONSUMPTION OF OFFICES*

Figures for global energy consumption in office buildings are available for three countries – the UK, Switzerland and France (see Table 2.3).

*BREAKDOWN OF DELIVERED ENERGY*

Data on the delivered energy in offices have been collected for the UK, France, Greece, Sweden and Switzerland. Table 2.4 gives data for different breakdowns of the office stock according to the national classification systems. Given that defined building clusters are different from country to country – for example, the UK reports according to building typology, while France reports according to the age of the buildings – direct inter-country comparisons cannot always be made.

In the UK, available energy consumption data are reported for four types of buildings: a naturally ventilated, cellular office; a naturally ventilated, open-plan office; a 'standard' air-conditioned office; and a 'prestigious' air-conditioned office.

In Greece, the National Classification System considers ten different types of building according to the energy system used and the quality of the envelope.

In Sweden, data are based on 1 kWh of electricity equalling 1 kWh of heat. Single office buildings from the 1980s have a total energy use of 110–190 kWh/m²/year, while older office buildings have a total energy use of 200–290 kWh/year/m². The typical office building energy use is around 220 kWh/m²/year.

Table 2.2. Office building stock in selected countries

| Country | Total stock | | Current increase | Built before 1945 | Built 1945– 1980 | Built 1980 – present |
|---|---|---|---|---|---|---|
| UK | 125 | km² | 3% p.a. | | | |
| France | 131 | km² | 2.6% p.a. | | | |
| Greece | 900 000 | units | | 28% | 67% | 5% |
| Sweden | 25 | km² | | 29% | 43% | 27% |
| Norway | 30 | km² | | 30% | 30% | 40% |

Table 2.3. Total energy consumption in the office sector

| Country | Total annual energy use | Notes |
|---|---|---|
| UK | 25 TWh | |
| Switzerland | 31 TWh | 14% of country use |
| France | 39.2 TWh | 3% increase p.a. |

Table 2.4 Delivered energy use

| Country | Total mean energy (kWh/m²) | Heating energy* (kWh/m²) | Cooling energy (kWh/m²)(mean all bldgs)* | Lighting energy (kWh/m²) | Office equipment energy (kWh/m²) |
|---|---|---|---|---|---|
| UK | 248–634 (depending on type) | 200–260 | 33–41* | 26–28 | 11–29 |
| France | 250–300 | 80–190 | – | 40 | 51 (inc. other uses) |
| Greece | 113–226 (depending on type) | 78–100 | 24 | 18–25 | 13–68 |
| Sweden | 110–290 (depending on age and type) | 135 | 10–15 | 15 | 18 |
| Norway | 190–235 | 59–73 | 7–10 | 51–62 | 23–30 |
| Switzerland | 220 | 90 | 30 | 35 | 45 |

* not including fans and pumps

In Norway, modern, energy efficient office buildings employing recent scientific and technological advances have an annual energy consumption as low as 105 kWh/m².

Energy use data for defined typologies of office buildings in Switzerland, are not fully available, but an estimated mean consumption is given in Table 2.4.

*ENERGY CONSUMPTION — HEATING*

Data on energy consumption for heating purposes are available for the UK, France, Greece, Sweden, Norway and Switzerland. Unfortunately, the various uses are not defined in the same way in all countries, so direct comparisons between countries should not be made.

Swedish office buildings constructed after 1975 are very well-insulated building envelopes and have rather high internal heat gains. This means that a typical new office building in Sweden does not need any heat energy during working days when the ambient temperature is above −10°C to −5°C. At these temperatures, any need to heat the ventilation air is covered by heat recovery.

In Norway, 27% of the total energy is used for heating, 8% for ventilation, 4% for hot water and 13% for the fans.

## REFERENCES

1   As referenced in: SBI - Rapport 140. *Kontormiljøets historiske udvikling - en registrering af kontorarbejdets og kontorbyggeriets udvikling* (English title: *A Historical Office Environment Review of Office Work and Office Buildings*). Susanne Mørch Flagstad & Susse Laustsen Statens Byggeforskningsinstitut (Danish Building Research Institute), 1983 ISBN 87-563-0456-0 ISSN 0573-9985.

2   Bluyssen P, de Oliveira Fernandes E, Fanger PO, *et al*, (1995), *European Audit Project to Optimise Indoor Air Quality and Energy Consumption on Office Buildings*, Final report edited by TNO, Delft, 1995. Information on this project can also be found in the proceedings of the *Healthy Buildings '96* conference, Milano, 1995.

3   Jagemar L, (1995), *Learning from Experiences with Energy Efficient HVAC Systems in Office Buildings*, CADDET Analyses Series No. 15, Sittard, The Netherlands, Centre for the Analysis and Dissemination of Demonstrated Energy Technologies & CADDET Analysis Support Unit, October 1995.

# — 3 —

# Retrofitting strategies and technologies

## 3.1 INTRODUCTION

The designers of a refurbishment are in an excellent position to improve the environmental performance of a building. Sections 3.2 to 3.8 describe the opportunities for passive energy saving and comfort enhancing actions, based on the best information currently available. Different buildings and sites offer different opportunities and particular clients and eventual uses of the building will dictate the options adopted. Some design tools which can help in this decision-making and refine designs for maximum effectiveness are described in Chapter 5. In order to measure the change produced by a refurbishment and to demonstrate the energy-saving potential of a design, an assessment or rating methodology can be used as outlined in Chapter 6.

Even where a designer is able to produce a passive and low energy refurbishment design satisfying the comfort and other design criteria, the environmental performance objectives may not be achieved when the building is eventually in use. This may be because use patterns are different to those predicted, or because of unskilled operation and maintenance of the building. The designer cannot directly influence the final use and operation of the building but Section 3.10 suggests how the designer can help to ensure that future building users understand the building and have the opportunity to operate it efficiently.

### 3.1.1 Objectives of a retrofit

When retrofitting a building the goals are:

- to increase the value of the existing building, or to restore its original value. This is often the main objective of the building owner;
- to adapt the building to new requirements or new use. This is the main objective of the building user. Office buildings

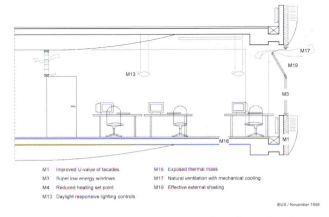

**Figure 3.1. Passive architectural strategy with mechanical cooling at Postbank Berlin, Germany**

| | |
|---|---|
| M1 | Improved U-value of facades |
| M3 | Super low energy windows |
| M4 | Reduced heating set point |
| M13 | Daylight responsive lighting controls |
| M16 | Exposed thermal mass |
| M17 | Natural ventilation with mechanical cooling |
| M19 | Effective external shading |

IBUS / November 1998

are often refurbished to accommodate changes in an organization or to adapt conditions for a new user;
- to improve the indoor environment. This may be the objective of the occupant; buildings suffering from Sick Building Syndrome should be retrofitted for this reason;
- to decrease energy consumption. This objective may be the long-term policy of governments and may be enforced by law.

The first two objectives are generally the prime mover for refurbishment. The second two objectives may at times seem contradictory, but a well-planned retrofit should achieve *all* these objectives at the same time.

The general strategy is to:

- reduce demand – for heating, cooling, airflow, artificial lighting, etc;
- supply demand as far as possible by passive means – passive solar heating, night ventilation cooling, natural ventilation, daylighting, etc;

- supply the remaining demand by efficient and well-controlled mechanical/electrical means.

### 3.1.2 The importance of an integrated strategy

The objectives of the retrofit can be achieved by following architectural strategies and by using appropriate technologies in a coordinated way, since there are strong interactions between them. Such a coordinated strategy, illustrated in Figure 3.2, includes the following six steps.

STEP 1. CONSIDER THE REQUIREMENTS OF USERS, CLIMATE, THE EXISTING BUILDING AND BUILDING PHYSICS

- The user's demands are of great importance but may not be fully achievable and feedback from the analysis is necessary to reach reasonable agreement.
- The building should be adapted to the local climate in order to maximize the use of passive measures and enhance occupant comfort (see Section 3.1.3).
- The existing building should be audited to reveal problems, weaknesses and opportunities.
- All requirements should be collected and considered at this first stage, including: thermal comfort throughout the year; indoor air quality and ventilation rates; lighting, including daylighting; acoustics, including noise protection and internal acoustics; general environmental requirements.

STEP 2. ANALYSE ALL REQUIREMENTS AND THEIR CONSEQUENCES

Interaction between these demands and their consequences should be borne in mind, for example, solar protection interacts with daylighting, passive cooling with ventilation and safety requirements, and local control by occupants makes the indoor climate control more complex.

If the consequences are incompatible or clearly unacceptable, the user requirements may need to be modified. When the consequences are clear and acceptable, they can be translated into technical demands.

STEP 3. CARRY OUT TECHNICAL ANALYSES

To improve both indoor and outdoor environments, passive solutions should always be considered first, and adopted whenever possible. Passive solutions favour appropriate architectural solutions backed up by limited use of mechanical equipment.

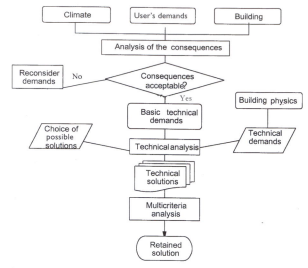

Figure 3.2. Design strategy for refurbishment

STEP 4. CONSIDER THE INTERACTIONS BETWEEN ALL THE COMPONENTS

STEP 5. CHOOSE THE BEST SOLUTION(S)

STEP 6. MULTI-CRITERIA ANALYSIS

A multi-criteria analysis, as described in Chapter 6, may be helpful.

### 3.1.3 Designing for occupant comfort

The main objective of building design is to provide good comfort levels for the occupants since this increases satisfaction and productivity. The commonly accepted parameters characterizing indoor environments are related to thermal comfort, indoor air quality, acoustic quality and lighting. However, general comfort conditions include more qualitative criteria which may be more difficult to satisfy, e.g. local control over conditions, views to outside, planting, colours, open-plan or cellular layouts, etc.

Many existing office buildings have relied on mechanical equipment to produce acceptable internal conditions, with little or no help from the building itself. The alternative approach is to take the outdoor climate and comfort criteria into account when designing the building and to adapt the building to the surrounding climate. Mechanical systems are then installed to compensate for remaining mismatches between free-running and required comfort conditions. The latter approach is likely to

Figure 3.3. Designed for occupant comfort – AVAX SA office, Greece

considerably reduce energy consumption and generally give better internal comfort conditions.

Some methods to reach acceptable levels for comfort are discussed below.

### THERMAL COMFORT

Thermal comfort depends mainly on the activity level of the occupant and on the clothing the occupants are expected to wear. Ideal comfort conditions vary between people and with external conditions, for example making comfort temperatures lower in winter than in summer.

Air temperature is not the only parameter. Mean radiant temperature, the temperature of neighbouring surfaces, is also very important. This should be considered in planning a retrofit, by taking into account the radiant effects of ceilings, walls and floors. Draughts and smaller air movements can also have a large effect on thermal comfort.

### INDOOR AIR QUALITY (IAQ)

Indoor air is polluted by internal sources of contaminants, including the building, the furnishings and equipment, and the occupants themselves. The polluted air is progressively replaced by outdoor air (assuming this is fresh and not polluted by vehicle and other emissions). Indoor air quality thus results from an equilibrium between the strength of contaminant sources and the fresh outdoor air flow rate. In order to ensure good indoor air quality, contaminant sources should first be avoided, then the outdoor air flow rate should be designed or adjusted to keep the concentration of contaminants below an acceptable level.

Most current ventilation standards do not take into account the strength of all the contaminant sources in the enclosure. However, the European draft standard prENV 1752,[1] proposes a list of air flow rates per floor area for various types of buildings, depending on their expected occupancy and a reasonable source rate for all likely contaminants in the building.

Audits of European office buildings have shown that IAQ standards are commonly not met, even with airflow rates higher than normally required standards. The reason in many cases is that the building itself is a larger contaminant source than the occupants. This can be avoided by careful choice of building materials and finishes, furniture, fittings and equipment, all of which should be chosen for low contaminant emission levels. This is particularly important when the retrofit takes place in a continuously occupied building.

### ACOUSTIC QUALITY

There are two components to acoustic quality: noise level and room acoustics. Buildings should be planned so that noise, coming from outside or from the building itself (equipment, neighbouring activity), does not disturb the occupants.

Room acoustics are particularly affected by reverberation time. Achieving a good acoustic quality for a theatre or a concert hall is not only good engineering but also an art, but it is much easier in office buildings, where the reverberation time should simply be less than 1 second. Installing sound absorbing materials, chosen in such a way that the reverberation time does not vary too much with the sound frequency, can reduce reverberation time. Care should also be taken that acoustic panels do not suppress the thermal mass where it is needed. (See Section 3.8 for more information on acoustic control.)

Figure 3.4. Acoustic ceiling panel at No. 1 Leeds City Business Park, UK

### LIGHTING

Daylight and artificial light strategies should take account of several parameters: light level and distribution, light spectrum, and glare. The light level should be adapted to the type of activity, the spatial distribution of the light should be relatively even, and the light spectrum should be as close as possible to that of sunlight. This last point is the main reason to promote daylighting, along with the other benefits of energy saving and reduction of heat load which can lead to overheating. For the same illuminance level, daylight brings with it less heat than any artificial lighting system.

Glare must be avoided by proper design and arrangement of light sources and by window shading systems. (See Section 3.5 for more details.)

### SPATIAL ARRANGEMENT

Spatial arrangement may have an impact on occupant comfort. Audits of European office buildings show significant differences in numbers of 'sick building' symptoms recorded between the two main types of office layouts, small cellular and open-plan, with cellular offices recording lower numbers. It was also recorded that people who were more than five metres from a window often considered that there was no window at their working place. However, user requirements for open-plan accommodation for operational reasons may outweigh other factors.

### LOCAL CONTROL AND ADAPTIVE OPPORTUNITIES

In audits, occupants have often complained when they could not open windows, or more generally, when they had no influence on their environment. Occupants are often more comfortable if they feel they have some control over their immediate surroundings, for example, to move their seating position, to adjust shading, lighting or heating. Designers should provide these 'adaptive opportunities' for occupants wherever possible.

### THE RELEVANCE OF EXTERNAL MICROCLIMATE

Local climatic and environmental conditions can vary greatly and need to be studied before deciding on retrofit actions. Rural and city centre locations will provide very different conditions, offering different refurbishment options.

Several areas should be considered:

- external air pollution from traffic, industry, etc. will affect natural ventilation design choices, including window opening, source of fresh air and the need for filters;
- external noise levels will affect window opening and the need for acoustic treatments;
- solar access to the building will affect passive solar design, the need for shading devices and the opportunities for active solar and PV installations;
- local wind effects will affect natural ventilation opportuni-

Figure 3.5. Microclimate of a London street

ties, canyon effects in urban areas requiring particular study;
- local temperature variation effects such as heat islands (the build up of temperatures in urban areas) may be important.

### 3.1.4 General environmental issues

The construction, refurbishment and use of buildings affects many aspects of the environment other than energy use and internal comfort. Retrofit planning should consider the range of environmental issues and include sustainable development opportunities wherever possible. For example:

- water conservation – reduce water demand by use of low flush toilets, spray taps, etc (Figure 3.5); consider the collection and use of rainwater for toilets and landscaping watering;
- use recycled, recyclable and renewable construction materials wherever possible;
- choose materials with low embodied energy, low pollution in manufacture, from sustainable sources;
- use building techniques which allow deconstruction and make recycling easy, instead of demolition which generates mixed waste material;
- avoid dangerous or hazardous materials, such as those containing CFCs or other ozone-depleting compounds, formaldehyde, heavy metals, toxic organic solvents, etc;
- provide facilities for storage of materials for recycling;
- provide bicycle storage and showers (to encourage cycling to work);

Figure 3.6. A water conservation toilet

- adopt site practices that minimize atmospheric pollution and energy and material waste.

## 3.2 SPACE HEATING

### 3.2.1 Strategy

In older office buildings the energy used for space heating constitutes a relatively large proportion of the total energy used. In new office buildings heating is often supplied by lights and equipment and the proportion of primary energy used directly for space heating is often small by comparison with that used for ventilation, lighting and equipment. Strategies for reducing space heating are therefore particularly relevant for many existing office buildings.

The following strategy should be followed:

- reduce the need for space heating as much as possible by limiting heat losses;
- supply heat by the use of passive solar technologies and heat recovery systems where appropriate;
- supply the remaining heating demand by efficient and well-controlled mechanical systems.

### 3.2.2 Reducing the need for space heating

Heat losses can be limited both by reducing the total area of surfaces contributing to the heat losses and by using appropriate insulation and ventilation strategies. The main strategies applicable in retrofitting are:

- building design: decrease surface area/volume ratio by adding attached structures to create buffer spaces and use internal zoning;
- insulation: increase insulation of walls and roofs; improve thermal performance of windows; add new envelope to the building;
- air-tightness: replace windows with low leakage units; seal cracks and holes in the envelope.

In a retrofit project it is often more difficult to alter the shape and layout of the building in order to reduce its total surface area, than to improve the thermal properties of the existing surfaces.

*OVERALL BUILDING DESIGN*
Buildings with low surface area to volume ratios, i.e. compact buildings, have less surface through which heat can be transmitted and therefore use less energy for space heating. Glass-covered spaces such as atria can be added on to existing buildings, can be made from existing light wells or can even be created in the middle of deep-plan buildings. Such spaces, which may be several stories high, can effectively insulate a structure against the outside climate, as well as providing daylighting and supporting natural ventilation systems.

*LAYOUT*
Thermal zoning of the floor plan can also reduce heat losses. Spaces that require lower temperatures, for example, storage and circulation areas, can be located together (on the north side of the building). However, the possibilities for changing the

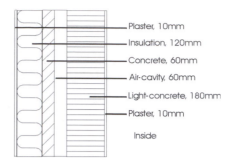

Figure 3.7. External wall insulation – Danfoss, Denmark

floor plan will be limited in many retrofit situations.

*ENVELOPE INSULATION*
Insulation will not only affect heat loss but will also influence the temperature of the walls and therefore the occupants' perceptions of thermal comfort. Increased insulation has been shown to be a prime factor in improving occupant comfort.

*WALLS, FLOORS AND ROOFS*
Insulation of walls, floors and roofs can be placed either on the outside or the inside of the existing structure. Insulation on the cold side of the building is preferred, as it: reduces thermal bridging; maintains a more stable structure temperature; en-

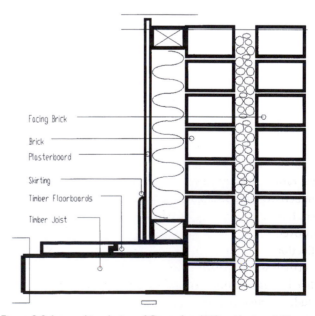

Figure 3.8. Internal insulation of Central and West Houses, UK. Internal insulation of brick walls in this project reduced heat loss by 45%, but at a high cost

Table 3.1. Key properties of different types of glazing

| Glazing types: | $U_i$ | $g_p$ | $g_g$ | $t$ |
|---|---|---|---|---|
| Single glazing (SG) | 5.60 | 0.82 | 0.84 | 0.90 |
| SG with selective coated | 4.30 | 0.66 | 0.69 | 0.73 |
| Double glazing (DG) with dry air | 2.90 | 0.69 | 0.75 | 0.81 |
| DG with argon | 2.70 | 0.69 | 0.75 | 0.73 |
| DG with selective coating and dry air | 1.60 | 0.62 | 0.67 | 0.78 |
| DG with selective coating and argon | 1.30 | 0.62 | 0.67 | 0.70 |
| DG with selective coating and xenon | 0.90 | 0.58 | 0.63 | 0.76 |
| Triple glazing (TG) with dry air | 2.00 | 0.62 | 0.70 | 0.74 |
| TG with argon | 1.90 | 0.62 | 0.70 | 0.71 |
| TG with 2 selective coatings and argon | 0.90 | 0.43 | 0.50 | 0.56 |
| Double window (two SG) | 2.70 | 0.69 | 0.75 | 0.81 |
| Glass paving | 3.00 | 0.60 | 0.65 | 0.75 |

Notes

| | |
|---|---|
| $U_i$ | thermal transmission coefficient |
| $g_p$ | global solar energy transmission perpendicular to glazing |
| $g_g$ | global solar energy transmission for global radiation in Europe |
| $t$ | light transmission |

sures that any condensation occurs outside; and keeps internal thermal mass high, allowing night ventilation cooling and a heat sink to even out temperature swings.

Insulation on the warm side of a building often results in thermal bridges, a risk of interstitial condensation (particularly with roofs) and reduced internal thermal mass. However, it is sometimes preferred in retrofitting as it may be easier and cheaper to install and does not change the appearance of the building. There again, a new external appearance may actually be a requirement in a commercial refurbishment.

## WINDOWS

Heat losses through transparent elements usually constitute a large part of the total heat loss in existing buildings, as old windows have relatively poor thermal properties. This is often the case both for the glazing itself and for the frames. The transmission losses of a window element can be reduced by a half or two-thirds if it is constructed of two or three layers of glass rather than of one, if the gaps are filled with a low conductivity gas, and if low-emissivity (low-e) coatings are used. It should be remembered, however, that the use of such improved glazing may result in decreased daylighting and collection of solar energy. The heat gain/loss ratio will, nevertheless, be greatly improved. Window frames should either be made from insulating materials, such as wood, or include thermal breaks.

At the Sentralbygg 1 office in Norway, replacement of old double-glazed windows by low-e-coated, argon-filled, double-glazed units reduced energy consumption by 50%, includ-

ing reduced air infiltration, estimated to account for two-thirds of the savings.

At the Aget office in Greece, replacing the single glazing with double glazing decreased the combined heating and cooling load by 10%.

Adding a new envelope to an existing building can provide a buffer space and give the building a new look. As well as reducing heat loss and preserving the existing structure, the second skin can provide a space for solar collection and/or passive ventilation, or for the location of shading devices.

At the Recamier office in France, the addition of a double-skin façade with winter pre-heat and summer ventilation reduced heating demand by 63%, although cooling and ventilation energy use increased.

### UNCONTROLLED VENTILATION

Uncontrolled infiltration of air through the fabric of a building results from holes in the envelope (such as chimneys and old ducts), gaps between building components, joints around movable elements such as doors and windows, and penetration of air through building components under pressure from wind. In older buildings the infiltration rates are usually much higher than in new buildings. Reducing infiltration will therefore significantly reduce heat loss in winter (and heat gain in summer).

The following actions can be taken to reduce infiltration:

- seal around door and window frames and other components with flexible mastic seal;
- block holes and seal old chimneys, structural cracks and

around ducts, pipes and cable entries;
* draught strip all doors and windows;
* provide a draught lobby on main doors;
* provide automatic door closers on all external doors.

Pressure testing of a building can be used to discover the extent of uncontrolled ventilation and to test the effectiveness of measures intended to reduce it.

However it is not necessary to cut out air infiltration entirely. The aim should be to minimize uncontrolled ventilation and provide adequate controllable ventilation sources. With mechanical ventilation systems it is also possible to reduce heat losses by using a heat recovery system. (See Section 3.3.5 for more information on mechanical ventilation.)

At the Danfoss office in Denmark, reducing air infiltration around windows reduced heat loss by 26% with a payback period of six months.

### 3.2.3 Using solar energy to heat offices

Thermal improvement of the building envelope reduces heat loss and therefore the length of the heating season. The heating season will consequently be concentrated in the period of the year when there is little solar gain. Nevertheless, solar energy may contribute to space heating energy (particularly in northern climates) if collection and storage devices are correctly designed. Increased heat loss in winter through larger glazing areas must also be considered.

Passive solar heating systems are used to reduce the need for auxiliary space heating by collecting, storing, and distributing solar energy using the basic building components. The collecting component is usually south-facing glazing, while the thermal mass inside the building absorbs the radiation and functions as storage.

Solar gains depend on the angle of incidence of the sun's rays. For vertical walls, orientations from south-south-east to south-south-west are most effective for collection in winter. Eastern and western orientations are more effective in mid-season and summer but can easily cause overheating. South-orientated walls are therefore most suitable both for passive solar retrofit and for reducing the risk of overheating.

There are two possibilities for the introduction of passive solar systems in refurbishment:

* windows: glazing with better solar transmission properties; increased window area on south façades;
* new glazed spaces: galleries, atria, second façades.

ACTIVE SOLAR SYSTEMS FOR SPACE HEATING

Active solar systems for space heating include solar walls and traditional solar air and water collectors. The types most suitable in refurbishment projects are:

* solar walls: traditional solar walls insulated with transparent insulation;
* solar collectors: transpired collectors for preheating ventilation air, traditional solar air collectors, solar water collectors.

In particular retrofit situations, the use of solar walls, i.e. the addition of glazing or transparent insulation to an existing façade, may be an attractive alternative to the addition of opaque insulation. In such cases the old, often non-insulated building structure is used as part of the solar system. At the same time the glazing protects the old façade from further deterioration, and it may also improve its appearance.

The prerequisite when constructing a traditional solar wall is that the existing wall has a high heat capacity. This is, fortunately, often the case in existing office buildings. In northern European climates it may also be necessary to use transparent insulation to prevent the night-time heat losses from the solar wall from exceeding the daytime heat gains, and care must be taken to avoid summer overheating.

An alternative is to use unglazed, transpired air collectors for solar preheating of ventilation air. This is an interesting way to renovate blind façades and the system does not require the existing wall to have a high heat capacity.

Traditional solar water collectors may also be used. The cost effectiveness of this option increases when they replace existing façade or roofing material in need of renovation. Solar water collectors may be effective if there is a local, water-based heating system in the building, otherwise the need for hot water in office buildings is probably too low to justify the investment.

### 3.2.4 Auxiliary heating

All office buildings require some form of auxiliary heating, at least on winter mornings. Heating systems frequently require replacement during a major refurbishment and when this occurs the following rules should be applied:

* use a fuel other than electricity if possible, to minimize $CO_2$ emissions and to prevent excessive running costs if the systems or building are mismanaged;

- install a new, efficient heat source such as a condensing boiler, at least as the lead boiler in multiple boiler installations;
- if electricity is to be the fuel, use a heat pump as the heat generator. This will improve efficiency over a direct resistance heater by a factor of 2–3;
- size heating systems to actual calculated maximum demand, rather than to traditional standards. Over-sizing is expensive in capital cost terms and normally reduces overall efficiency;
- insulate pipework and related equipment to reduce waste of heat. Heat loss to the boiler room, the outside and to spaces that do not require heating can be large;
- install a control system that ensures that heat is only supplied when and where required. Provide local temperature control via room thermostats and thermostatic radiator valves and use zoning if different areas require different periods of heating. (See discussion of building energy management systems [BEMS] in section 3.7);
- consider a co-generation plant if the heat generated can be used in the building, for example for absorption cycle chillers. An expert analysis is needed for each such installation;
- install heat recovery equipment on the ventilation system (see Section 3.3);
- install heat recovery on the boiler flue stack if the existing boiler is to be kept;
- provide local controls that are readily understood by users, labelled and local to the demand.

At Central and West Houses, UK, replacement of the existing heating system with a condensing gas boiler, optimal start and thermostatic radiator valves reduced energy consumption by 41% with a payback period of eight years.

At the AGET office in Greece, installation of a boiler flue heat recovery system was estimated to reduce energy use by 29%.

## 3.3 VENTILATION

### 3.3.1 Strategy

The purpose of ventilation is to maintain indoor contaminant concentrations at an acceptable level. This can be achieved in most cases by increasing the fresh air ventilation rate, however this wastes energy in heating and possibly cooling the air, and in fan power when mechanical systems are used.

The energy efficient strategy for ventilation is:

- reduce contaminant sources in the building;

- keep particular sources in specific zones (e.g. photocopiers, toilets, smoking areas) and extract from these zones;
- provide fresh air to all areas using natural ventilation as far as possible;
- provide fresh air by carefully controlled mechanical ventilation at the minimum volume compatible with acceptable indoor air quality.

### 3.3.2 Reducing contaminant sources

Contaminant sources in offices include:

- the occupants (producing $CO_2$, smells, water vapour, heat and, possibly, cigarette smoke);
- the building itself and the finishes, particularly paints (off-gassing formaldehyde and other toxic, volatile organic compounds);
- the furniture, fittings and carpets (as above);
- the office equipment (photocopiers and printers emitting heat, ozone, etc.);
- cleaning materials (leaving smells and other air contaminants).

Existing buildings may also contain other toxic materials such as asbestos in insulation and fire protection materials and lead in paint and pipes. These must be removed by specialist services.

The designer can frequently only affect the contamination from the building and finishes, and not from equipment (though equipment location can affect general office contamination (see Section 3.10) and they will need to take into account other likely sources of contamination when designing air change rates. The designer should specify the use of building materials that do not emit contaminants such as formaldehyde or other toxic, volatile organic compounds. This applies particularly to the choice of paints and other finishes; water-based paints should be specified where conditions allow their use.

### 3.3.3 Removing local pollution

Some contaminants, in particular those produced by photocopiers, printers and some other equipment and activities, cannot be avoided in offices. To avoid high overall ventilation rates, these contaminants should not be allowed to mix with other indoor air but should be extracted as close as possible to the source. The following methods can be used:

ZONING

The occupied space is divided into zones, separating the zone where the contaminants are produced from the remaining space which can then remain clean. Examples of zones are smoking and non-smoking areas, kitchens and toilets.

HOODS

Contaminants can be extracted close to the source by the use of hoods, ducts and fans. These are efficient only when the source is either in the hood or at least very close. Efficiency of hoods may be increased by using a combination of blown and drawn airflows.

### 3.3.4 Natural ventilation

Many existing office buildings are naturally ventilated and if this can be maintained with adequate indoor air quality after refurbishment, a low energy and comfortable solution should result.

Wind effects and temperature differences between the internal and external environments induce pressure differences across the building envelope. These pressure differences move air naturally through the building by envelope leakage (infiltration) and through ventilation openings and ducts (ventilation).

As there is great variation in these natural forces, there is a need to control the amount of air movement. This is best achieved by minimizing infiltration, by making the building envelope as airtight as possible, and controlling ventilation by operating the openings installed for that purpose.

WIND PRESSURES AROUND BUILDINGS

The wind exerts a pressure on a building that can naturally ventilate the building. Wind velocity increases with height above ground and is also affected by the terrain, being fastest above sea, slowest in a built-up area.

The distribution of wind pressure depends strongly on the wind direction but can be dramatically modified by the presence of surrounding buildings, and other obstructions including vegetation.

NATURAL VENTILATION DRIVEN BY STACK EFFECTS

In the absence of wind, the difference between inside and outside temperatures results in differences in air density and pressure causing a stack effect. Internal stratification of air resulting from temperature differences also causes a stack

effect, though it is generally less important. A part of the building, usually the upper part, is over-pressurized, while the other, lower part is under-pressurized. The level at which pressures are equal is called the neutral pressure level, or neutral level. This determines the direction of airflows through the building openings. Below the neutral level, there is an inflow of external air, while warmer inside air tends to flow outward above the neutral level.

For equal opening areas the neutral level is situated halfway between the openings, but a temperature gradient within the building tends to push the neutral level up. Such temperature gradients often occur in large spaces such as atria.

Making the outlet at the top of the building, e.g. at the top of an atrium, significantly larger than the total of the openings at lower levels, can ensure that outdoor, colder air will be drawn into the building at all lower levels, where it is needed. Stack ducts or chimneys may be used to reinforce this effect.

COMBINED WIND AND STACK EFFECTS

The pressure distributions due to wind and stack effects can be combined. For multilevel buildings the wind will reinforce the stack flow as long as the wind pressure is in the same direction as the stack pressure (Figure 3.9). It is recommended that the outlet is situated on the leeward side. An unfavourable situation can arise when the air outlet is situated on the windward side (Figure 3.10).

The following principles should be followed for efficient natural ventilation.

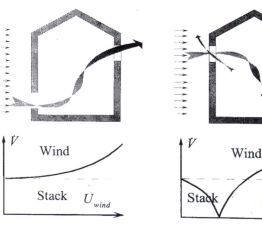

Figure 3.9. Synergy between wind and the stack effect

Figure 3.10. In some cases, wind may counteract the stack effect

- Natural ventilation should not be used in noisy and/or polluted areas, without specific design, nor where the air is frequently uncomfortably hot and humid.
- The building envelope should be airtight, except for the ventilation openings which should be adjustable to provide the required airflow rate with variable pressure differentials. There are several controllable ventilators on the market
- Ventilation openings should be carefully located and sized, using either good practice or computer modelling. Special care should be given to design at the 'neutral level'.
- Cross ventilation of all rooms should be planned. Single-sided ventilation cannot efficiently ventilate rooms that are two to three times deeper than their height, whilst cross-sided ventilation can ensure large airflows through the building.
- It is possible to ventilate using atria, double-skin façades, or other glazed areas where they are included. This requires careful design to avoid overheating and possible transfer of pollutants.
- Computer analysis of natural ventilation air movements is advisable in all but the most simple situations.
- In colder countries, external air may be too cold for ventilation without preheating. Care must be taken to avoid cold draughts.

In the Danfoss office in Denmark, using natural ventilation via opening windows to replace the mechanical ventilation system in summer reduced total annual electricity demand by 16% and ventilation energy by 29%, with only a small increase in overheating hours.

### 3.3.5 Mechanical ventilation

Natural ventilation may not provide acceptable indoor air quality in noisy or polluted environments, in deep-plan office buildings or in very sheltered urban locations. Outdoor summer temperatures in hot regions may require cooled ventilation air to provide acceptable indoor temperatures. Where a mechanical ventilation system exists, its performance and efficiency can be improved during refurbishment, or where a mechanical system is thought necessary in a previously naturally ventilated office, an efficient system can be installed. Natural ventilation may be supplemented by mechanical ventilation or fully replaced by it at certain times of the year or in certain parts of an office building. Year-

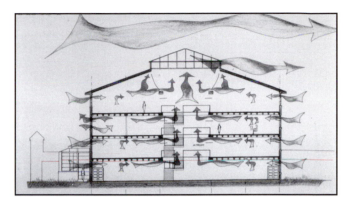

Figure 3.11. Atrium used for ventilation at Anglia Polytechnic University, UK

round mechanical ventilation should be avoided if possible for reasons of energy consumption, but if provided, a requirement for opening windows at least is now common.

Existing mechanical ventilation systems should be checked before retrofit, if it is intended to keep a system or a part of it. Leaky ducts decrease the ventilation efficiency and increase the fan motor energy consumption. It may be cheaper and simpler to completely change the ducts than to try to make them airtight. Air handling units may not function as designed, so airflow rates, leakage and shortcuts should be measured, for example by tracer gas testing.

#### MECHANICALLY ASSISTED NATURAL VENTILATION
Where fresh external air is available but natural forces are not considered sufficient to produce the required air change rates, ventilation may be mechanically assisted. Such systems can be controlled so that they only operate when necessary. For example, extraction fans in atria or chimneys can be used to increase ventilation rates when necessary; fresh air can be blown into a duct system and extracted by natural pressure difference.

At Central and West Houses in the UK, extraction fans installed in existing chimneys increased ventilation rates to maintain minimum ventilation rates in winter and to remove unwanted heat gains in summer.

#### FULL AIR-CONDITIONING SYSTEM
In a full air-conditioning system, airflow is used not only to eliminate contaminants and bring in fresh air, but also to provide or remove heat. Since the heat capacity of air is 4000 times less than that of water, large airflow rates may be

necessary to transport heat in poorly insulated offices or to remove heat from buildings that overheat. Energy efficiency can be built in or retrofitted by:

- installing heat recovery to existing systems;
- adding controls so that both heating and cooling cannot be applied to the same air;
- where there is a requirement for opening windows, installing cut off switches for rooms when windows are open;
- replacing existing systems with displacement ventilation systems (see Section 3.3.6);
- replacing old fans and ductwork with efficient fans and low resistance ductwork;
- reducing airflow rates to the minimum required.

Recirculation of air is not recommended, although it is often used to save energy, as it distributes contaminants throughout the whole building.

At the Danfoss office in Denmark, replacing the old fan system (motor, impeller and fan drive) with modern equipment saved 48% of energy use, with a payback period of 12 years.

At the City West building in Switzerland, replacing the fans and reducing the airflow rates reduced fan energy consumption by 70%.

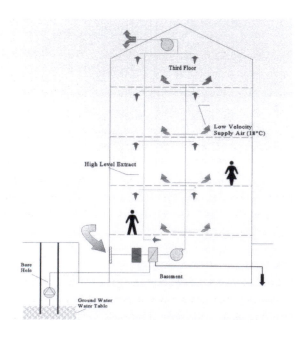

Figure 3.12. The principle of the displacement ventilation as it is used in Central and West Houses, UK (reproduced with permission from Ove Arup & Partners)

HEAT RECOVERY

There are several means of recovering heat from exhaust air and delivering it to some useful place, in most cases to outdoor air entering the building. Such systems can be used either in winter when heat is recovered from exhaust, or in summer when the warm outdoor air is cooled by giving heat to the cold exhaust air. Heat recovery can often be installed when retrofitting existing mechanical ventilation systems.

The most commonly used technologies are plate heat exchangers, rotating heat exchangers or 'heat wheels', and 'run around coils'.

At the Danfoss office in Denmark, air-to-air heat recovery on the existing ventilation plant reduced the heating energy consumption by 23%, although fan electricity use increased by 10%. Overall the payback period was ten years.

### 3.3.6 Displacement ventilation

Displacement ventilation can be a low energy method of ventilating office buildings. The fresh air, a little colder than the required room temperature, is blown at low speed close to the floor. The internal heat sources provide the necessary buoyancy to push the 'old' air up to ceiling exhaust outlets. (See Figure 3.12.) Displacement ventilation cannot by itself be used to provide cooling.

### 3.3.7 Controls

Occupants generally prefer some control over their environment and this allows them to tolerate greater variations in conditions, although it may not optimize energy efficiency. Natural ventilation and mechanical systems can have manual or automatic control systems or a mixture of the two.

The following controls are recommended singly or together:

- occupants manually open windows and wall vents and operate switches;
- wall vents are pressure controlled, automatically reducing the size of opening with increasing pressure;
- a minimum or base ventilation rate is ensured through automatically controlled openings, with the occupant opening the windows when large airflow rates are necessary;
- automatic sensors operate fans, high-level window opening, etc. These sensors include room presence detectors, $CO_2$ concentration monitors (as indicators of occupancy levels) and multi-gas pollution sensors;

- time clocks operate mechanical systems for defined occupancy patterns;
- in full air-conditioning systems, window sensors shut off supply adjacent to an open window.

Whole building control by building energy management systems (BEMS) is discussed in detail in Section 3.7.

## 3.4 AVOIDING OVERHEATING AND PROVIDING COOLING

### 3.4.1 Strategy

Retrofitting should employ the following strategy to avoid overheating and provide cooling:

- reduce all heat gains, including unwanted passive solar gain;
- remove remaining heat gains by natural ventilation, use of thermal mass and air movement;
- provide efficient active cooling if, when and where necessary.

Retrofitting actions can include:

- improvements to the building envelope, insulation and solar shading;
- improvements to the lighting system, type of lights, installed power and controls;
- the use of passive cooling systems and techniques;
- improvements to the efficiency of the active cooling system.

The retrofitting strategies applied to avoid overheating are closely related to those aiming to improve space heating (Section 3.2), ventilation (Section 3.3) and lighting (Section 3.5).

### 3.4.2 Reducing heat gains

The main heat sources in an office are solar heat gain (through windows and the structure), electric lighting, office equipment (mostly computers and related equipment) and the occupants. The designer can reduce the first two directly.

#### INSULATION OF THE STRUCTURE
Insulation of the external opaque elements, or use of additional insulation to the façades and the roof, is one of the simplest methods of reducing external heat gain to a build-

ing. Insulation has already been discussed in Section 3.2. Of particular importance for reducing overheating are roof insulation, to reduce heat gain to top floors, and external insulation so that thermal mass is retained inside the building (see Section 3.4.3).

The cost effectiveness of insulation varies with building type and existing insulation levels, the reduction of the cooling energy consumption typically in the range of 3–6%. However, the impact on cooling and comfort when insulation is combined with other actions on the building envelope can be significant.

At the City West building in Switzerland, the number of hours per year during which the internal building temperature exceeded 26°C was halved when insulation levels were improved in combination with a reduction of air infiltration and replacement of the existing windows with new, energy efficient ones.

#### WINDOWS
Glazing has a major impact on the heat gain and energy consumption for cooling in a building. Heat transmission is much greater through glass than through most opaque walls. Therefore, the ratio of window area to opaque wall area should be optimized, taking into account daylighting, heat loss in winter and heat gain in summer (and winter).

Window insulation has already been discussed in Section 3.2. High performance glazing, such as super low-e, can have a significant effect on heat gain, due to its low transmittance of solar radiation.

At the Danfoss office in Denmark, replacement of double glass windows with super low-e windows gave a reduction of 6–17% in the number of hours exceeding 24°C, with a cooling energy cost payback period of 16 years.

In southern Europe, replacement of single-glazed windows with double-glazed ones at the AGET and Cassa di Risparmio offices, produced a reduction in energy consumption for cooling of up to 16% and a reduction of 12% in the number of overheating hours.

#### SOLAR SHADING
Shading reduces solar heat entering the office via the windows and causing overheating in summer, while some direct solar gains may be beneficial in the heating season. Additionally, shading is often used to reduce glare, improving the visual comfort in the working spaces. Solar shading can be external, interpane and/or internal.

Figure 3.13. Exterior elevation of the Berlaymont Building, Brussels, with moveable shading louvres

Figure 3.15. Ceiling fan at Leso, Switzerland

## EXTERNAL SHADING

External shading includes fixed or movable devices: fixed horizontal overhangs and louvres, vertical side fins, reflective window films, movable horizontal or vertical louvres, awnings and vertical roller shades.

All fixed devices reduce daylighting and views and usually provide only partial shading. They are of little use on east and west elevations due to low sun angles (unless the view out is completely stopped), but can be effective on the south elevation (except in northern latitudes), letting low winter

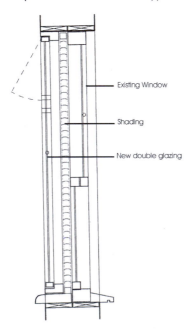

Figure 3.14. Interpane shading at City and West Houses, UK

Existing Window

Shading

New double glazing

sun in but excluding high summer sun when overheating is most likely.

Movable systems are more flexible, since they can be adjusted, either manually or automatically, to cut out sun when and only when it is unwanted. Fritted or laminated shades that allow some light to penetrate are recommended as they help to maintain adequate internal daylight levels.

At the Danfoss office in Denmark, an automatically controlled, external shading system reduced the number of hours with temperatures exceeding 24°C from 103 to 44 hrs/year.

At the AGET office in Greece, the use of additional external shading devices on the first and second floors gave a reduction of the energy use for cooling of 29%, while the number of overheating hours was reduced by 24%, with a payback period of seven years.

## INTERPANE SHADING

Interpane shading usually consists of adjustable and retractable venetian or roller blinds, or films which are placed within the glazing. If placed between the outer two panes of triple glazing they can be very effective in stopping heat gains entering the office. There is little maintenance or cleaning required.

At the Sentralbygg I office in Norway, an interpane venetian blind system provided solar shading in summer and improved daylighting resulting in a 15% reduction in lighting energy.

## INTERNAL SHADING

Internal shading is very common, offering occupants local control with easy and low cost installation, accessibility and maintenance. However, it is not an effective method of excluding solar heat gain as heat is trapped inside the building after hitting the shade.

Other shading methods include shading of roofs exposed to direct sunshine and, for offices in the suburbs or in rural areas with available space, natural growth can provide shading. Deciduous trees can provide shade during the summer and solar access in winter for buildings of up to three storeys, and exterior walls and roofs covered with creepers can reduce direct solar gains.

### DAYLIGHTING AND EFFICIENT LUMINAIRES

Electricity for lighting is a major use of energy, in the energy required to operate the luminaires and in increasing the internal heat gain, and consequently, the cooling load. To reduce lighting energy use, daylighting should be optimized and the installed lighting power and time of operation should be minimized. Efficient practices to increase the use of daylighting and reduce the installed power and number of operating hours are described in Section 3.5.

At the AGET office in Greece, installation of more efficient luminaires with electronic ballasts and the use of a daylight compensation system reduced the cooling energy consumption by 26%, which, with the energy used for lighting reduced by 63–66%, gave a simple payback period of three years.

### OFFICE EQUIPMENT

There is likely to be little the designer can do to reduce the heat generated by office equipment which can add significantly to the energy required for cooling in office buildings. Some possibilities are discussed in Section 3.10.

## 3.4.3 Passive cooling using natural ventilation, thermal mass and increased air movement

### NATURAL VENTILATION

If the outdoor air temperature is lower than or equal to the design temperature for the office building, ventilation can be used as a means to remove excessive heat gains from the indoor spaces to the atmosphere. Natural ventilation techniques have been discussed in Section 3.3. In cases where the use of natural ventilation is unfavourable, mechanical ventilation can be used to remove unwanted heat gains.

### USING THERMAL MASS

Heat storage within the building structure acts as a temporary heat sink providing a means for the control of indoor tempera-

ture swings during the daytime. Internal thermal mass in floors and partition walls can store heat during the day which can be dissipated by night ventilation using cool air. The cooled surfaces then act as cool radiators during the daytime.

External walls and roofs can serve the same function as long as they do not absorb solar heat from outside, as the time lag may mean that the heat is transmitted to the inside many hours after the sun sets. External insulation is recommended to reduce this effect.

For effective use of thermal mass:

- remove suspended ceilings to expose the concrete where possible;
- if necessary, use free hanging ceiling panels that allow air to circulate across the concrete;
- avoid raised floors where possible, as these insulate the mass of the floor against heat transfer;
- use external insulation on walls and roofs, but avoid internal insulation unless there is sufficient other thermal mass inside the offices;
- use specially designed windows with top openings, if possible, for natural night ventilation;
- use protection bars and special screens in the windows that are open to provide security;
- if for security, privacy or climatic reasons, natural ventilation during the night is not possible, a mechanical ventilation system may be used (but the necessary use of electricity should be taken into account);
- use an automatic controller to open and close windows or vents; to start the mechanical ventilation system if one is used; to start cooling when the outdoor air temperature is lower than the indoor air temperature and to stop cooling before the indoor temperature at the time of occupation is below the comfort level.

Night ventilation is one of the most efficient passive cooling techniques and is suggested as a retrofitting strategy in most office buildings. Peak daytime temperatures can normally be reduced by around 2°C, with up to 5°C reduction possible under ideal conditions. The effectiveness of night ventilation increases with increasing difference between indoor and outdoor air temperatures and with increasing velocity of the air passing over the surfaces. Ceiling fans can be used to increase air velocities at night.

When only natural ventilation is used, the running cost is zero and the capital payback period usually short. When night ventilation is achieved through mechanical means, the extra electricity used by the fans must be taken into account and may significantly reduce the cost effectiveness.

At the naturally ventilated Central and West Houses, UK, night ventilation reduced overheating hours above 27°C by 20–25%.

### USING MOVING AIR

Moving air creates a sensation of thermal comfort even when the indoor temperature exceeds the design air temperature. This can be achieved by air from an open window or by the use of ceiling fans. Ceiling fans can extend the comfort zone, up to 27 or even 29°C in some climates, when operated with an air speed of 1.0 m/s which avoids drafts and noise. The increased cooling set-point can result in a reduction of the operation time and cooling load to be covered by the mechanical system. The cost of ceiling fans permits a short payback period of between a half and seven years, based on the cooling load reductions against the initial investments. The use of ceiling fans may not be acceptable in 'prestige offices' in some countries.

At the AGET office in Greece, the installation of ceiling fans reduced the energy consumption for cooling by 30% with a payback period close to three years.

## 3.4.4 Efficient air conditioning

### FREE COOLING USING OUTDOOR AIR

Cooling requirements can be totally or partially satisfied using outdoor air during some parts of the year, especially during autumn and spring when outdoor conditions are favourable. This is commonly called 'free cooling'.

At the Aget office in Greece, the introduction of an economizer cycle control in the mechanical ventilation system resulted in a reduction in cooling energy consumption of 4%, with a payback period of six years.

### GROUND OR RIVER WATER COOLING

Ground water can provide another source of 'free' cooling, either using a closed loop or by drawing water from a bore hole and discharging it elsewhere after use. Ground water temperatures vary around a mean of 12°C depending on climate, the depth of the bore hole and the season, and can be passed through a heat exchanger or support a chiller unit to cool ventilation air. River water can also be used to the same effect. At the Krokslatt office in Sweden, the use of river water reduced the electricity used for cooling by 35%.

### ABSORPTION HEAT PUMPS

Absorption chillers are heat-operated refrigeration machines, typically using waste heat (e.g. from a CHP system) or a gas-fired burner, rather than electricity, as the energy source. They produce cooling at lower efficiency than conventional chillers in terms of delivered energy, with larger machine size, but they can be more efficient in primary energy terms and very efficient if waste heat is used.

### EVAPORATIVE COOLING

The operation of evaporative cooling systems is based on the principle of phase change of water into vapour. The latent heat which is necessary for this phase change is provided by the air, which is thus cooled. Indirect evaporative cooling systems can be used as pre-coolers of fresh air before it is introduced to the working spaces of an office building. They are recommended as a low-energy retrofitting option, as neither humidity control nor dehumidification is necessary for the air supplied to the building.

At the AGET office in Greece, the introduction of an indirect evaporative cooler resulted in a 10% reduction in the cooling energy consumption, with a payback period of six years.

### DESICCANT COOLING

Desiccant cooling systems can be either single-bed, fixed units or rotary-type units, similar to thermal wheels. With desiccant wheels, the system utilizes a disc-shaped, heat retentive, honeycomb material which is chemically treated to absorb moisture. This slowly rotates, allowing both supply and outgoing airstreams to pass through separately. The outdoor air supply is heated and passes through one section of the wheel, evaporating the moisture trapped in the wheel's material and discharging it to the atmosphere. The dried wheel material is then rotated and comes into contact with the humid indoor airstream, allowing vapour to condense and be trapped by the wheel, while the dry air is returned to the space.

Desiccant dehumidification can be used to maintain acceptable humidity levels in working areas with high internal latent heat gains or where high percentages of untreated outdoor air are introduced if this air is humid.

## 3.4.5 Chilled ceilings

Chilled ceilings and beams can be retrofitted to existing offices and may be particularly useful if there are low floor-to-ceiling heights. They provide radiant cooling to assist passive cooling

Figure 3.16. A chilled ceiling panel at the Enschede Tax Office, the Netherlands

and absorb peak cooling loads. To ensure air quality and avoid condensation, radiant cooling panels need to be used in conjunction with a low-volume, low-velocity ventilation system, usually a displacement ventilation system. Since radiant cooling systems do not use forced airflow to facilitate cooling, a uniform temperature gradient can be created, providing a very comfortable environment for the occupants. Generally, cold ceilings are able to handle around 100 W/m$^2$ with up to 50% of the ceiling space utilized for cooling.

Some advantages of chilled ceiling systems are:

- as chilled ceilings operate at relatively high temperatures (average surface temperatures of 16°C), the chillers can operate at higher temperatures resulting in an increase in efficiency and reduction in energy costs;
- cooled ceiling and displacement ventilation systems are silent and virtually draught free since air flow volumes are reduced compared to conventional systems (2–3 air exchanges per hour compared to 6–10 with conventional systems);
- radiant cooling panels can be retrofitted into the false ceilings of older buildings, as the space requirement is smaller than with ducted systems, making more room height available;
- radiant panels can be used as both heating and cooling panels reducing the amount of equipment required compared to conventional heating and cooling systems;
- 'free cooling' is possible by using ground or river water in the panels (via a heat exchanger).

However, care is needed in the design of chilled ceiling systems.

- Operating temperatures and humidity levels must be carefully designed to avoid condensation on the panels under extreme conditions. When used with opening windows, cut-off switches may be necessary for adjacent panels.
- The buoyant flow of displacement ventilation systems may be disturbed by the presence of cooling ceiling panels and partial mixing may be induced. Continuous ceilings, made of jointed panels, cause fewer disruptions of the airflow than discontinuous cooling ceilings where panels or pipes are separated by an air gap.
- Radiant metallic panels reflect sound waves. Therefore, in order to maintain the acoustics in the rooms within comfortable limits, they should be combined with sound absorption.

## 3.5 LIGHTING

### 3.5.1 Strategy

Energy use for artificial lighting in offices can account for up to half of their primary energy use. Since the office working period is largely in daytime, a large proportion of this energy load can be eliminated by using daylight. Experience has shown that the use of daylight can introduce energy savings in the range of 35–75% of lighting costs, provided that the artificial lighting is controlled in such a way as to take the increased daylight level into account.

However, the admission of daylight into offices is associated with a number of problems, particularly heat loss and/or overheating, glare and, sometimes, fire protection and security. All these potential problems need to be addressed.

The following low energy lighting strategy should be followed:

- optimize daylight admission through windows, skylights and atria, taking into account heat loss in winter and heat gain in summer;
- design a solar shading system to avoid overheating in summer (see Section 3.4);
- check and adapt for potential glare problems;
- maximize daylight distribution from the perimeter deep into the office space;
- provide energy efficient luminaires;
- provide efficient and effective control of all artificial lighting.

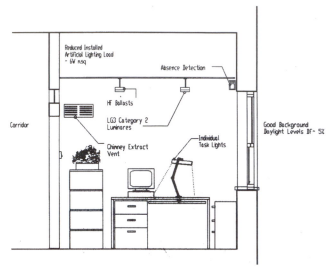

Figure 3.17. Lighting strategy at Central and West Houses, UK

Figure 3.18. Daylight and vision windows at the Enschede Tax Office, the Netherlands

### 3.5.2 Optimizing daylight admission

*WINDOWS*

Refurbishment frequently includes replacing the windows. It is important to choose a glazing with a high light transmission and if the existing window openings are large, it may be a good compromise to use slightly reflective glazing instead of a clear glazing. In this way, a balance can be obtained between daylight admission, solar gain admission and heat loss.

Where major layout changes and interventions in the façade are possible, glazing location may be one of the most important considerations in daylight design and the control of direct sunlight. North-oriented openings may be preferred in southern regions, while in temperate and cold climates, where the sun can be used for passive heating, the south-facing orientation is generally preferable.

The shape and position of daylight openings has important implications for daylighting and internal distribution, as well as view. The following points should be kept in mind:

- for a given size, a narrow high window will admit more light to the depth of the room than a wide low window;
- a view of the sky is important for light intensity, but too large a proportion of sky can limit views and is very likely to cause glare;
- the first metre of window above floor level gives little daylight (mostly solar gains and transmission heat loss).

An efficient solution is to divide the window into a lower part,

the vision window, and a higher part to allow daylight deep into the building. This division also makes it possible to use a different shading strategy on the upper and the lower windows in line with the different functions (see Figure 3.18).

*SKYLIGHTS*

Skylights are very efficient in admitting daylight to the top floors of buildings, the one drawback being that visual contact with the outside is limited to general information about the weather. A good solution is to use skylights to illuminate core areas (e.g. corridors) which usually have no access to daylight, or to use them to supplement daylighting in deep-plan rooms.

In the AGET office in Greece, admitting daylight through the roof reduced energy use for daylighting by 8%, with a payback period of 11 years.

*ATRIA*

One way of admitting daylight into deep-plan, multi-storey buildings is to add an atrium into the building. In this way, the advantages of a compact building with respect to heat loss (see Section 3.2) can be combined with the advantages of a narrow building with respect to daylighting, ventilation and cooling.

Atria can be added in several ways:

- as a core atrium cut into the centre (where the atrium is surrounded by the building);
- as a linear atrium (where the atrium separates two parts of a building);

Figure 3.19. Lightshelves at Anglia Polytechnic University, UK

- as an attached atrium (where the atrium is connected to the building on one or more façades), although this will reduce daylight levels through existing windows.

Atria should be designed so that they do not require heating or cooling as this will consume considerable energy. Blinds will usually be required to reduce solar gain and glare, but internal blinds are usually satisfactory since heat gains can be exhausted directly from the top of the atria via opening windows.

SOLAR SHADING

An ideal shading device will block the maximum amount of unwanted solar radiation and still permit daylight, views and breezes to enter the window. Shading devices have been discussed in Section 3.4.

### 3.5.3 Maximizing internal daylight distribution

DAYLIGHT SYSTEMS

A typical office daylight intensity falls off rapidly with distance from the window, making the backs of rooms gloomy in comparison to areas next to the window. Lightshelves are one retrofit solution which reduces light levels at the window and increases levels away from the window, in a way that at the same time reduces glare from the sky. Lightshelves are flat or curved elements in the window aperture, either inside or outside and above eye level, which redirect incoming light and thus protect occupants below from direct sun to some extent. The lightshelf divides the window into a view-window below the shelf and a daylight window above the shelf. Only the exterior part of the lightshelf contributes to a higher light level in the space, whereas the interior part mainly reduces the sky component and therefore contributes to the distribution of light in the space. It is important to combine the lightshelf with a highly reflective ceiling in order to achieve the best efficiency.

Prismatic panels and holographic optical elements can also be used to redirect daylighting. Prismatic panels control transmitted light by refraction, while holographic optical elements bend light by diffraction. Neither are well enough developed at present to be used commercially.

REFLECTANCE OF INTERIOR SURFACES

Reflectance of the interior of an office has a considerable effect on daylight distribution, particularly in large interiors. Light-coloured ceilings and walls (and furnishings) improve the penetration of daylight deep into the interior and reduce the contrast between the bright windows and the other surfaces. It is recommended that:

- internal surfaces, especially ceilings and walls, should be repainted in light colours;
- window walls should be at least as reflective as the other walls to reduce the contrast between the windows and their immediate background;
- shiny surfaces should be avoided whenever possible, particularly on or near working surfaces, to reduce glare.

### 3.5.4 Visual comfort

Glare occurs whenever one part of an interior is much brighter than the general brightness in the interior. The most common glare sources are luminaires and windows, seen directly or by

Figure 3.20. Interior fabric sails to optimize shading, Anglia Polytechnic University, UK

reflection. Glare can have two effects. It can impair vision – called 'disability glare' – and it can cause discomfort – called 'discomfort glare'. Disability glare and discomfort glare can occur simultaneously or separately.

Disability glare is most likely to occur when there is an area close to the line of sight which has a much higher luminance than the object being observed. The following parameters increase discomfort glare: a high source luminance; a large source area; low background luminance; and/or a position close to the line of sight.

Veiling reflections are high luminance reflections which overlay the detail of the task, they may therefore affect task performance and cause discomfort. The most common source of veiling reflections are as before, windows and luminaires. To avoid veiling reflections:

- use matt materials in task areas;
- arrange the geometry of the viewing situation so that the luminance of the offending zone is low;
- reduce the luminance by curtains or blinds on the windows.

### 3.5.5 Energy efficient artificial lighting

As daylight cannot be expected to meet all lighting requirements in an office, the interior needs to be equipped with an efficient artificial lighting system which can be used when daylight is insufficient for a specific task. Redesigning artificial lighting systems involves:

- designing the general lighting system for minimum acceptable illuminance levels;

- including task lighting;
- using the most efficient lamps, luminaires and ballasts.

#### REDUCING LIGHTING LEVELS

Existing artificial light levels may be unnecessarily high, especially if combined with task lighting. To reduce installed lighting loads:

- luminaires can be replaced with more efficient types;
- lamps can be removed from fittings to reduce unnecessarily high lighting levels;
- lamps can be replaced by more efficient light sources.

Once background lighting levels have been minimized, compact fluorescent task lighting on individual desks under the control of the user are recommended as part of the strategy.

#### LAMP TYPES

In lighting refurbishment, all incandescent filament lamps should be replaced by fluorescent lamps with compact or traditional tubes. Older tubular fluorescent lamps, usually 38mm (T12), can be directly replaced by more efficient smaller sources, 26mm (T8) lamps in conventional switch start applications. This can save up to 10% of energy consumption, while offering longer life and equivalent light output. For highest efficiency, a full replacement of luminaires is recommended.

#### LUMINAIRES AND HIGH FREQUENCY BALLAST

Luminaires should be replaced by those suitable for fluorescent lamps, either compact or tubular, with high frequency electronic ballasts, which can save up to 30% of circuit power, are lighter in weight, silent in operation and virtually eliminate flicker and stroboscopic effects.

In the selection of luminaires, the efficiency of the fitting in terms of its light distribution should also be considered as there is little sense in placing an efficient lamp in an inefficient luminaire. Luminaire efficiency is dependent on its maximizing reflection which in turn is dependent on materials and design. Anti-glare diffusers are also an important aspect of luminaire design. Selection depends on the task – in VDU environments it is critical to eliminate glare, whereas for other tasks this may not be critical.

At Central and West Houses in the UK, reduced lighting levels with provision of task lighting gave a saving of 20% in energy use with a four-year payback period.

## 3.5.6 Controlling artificial lighting

To maximize the use of daylight and minimize the use of electricity for artificial lighting, automatic control systems should be installed. Even in small, cellular offices an appropriate automatic control system will save energy by turning off the lights when they are not needed, either due to sufficient daylight or if the room is unoccupied. There are two common systems:

### AUTOMATIC LIGHT LEVEL CONTROL SYSTEMS

Automatic light level control systems are based on photoelectric cell sensors which measure the light level and reduce the artificial lighting levels as necessary. Systems for controlling artificial lighting output can be divided into three categories: on-off step regulation, continuous regulation and a combination of the two. In the simple form, in small offices, an on-off control switches off all lights in the room as daylight exceeds the pre-selected level. In a more sophisticated form, appropriate in large offices, individual lights in multi-light fixtures are switched off in sequence until ultimately all the lights are off. Alternatively, the output from individual lamps can be reduced by reducing the voltage, but this type of control cannot be applied to all lamp types.

### PRESENCE DETECTORS

Presence detectors sense whether a room is occupied. Their typical operating method is to detect movement of mass by sensing reflected beams (infrared, radar or ultrasound). A system that turns lights off when the room is unoccupied and leaves it to the occupant to turn the lights on if required, is likely to be the most efficient. Energy consumption can be reduced with this system compared to a conventional presence detection system, by eliminating the possibility of the lights being switched on by small movements such as wind, even when the room is unoccupied.

It is important to be aware of occupant reactions to these control systems. If the control system is purely automatic with no possibilities for the occupants to override it, user satisfaction is often low and generally energy is wasted. Energy waste can occur when occupants block the sensors to ensure that artificial light is not turned off, even when the amount of daylight is sufficient.

At Central and West Houses in the UK, occupancy detection gave a 40% reduction in energy use with a payback period of six years, whilst photocell control gave a similar saving but with a payback period of 20 years.

## 3.6 DOMESTIC HOT WATER

### 3.6.1 Strategy

Where hot water is provided for washing in offices, considerable energy may be wasted compared with the amount of hot water actually used. The energy efficient strategy recommended is:

- provide hot water only where necessary;
- use water-saving devices such as spray taps, spring loaded taps, etc;
- provide local hot water generation;
- control hot water generation by time and temperature.

Hot water is generally only considered necessary in offices in northern European countries. Centralized generation of hot water often utilizes the central heating boiler, which can be particularly wasteful in summer due to the low demand. It may also contribute to overheating in summer due to heat losses to the space. Local generation and storage of hot water in toilets and kitchens avoids long pipe runs and consequent waste of water and energy. Water-saving taps control the use of both water and energy.

During refurbishment, existing centralized systems can be cut off and local generators fitted. New taps can also be fitted to control the quantity of water used or wasted.

### 3.6.2 Reducing the use of hot water

Taps that give a small flow of hot water and that cannot be left running after use will ensure efficient use of hot water. The following systems are recommended: spray taps with automatic temperature control; hand presence activated taps; spring-loaded push or turn taps.

### 3.6.3 Efficient generation and storage

A central hot water generation and distribution system can be replaced by individual point-of-use heaters. Dedicated generators of hot water should be located adjacent to toilets and canteens to avoid long pipe runs. Gas-fired boilers will be the most energy-efficient, either for instantaneous generation or coupled to storage cylinders, and may serve several toilets if in a stack or close together. Time control should be provided to stop out-of-hours heat loss and temperature control provided to stop scalding and energy waste.

Electric storage heaters can be an acceptable option for very small usage, say up to four basins. They provide a low capital cost option and if usage is controlled and small, they can have minimal running costs. Off-peak storage will provide the lowest running cost, but on-peak boost may be necessary.

At Central and West Houses in the UK, conversion of the central generation and distribution of hot water to instantaneous local electric generation was calculated to reduce the energy consumption from 12.3 kWh/m²/yr to 1.1 kWh/m²/yr, a saving in primary energy of 73%.

If central generation of hot water is necessary for any reason, ensure that pipework and storage vessels are well insulated and that controls are provided. To minimize summer energy waste by an (effectively) over-sized boiler, provide a wide margin between 'on' and 'off' thermostat settings on the storage vessel.

### 3.6.4 Catering hot water

Catering facilities can be large hot water users. Most of the recommendations above apply, except that electric heating should not be used. In addition, active solar water heating (or preheating) can be economic due to the daytime use of hot water and the year-round requirement for catering hot water.

## 3.7 BUILDING ENERGY MANAGEMENT SYSTEMS (BEMS)

### 3.7.1 Controls strategy

Office heating, cooling, solar shading, ventilation and lighting equipment can be controlled manually (e.g. window opening), by local automatic control (e.g. presence detectors for lighting) or by centralized automatic control. Most offices operate on a mixture of all three. Whilst BEMS were originally developed to control mechanical equipment, they are becoming practically essential to operate the complex passive systems currently recommended for offices.

The following strategy should be used to design a BEMS:

- decide what actions and systems the BEMS will control;
- design an appropriate system which will be simple to understand (taking the occupants' wishes into account if known);

- write a manual for the operator and occupants and clearly label the parts of the system;
- commission the system and check that all actions operate correctly.

Installing a BEMS during a retrofit is likely to improve energy performance except in the most basic of buildings, as long as it operates correctly.

### 3.7.2 BEMS for controlling passive measures

In addition to control of mechanical equipment, BEMS can be used to promote comfort with energy efficiency by controlling passive and natural operations:

- natural ventilation, including the opening and closing of high level vents, e.g. atria vents, and air inlet vents, and implementation of the fire control strategy;
- night ventilation, including the decision of whether night cooling is required, window opening and closing, fan-assisted cooling;
- overall timed lighting control;
- external solar shading systems.

### 3.7.3 BEMS design

An office BEMS is composed of four main parts:

- sensors to measure the parameters required for the implementation of any control strategy, including indoor and outdoor temperatures, $CO_2$ or air quality sensors, wind velocity and direction, rain, solar radiation and humidity;
- actuators to adjust mechanisms and operate switches;
- a controller, the heart of the control system, to receive and treat data from the sensors and send orders to the actuators. The control strategy is programmed into the memory of the controller and continuously implemented at fixed time intervals;
- a supervisor may be necessary to supervise control decisions from outside controllers and possibly override local decisions (for example, to decide which windows to open according to wind direction, or to close all windows in case of fire).

The main elements of control for heating, cooling, ventilation etc., are contained in the individual sections of this Handbook. However, there are some general points to be made:

- the BEMS should ensure that the different components of the building are working in harmony and not in opposition, for example, heating and cooling at the same time, night ventilation causing the need for heating the day after or air conditioning working in rooms with open windows;
- the BEMS should allow the user to input his/her local wishes with respect to temperature, lighting and shading (otherwise the user may act against the automatic operation);
- the BEMS should incorporate safe and energy efficient fall-back positions and settings, which should be clearly displayed when the system is interrogated;
- the BEMS must be designed to be transparent so that new operators can understand how to operate it.

### 3.7.4 The manual

The designer must specify that a simple manual be written and left attached to the BEMS, referring to labelled components of the system to help the new operator to understand, use and change the system as necessary. Frequently BEMS are found to be the cause of considerable energy waste as they are not understood by the operator and/or cannot be changed to suit a particular situation.

### 3.7.5 Commissioning and testing

Frequently BEMS do not operate in practice according to their design. The designer must specify that the system be commissioned and tested to check that it is operating correctly and test certificates should be obtained.

## 3.8 ACOUSTIC CONTROL

### 3.8.1 Strategy

Consideration of the transmission of sound in an urban environment from the street to an office is especially important when designing passive ventilation systems, particularly with windows that open. Inside the office, the principal acoustic design factor is the reverberation time and certain aspects of low-energy passive design, such as open-plan spaces and exposed thermal mass, are likely to have a negative effect.

The appropriate design strategy is to:

- reduce external noise transmission as much as possible;
- contain internal noise in particular spaces within the office;
- minimize internal noise from ventilation and air-condition-

ing systems;
- reduce internal reverberation as necessary;
- reduce noise transmission between adjacent rooms.

### 3.8.2 Dealing with external noise

In urban areas, external noise from roads enters an office through façades and open windows and may be a serious problem. Transmission through façades and windows will alter the frequency spectrum so that indoor noise will be more dominated by noise at low frequencies.

The following retrofit strategies can be adopted:

- seal any cracks in façades;
- eliminate window opening on the noisiest façades and draw in air from quieter areas;
- shield windows that open from direct noise inlet;
- use double- or triple-glazed windows with different weights of glass to counter vibrations;
- provide noise-baffled air inlet vents.

### 3.8.3 Internal noise containment

In open-plan offices, redesign sufficient meeting rooms, or separate meeting areas, e.g. coffee machine areas, so that discussions do not affect the whole office space.

### 3.8.4 Reducing noise from ventilation and air-conditioning systems

Ventilation and air-conditioning systems can produce two sorts of noise problems. 'Structure-borne sound' is sound produced by the fan, motor and compressor. 'Aerodynamic noise' is produced by turbulent, high velocity air in the ducts and passing through grilles, diffusers and air inlets. Aerodynamic noise is transmitted via the ducts to other parts of the building.

Motors, fans and compressors should be placed as far as possible from the areas which are liable to be sensitive to noise and the machinery should be isolated from the main structure of the building by means of anti-vibration mounts. Short lengths of flexible, resilient hosing should be inserted between the machinery and the ductwork.

To reduce the aerodynamic noise transmitted by the ducts, a number of techniques may be employed, such as:

- replacement of high pressure, high velocity systems by low

Table 3.2. Noise acceptability levels (dB)

| Type of space | 125 Hz | 500 Hz | 2000 Hz |
|---|---|---|---|
| Restaurant | 65 | 55 | 50 |
| Office room | 50 | 45 | 40 |
| Conference room | 44 | 30 | 25 |

velocity systems;

- replacement of small nozzles by larger ones;
- lining the ducts with sound-absorbing material;
- inclusion of a plenum chamber in the system;
- provision of bends and smooth changes of cross-sectional area of the ducts;
- insertion of ready-made, commercially available attenuators;
- the use of vanes for maintaining a non-turbulent air flow;
- the use of high acoustic quality air inlet vents.

### 3.8.5 Controlling reverberation

Noise disturbance varies with type of sound, the level/volume and the spectrum. The current values of noise acceptability levels in decibels (dB) are given in Table 3.2.

The well-known relationship between reverberation time and absorption of sound is given by the Sabine formula:

$T = 0.16V/A$

where

$T$ = reverberation time

$V$ = volume of the auditorium in m$^3$

$A$ = total absorption of the auditorium in m$^2$ sabins

In offices without false ceilings, with solid walls and uncarpeted floors, noise reverberation from any source is likely to be a problem. Reverberation can be reduced, with consequent effects on average noise levels, by installing sound absorbing

Figure 3.21. Acoustic ceiling panels at the Enschede Tax Office, the Netherlands

panels on ceilings (best) and walls. Reverberation times for speech should be around one second.

### 3.8.6 Sound insulation

Where two rooms have a common dividing element, a noise source operating in one room will produce a reverberant sound field which impinges on all surfaces of the room. The sound energy incident upon the dividing wall will depend on the sound power output of the source and the total sound absorption in the room. This incident sound energy will be partly reflected back into the room and partly absorbed by the wall, which then radiates acoustic energy into the adjoining room. The amount of radiation from the wall, and hence the sound insulation provided by the wall, depends on the frequency of the sound, the construction and material of the wall and, above all, on its density.

In a building, there is almost always a certain amount of indirect or flanking transmission. Besides the structure-borne paths, there could also be transmission through air ducts, air inlets and leaks around doors, for example.

To reduce sound transmission from one room to another, the following rules should be followed:

- seal all cracks and openings, both large and small;
- use double-glazed windows;
- use heavyweight or multi-layer partition construction;
- provide sound attenuation material inside the noise generating room.

## 3.9 FIRE SAFETY IN REFURBISHED OFFICES

### 3.9.1 Fundamentals of fire safety

Certain aspects of passive and low energy offices generate new problems with respect to fire safety, particularly open-plan, naturally ventilated offices, new types of glazing, and atria. These need to be addressed during a refurbishment which incorporates these features.

The principal objectives of national fire safety regulations are more or less the same throughout the world:

- to reduce the potential for fire incidence;
- to control fire propagation and fire spread;
- to provide adequate means of escape for the occupants in the building.

The means used to accomplish these overall objectives vary according to building type and from country to country, but six main strategies can be identified (which correspond to the different phases in a fire):

- fire prevention (prevention of fire ignition);
- design to slow early fire growth;
- fire detection and alarming;
- evacuation of occupants;
- fire suppression;
- confinement of fire.

## 3.9.2 Fire safety and natural ventilation

As most natural ventilation systems are based on low pressure driving forces, the building must be very open allowing for free flow of the air. In deep-plan buildings, the airflow path could go from grilles in the façade to exhaust ducts in the core of the building or to an atrium. In narrow-plan buildings the flow path could go from façade to façade, a simple cross ventilation system. Common to both systems is the absence of any barriers, with the consequent danger of the rapid spread of fire and smoke. To compensate for this, it is important to apply effective fire detection and alarm systems, to give an early warning for the occupants, and that the evacuation time of the building is short. It may also be possible to use fire and smoke dampers to confine spread, for example in ducted extract systems. Another solution where corridors are the main flow path is to use fire doors as a blocking mechanism.

## 3.9.3 Fire safety and glazing

Low energy buildings frequently use low transmission and low emissivity glazing, making it possible to design buildings with large glazed areas without undermining the stability and the heat balance of the building. Examples of such large glazed areas are double façades and atria. However, glass does not have good fire resistant qualities, and therefore buildings should be retrofitted in such a way that the glazing is not used as a fire barrier.

Another potential problem is the danger of fallen glass, broken by the heat of a fire. To avoid casualties, escape routes should follow routes away from glazed areas, or be protected from fallen glass by some kind of structure.

## 3.9.4 Fire safety in atrium buildings

The problem of fire safety in atria is that, by their very nature, atria usually penetrate several floors, thus running contrary to one of the six important strategies described in Section 3.9.1 – confinement of fire involving horizontal as well as vertical compartmentalization. Therefore it is necessary to apply special techniques in an atrium, when fire safety has to be assured.

The main fire safety problem in atria is that the room/atrium boundary is either glazed or open, allowing smoke, hot gases and even flames to travel from rooms into the atrium and then affect other areas which would have remained unaffected in the absence of an atrium. The ideal option would be to prevent any smoke from a room fire entering the atrium at all, by ensuring that the boundary between the room and the atrium, is both unbroken and fire-resistant, and that the atrium base only has restricted use, e.g. acting as a circulation area. This solution, called the 'sterile tube', has frequently been used, but because of the many restrictions on atrium design and use, it is not favoured by designers. For example, it precludes the use of natural ventilation driven by the buoyancy in an atrium.

To design an atrium building with an open boundary between the atrium and the adjacent floors, an effective smoke control system must be adopted to prevent smoke from entering the atrium and/or smoke in the atrium from entering the adjacent floors. Some of the strategies which can be applied, are outlined below.

### SMOKE CONTROL ON THE FLOOR OF THE ORIGINATING FIRE
### SMOKE CONTROL WITHIN THE FIRE ROOM
To prevent smoke from the surrounding compartments entering the atrium, a down-stand barrier can be attached at the atrium boundary edge to create a reservoir within the compartment. A similar solution is to use a high-powered exhaust slot at the boundary edge.

### VENTILATION OF BALCONY SPACES
If the atrium is designed with a balcony space for circulation, the space can be used as an extra smoke reservoir with a smoke screen around the balcony perimeter, to prevent the smoke from flowing into the atrium. The smoke can then be extracted either mechanically or ducted to the outside or into the ceiling reservoir of the atrium.

Figure 3.22. Down-stand barrier at Anglia Polytechnic University, UK

### SLIT EXTRACT

When removing the smoke from a common balcony reservoir, in a situation where there is no possibility of using down-stand screens to prevent the passage of smoke into the atrium, a slit extract system may be employed over the length of the flow path to supplement the exhaust system and replace the screens. Similarly, a slit extract system can be used across room openings, to prevent any outflow of smoke.

### SMOKE CONTROL WITHIN THE ATRIUM
### SMOKE VENTILATION IN THE ATRIUM

When the smoke and heat cannot be confined and removed from the room of origin or associated balcony space, the use of 'through flow' or steady-state ventilation from the atrium itself can be considered.

### CHANNELLING SCREENS

When smoke is able to flow unrestricted under, for example, a balcony, it will flow sideways towards the balcony and then rise into the atrium space as a very long line plume. This results in large quantities of air being entrained, and hence a very large mass flow rate of smoke entering the layer in the atrium roof. In addition, the temperature of the smoke layer will fall, hence reducing the buoyancy. This may cause the smoke to accumulate further down in the atrium, blocking escape routes on the abutting floors and on the atrium base. This can be reduced by making channelling screens which restrict the sideways travel of the smoke.

### VOID FILLING

Some atria provide large available volumes in which any smoke from a fire could be contained, such that smoke control/ventilation may be unnecessary.

### DE-PRESSURIZATION VENTILATION (NATURAL OR FAN-POWERED)

If the atrium is de-pressurized, the smoke will be prevented from flowing from the atrium to the neighbouring spaces.

## 3.10 OCCUPIER ISSUES

However well the designer incorporates energy efficiency into a refurbishment project, the final operation of the building will have a major effect on both energy use and internal comfort. This section will focus on what the designer can do to encourage the owner to use the building in an energy-efficient way and to improve the indoor environment.

### 3.10.1 Strategy

The strategy for the designer is to:

- understand the likely future operating conditions of the office and the wishes of the occupants;
- make the systems and their control as simple as possible;
- build in opportunities for the occupants to have local control;
- have controls clearly labelled with function and normal set points;
- provide an information manual on efficient building and systems operation;
- ensure that there are safe and low-energy fall-back positions;
- ensure that the systems are adequately commissioned;
- propose that low-energy appliances are used by present or future owners and occupants.

### 3.10.2 Design aspects

The designer should seek information on the likely facilities management of the office and design systems, particularly controls, so that they can be operated by the level of management proposed. A complex BEMS will not operate efficiently except when professional staff are involved. Mixed mode

Figure 3.24. The European ecolabelling symbol, to be found on environmentally friendly furnishings and equipment

Figure 3.23. The AVAX office, Greece, in operation

systems operating active cooling only in high summer for example, will need professional management. Thus, in general, it is only in the larger offices where it is cost-effective to employ an energy professional that complex systems and controls should be considered.

Simple systems and basic control systems are likely to be operated for maximum efficiency since they are easily understood by users. All controls, both local and centralized, should be labelled as to their function, e.g. 'Boiler time clock', 'Atrium ventilator override switch'. Graduated controls such as time clocks and thermostats should have their 'normal' settings clearly marked. This allows users to adjust settings within reasonable limits and others to check settings easily.

The designer should have a manual written for the occupiers explaining how the building and the mechanical systems operate. The following information should be included, as appropriate:

- ventilation systems – principles, vents, opening windows, mechanical systems and potential conflicts, $CO_2$ level control systems, use of ceiling fans;
- shading systems and their efficient use, anti-glare systems;
- heating system, control settings;
- night cooling operation;
- active cooling operation;
- location and description of local and centralized controls, BEMS, etc;
- lighting control systems;
- any special features, e.g. the need not to restrict cross ventilation, the need to leave thermal mass exposed, etc;
- maintenance requirements and schedules;
- energy saving suggestions.

## 3.10.3 Commissioning and checking consumption

The designer needs to write into the contract the requirement to commission all the mechanical and electrical systems, and to supply proof that once installed they are operating according to the design.

Monitoring of energy consumption and temperatures of the building in use will show up any problems in terms of settings, malfunctions, missing insulation, poor programming, etc. The designer should supply the occupier with calculated gas and electricity consumption figures and recommend monitoring to check actual performance.

## 3.10.4 Equipment and furnishings

Where the designer is able to make recommendations to the future occupier, the following are suggested:

- low energy office equipment, computers and networks, copiers, printers, etc;
- environmentally-friendly furnishings, excluding those emitting volatile organic compounds, particularly carpets.

### REFERENCES

1   prENV 1752, (1996), *Ventilation for Buildings – Design Criteria for the Indoor Environment*, draft submitted by TC 156 to CEN for formal vote.

# — 4 —

# Design standards

Each country has its own standards, and in this Handbook we cannot give specific country details. Presented below are some European standards, or draft standards, which are often adopted in European countries when retrofitting office buildings.

## 4.1 THERMAL COMFORT

Today's generally accepted criteria for thermal comfort come from Fanger's theory, which lead to several national and international standards, such as EN-ISO 7730.[1] This theory relates the occupant's mean vote for comfort to physical parameters, the most important being:

- the activity of the occupants;
- their clothing;
- the operative temperature, which is a combination (usually the average) of the mean radiant temperature and the air temperature;
- the air velocity;
- the air moisture content, but only if it is outside the range 30–70%.

Applying the theory shows that optimal winter operative temperature in offices (light activity, seated, that is, 1.2 met, clothing 1 clo) is 22°C, with a tolerance of $\pm 2$°C. This means that, statistically, 5% of the occupants will be dissatisfied at 22°C, and 10% dissatisfied at 20°C or 24°C.

The optimal summer temperature for the same activity, but with summer clothing (0.5 clo) is $26 \pm 1.5$°C.

## 4.2 VENTILATION

### 4.2.1 Minimum ventilation rate

There are few good standards for ventilation levels. Today's standards are based on common practice rather than on contaminant source strengths. Most of them propose specific air flow rates, or air change rates, being the air flow rate divided by the volume of the ventilated space. For a given air change rate, the larger the volume, the larger will be the air flow rate. Therefore, the 'specific air flow rate method' is not valid for large enclosures, since it would require unnecessarily large ventilation rates, or for rooms with dense occupancy, where it would result in insufficient ventilation rate.

*EUROPEAN DRAFT STANDARD PRENV 1752*
The European draft standard prENV 1752,[2] proposes a list of air flow rates per floor area for various types of buildings, depending on their expected occupancy and a reasonable contaminant source rate from the building.

This standard offers a choice of three classes, A, B and C. These correspond to high, medium and minimum requirements and aim to satisfy, respectively, 85%, 80% and 70% of the occupants. It is basically valid for clean buildings, since it assumes that occupants are the main contaminant source. Values given in Table 4.1 are valid for 100% ventilation efficiency. They should be doubled in rooms with complete mixing.

### 4.2.2 Draught risk

Requirements related to draught are also important. Occupants complain about draught when air velocity exceeds a limit which depends on air temperature and on turbulence. Figure 4.1 shows the mean air velocity that results in 10% dissatisfaction, that is, 10% of occupants complaining of draughts, as a function of temperature and turbulence intensity.

PrENV 1752[2] provides various figures for acceptable air velocity for the three levels, A, B and C, in summer and winter, and for the various types of buildings. As a rule of thumb, the air velocity in an occupied area should not

Table 4.1 Air flow rates per square metre floor area [l/(s·m²)], as recommended by prENV 1752 (1994 draft)[2]

| Building type | Occupancy (person/m²) | Ventilation rate [l/(s·m²)] | | |
|---|---|---|---|---|
| | | A | B | C |
| Individual office room | 0.1 | 2.0 | 1.4 | 0.8 |
| Open office room, no smoking | 0.07 | 1.7 | 1.2 | 0.7 |
| *ibid*, smoking | 0.07 | 2.4 | 1.7 | 1.0 |
| Conference room | 0.5 | 6.0 | 4.3 | 2.4 |
| *ibid*, smoking | 0.5 | 11 | 8 | 4.4 |
| Auditorium | 1.5 | 16 | 11 | 6.4 |
| Cafeteria | 0.7 | 13 | 11 | 6 |
| School room | 0.5 | 6 | 4.3 | 2.4 |
| Kindergarten | 0.5 | 7 | 5 | 2.8 |

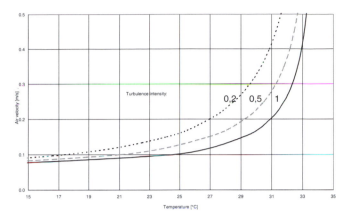

Figure 4.1 Combination of air temperature, velocity and turbulence which results in 10% of occupants complaining of draught

exceed 0.2 m/s in winter. This upper limit increases to 0.25 m/s in summer.

## 4.3 ENERGY USE

### 4.3.1 Heating

The European standard EN 832[3] provides a calculation method based on a steady state energy balance, which takes account of internal and external temperature variations and, through a utilization factor, of the dynamic effect of internal and solar gains.

This method allows the calculation of heat loss coefficient, equivalent solar collecting areas, heat loss, solar heat gains, internal gains, heat use and the heating energy requirement. It is a simple but powerful tool to estimate the heat requirement of various retrofit measures or scenarios for a given building.

This method can also be used for the following applications:

- judging compliance with regulations expressed in terms of energy targets;
- optimization of the energy performance of a planned building, by applying the method to several possible options;
- displaying a conventional level of energy performance for existing buildings;
- predicting future energy resource needs on a national or an international scale, by calculating the energy uses of several buildings representative of the building stock.

The user may refer to other European standards or to national documents for input data and detailed calculation procedures not provided by this standard.

Recommended maximum limits for heat use are not provided by a European standard, but should be given in national regulations.

### 4.3.2 Cooling

There is no international standard with a simplified method for assessing cooling requirements. However, CEN/TC89 is preparing a standard to evaluate any calculation method.

## REFERENCES

1 EN ISO 7730, (1993), Ambiances thermiques modérées. Détermination des indices PMV et PPD et spécifications des conditions de confort thermique (Moderate thermal environment – Determination of the PMV and PPD indices and specification of the conditions of thermal comfort), CEN, Brussels and ISO, Geneva.

2 prENV 1752, (1994), Ventilation for buildings – Design criteria for the indoor environment, draft submitted by TC 156 to CEN for formal vote.

3 EN 832, Thermal performance of buildings – Calculation of energy use for heating – Residential buildings.

# — 5 —

# Design tools

## 5.1 THE NEED FOR DESIGN TOOLS IN LOW ENERGY REFURBISHMENT

Different types of design tools have been used in building design for many centuries, varying from simple tools such as nomographs to complicated computer-based simulation tools.

Today sophisticated design tools have become a vital element in the design process of low energy buildings. This is because of the complexity of the parameters influencing the performance of such buildings, making it very difficult to find an optimal design solution using traditional methods or rules of thumb.

## 5.2 USING DESIGN TOOLS

The use of design tools requires a knowledge of building physics and building technology, and the design tool alone cannot be used to solve the design problems and present the user with the optimal solution. Design tools should be considered as design aids, not as a designer.

It is crucial that the user of the design tool knows the theoretical basis of the tool, and so is aware of its limitations. All design tools, from the most simple to the most complex, are developed with a number of limitations inevitably built into the program.

The process of using design tools can be divided into five phases: problem definition; selection of a tool; data input; processing; and result analysis.

### 5.2.1 Issue definition

The first step will always be to define the design problem or issue, then to decide which kind of output data are needed. Examples of design issues and outputs:

ISSUE: THE OVERALL ENERGY DEMAND OF A BUILDING
Output could be given in net or gross energy demand, as energy demand per year, month, week or day, and as total energy or energy divided by energy types (e.g. electricity and natural gas) or by services using the energy (heating, cooling, ventilation etc.).

ISSUE: THE THERMAL ENVIRONMENT
Output could be given as hours per year where the room temperature exceeds a given set-point, as accumulated frequency curves or as hourly representations for typical days.

ISSUE: THE PERFORMANCE OF A SPECIFIC BUILDING ELEMENT
Output could be given which refers specifically to the examined building element (e.g. for the ventilated solar wall, kWh/year produced or temperature rise in inlet air) or which relates to the whole building.

### 5.2.2 Selection of an appropriate tool

Having determined the type of design issue to be studied, the type of output and the level of accuracy desired, the design tool can be chosen. Different design tools may be able to provide these calculations, but give different results. It is therefore also important to know the viability and validation background of the tool. In general, always use well known and well validated tools, but if a new tool is to be used, it is recommended that an in-house quality control exercise be undertaken.

### 5.2.3 Data input

Remember that you can never expect results of better quality than the quality of the input data. Therefore great attention should be paid to the data input phase. The level of accuracy of the input data required depends on the design problem, the type of output required and the specific tool. Some design tools only need raw data to be able to present usable results, while other complex tools need very detailed, pretreated data.

### 5.2.4 Processing

The processing phase can be either computerized or manual (e.g. reading tables and graphs), but today most tools run on PCs or workstations. Depending on the tool and the computer used, this phase can take anywhere from a fraction of a second to several days (as in the case of some computerized fluid dynamics [CFD] programs).

### 5.2.5 Result analysis

To be able to extract design recommendations from the processed data, the output needs to be analysed and interpreted. Correct interpretation of results requires great care and understanding of the building type, use and previous experience.

### 5.3 CLASSIFICATION OF DESIGN TOOLS

Design tools dealing with energy efficiency and indoor quality in buildings, can be classified in two major categories, specific and global.

### 5.3.1 Specific computational tools

Specific computational tools are tools which are used to calculate the performance of specific building components (e.g. thermal bridges), specific techniques (e.g. natural ventilation)

or specific parts of the building environment (e.g. temperature distribution in a space).

Specific computational tools can be divided into 13 different classes based on their purpose. The classes are shown in Table 5.1, together with examples of tools currently available in each of the classes.

In the OFFICE project, the following specific computational tools have been used: SUPERLITE, RADIANCE and MATHLAB for daylight calculations and TRYCV for preparation of weather files for the global computational tool Tsbi3 (see Section 5.3.2 below). LESOCOOL was used to check cooling strategies.

### 5.3.2 Global computational tools

Global computational tools are used to calculate the overall performance of a building in terms of energy demand and thermal environment and may use simplified or detailed methods.

Simplified tools are based on empirical or statistical algorithms which are only valid under certain conditions. These programs do not calculate the dynamic nature of a building and must be used strictly within limits. Examples of simplified tools are the European standard EN 832 and the LT-Method.

Tools based on detailed simulation codes aim to describe most physical processes in a building and thus predict its dynamic performance. To secure reliable results, most of the detailed simulation tools are validated against real measured data from experimental buildings and/or against data from test cells. However, most detailed simulation tools are complicated to use and should therefore only be used by trained professionals.

Well known, detailed global simulation tools are TRNSYS,

Table 5.1 Classes and examples of specific computational design tools

| Class | Description: Tools dealing with ... | Examples of tools |
|---|---|---|
| 1 | transfer phenomena in opaque elements | KOBRA |
| 2 | transfer phenomena in transparent elements | WINDOW-LBL, WIS |
| 3 | mass transfer phenomena (ventilation, infiltration) | AIOLOS, AIRNET, BREEZE, CONTAM96, PHOENICS, COMIS, FLOVENT, FLUENT |
| 4 | solar control problems | SHADOWPACK, SUMMER, LAMAS, PEM |
| 5 | microclimate around buildings | CPCALC |
| 6 | lighting <–> daylight in buildings | LT-METHOD, SUPERLITE, RADIANCE, PASSPORT-light, GENELUX, Daylight, MATHLAB |
| 7 | HVAC systems | |
| 8 | the specific performance of passive heating components | SLR Method, Method 5000 |
| 9 | thermal comfort in buildings | COMFORT, SUMMER |
| 10 | climatic and solar data | TRYCV, TRY, SOLRAD |
| 11 | indoor air quality in buildings | AIR |
| 12 | post-evaluation of the building's performance | PRISM |
| 13 | the specific performance of passive cooling techniques and components | SINK, SUMMER |

ESP-r, TAS, DOE, SUNCODE and Tsbi3. PASSPORT+ is also a useful dynamic modelling tool. All these were used by the participating groups in the OFFICE project.

## 5.4 PHYSICAL MODELLING

As a supplement to manual or computer-based design tools, physical models can be used to test different design options. Physical models are particularly recommended to test new unproven designs. Depending on the design problem, scale or full-size models may be used.

### 5.4.1 Scale models

Physical scale models have been used by architects for centuries to study various aspects of building design and construction, as well as communication tools between clients and consultants. However, not all types of problems are suited to testing in scale models; for example, room temperature patterns and natural ventilation configurations are best tested in full-size models.

One parameter well suited for scale model testing is lighting. No scaling corrections are needed because the wavelength of visible light is so short that the behaviour of light is largely unaffected. Therefore rooms accurately modelled in terms of geometry and surface reflectance will provide the same quantity and quality of illumination as the real space.

Limitations of scale models arise when materials which cannot be scaled easily (e.g. fabrics) are involved.

### 5.4.2 Full-size models

Tests using full-size models give the best and most accurate results because no scale corrections are necessary and they give the best impression of the design solution from the real point of view. They are therefore well suited for communication between architects, engineers, building owners and future occupants.

The disadvantages of full-size models are the cost of the model and the cost of changing test parameters, but full-size may not be necessary for retrofit projects if on-site tests can be arranged. However a disadvantage then is that the boundary conditions (e.g. wind and temperature) can be difficult to control in on-site models, so full-size laboratory models might be better in some cases.

# — 6 —

# ORME:
# Office rating methodology for Europe

## 6.1 WHAT IS A RATING METHODOLOGY?

Rating or ranking techniques are used for checking compliance with regulations, evaluating the efficiency of a retrofit or even for labelling a building. However, the building is, in most cases, rated on very few parameters among the many that should be taken into account in making an assessment.

Within the OFFICE project two methods were developed: a multi-criteria ranking method, based on the ELECTRE family of algorithms, and a rating method based on main component analysis. Together, the two methods aim to rate and sort office buildings or retrofit scenarios according to an extensive list of parameters, including energy use for heating, cooling and other appliances; impact on the external environment; indoor environment quality; and cost.

A typical application of such a method is to determine if one retrofit scenario is globally better than another for a given building. Figure 6.1 shows that it is not easy to decide if a

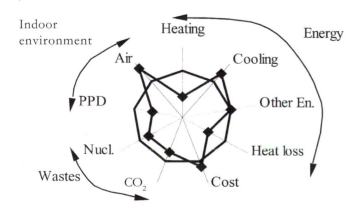

**Figure 6.1** Ratio of value after and before retrofit for nine criteria in a Swiss building. The building is better, according to a given criterion, when inside the polygon

strategy improves the building in all aspects. It is however possible, using modern tools, to rank buildings according to several criteria.

This chapter briefly presents the principles used in the method, and some examples of its application on real buildings. More information is given in the complete report,[1] and in other publications.

A rating or ranking methodology should contain:

- the list of parameters to be considered and why;
- the methods to assess the considered building parameters;
- the method to compare the assessed parameters to criteria and to rate or sort the buildings.

The methodology should be applicable to existing buildings before and after retrofit, and should be able to assess the improvement achieved by a retrofit.

A common approach uses the multi-attribute utility theory to provide a method giving a type of grade to the building, taking account of the most important parameters of the building. A typical example is the average value of grades describing how each criterion is fulfilled. This method is useful when a single value should be given to a building or a retrofit scenario. Most existing multi-criteria methods, as well as the rating method presented here, are based on this technique.

However, this approach has the disadvantage of allowing the compensation of a poor performance against one criterion by fair results against another. In addition, the mathematics give an apparent objectivity to the judgement that does not correspond to reality, as the methods always include subjective aggregation of the rates obtained for each criterion.

To overcome these problems, a multi-criteria ranking method based on a holistic approach was developed. This method uses fuzzy logic on a set of indices, each one addressing

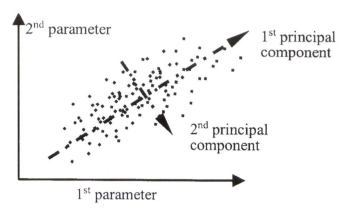

Figure 6.2 Illustration of a principal component analysis

a particular aspect of the building's performance, the analysis of which allows the ranking of the buildings with respect to standards, best practice or performance before and after retrofit.

## 6.2 THE RATING METHOD

### 6.2.1 Purpose of the rating method

The rating method aims to qualify and sort various retrofitting scenarios, based on their energy use and thermal comfort achieved. The method is based on the use of 'principal component analysis' to develop a single indicator that characterizes the overall performance of the building. This single indicator is then used to compare the performance of the building under different retrofitting scenarios, taking the existing situation before retrofitting as the low score and the situation after retrofitting as the (hopefully) high score.

### 6.2.2 Parameters considered

The method uses five energy and comfort parameters to define the indicator:

- annual heating energy use (kWh/m³);
- annual cooling energy use (kWh/m³);
- annual lighting energy use (kWh/m³);
- discomfort hours during the winter period (hours);
- discomfort hours during the summer period (hours).

These parameters can be assessed either by measurement or by simulation. Other parameters can be added or replace existing ones, as far as data are available and the parameter is important

in defining the environmental performance of the building. As the variables are expressed in different units, it is preferable to homogenize them by dividing each one of them by the corresponding standard deviation value.

### 6.2.3 Principal component analysis

Each building to which a retrofit measure or set of measures is applied can be represented as a point in a multidimensional space defined by the parameters chosen to describe the building. The buildings are then represented by a 'cloud' of points.

Principal components are the main inertia axes of this cloud, the first component is the longest axis, and so on. In most cases, the first two principal components suffice to explain most of the variability of the building set, and then 'summarize' a larger set of parameters. (See Figure 6.2.)

### 6.2.4 The energy efficiency retrofitting score (EERS)

A target building can be defined as the building having the best values for all chosen parameters, and the distance between each building and the target can be calculated. On this basis, the energy efficiency retrofitting score (EERS) was defined. This score is a dimensionless parameter which defines the potential for energy retrofitting of office buildings. It is defined by the expression:

$$EERS = 1 - \frac{Distance_i}{Distance_{base\,case}}$$

The EERS is a measure of the specific potential of a retrofitting scenario $i$. It is equal to zero for the existing building, and to one for the target building.

### 6.2.5 Example of application

The method is illustrated using the Norwegian case study. Twenty-four retrofitting measures and scenarios were analysed and values for the five parameters were estimated. The original building and the virtual buildings on which each measure or scenario is applied, are represented as points in the five-fold space of the parameters. The principal components of this cloud of points were determined.

As can be seen in Figure 6.3, the two principal components represent almost 80% of the variability of the system. These

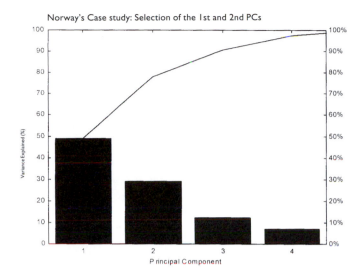

Figure 6.3 Variability represented by each principal component for all ten considered buildings

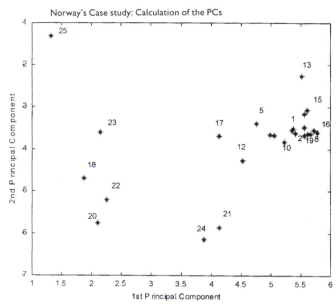

Figure 6.4 Relative position of all the considered scenarios with respect to the calculated first and second principal components. Point 1 represents the original building, and point 25 represents the virtual building with all retrofit measures applied

two of the five parameters define a new two-dimensional space in which each 'building' can be represented, as in Figure 6.4.

Figure 6.5 shows the energy efficiency retrofitting scores of all measures and scenarios, the references being the original building and the full retrofit.

## 6.3 THE RANKING METHOD

### 6.3.1 Description of the method

The holistic approach presents several important advantages and ORME was developed to incorporate these:

- information from the evaluation of each parameter is not 'lost' in a single figure indicating the overall performance, so small improvements in many parameters cannot cover up a bad performance in one parameter;
- the outranking relation takes into account several qualitative principles, such as thresholds of preference, indifference or veto on the comparison of a pair of objects, and also takes into account uncertainty in the attribute evaluation, vagueness in the human preference expression and the indiscernability of very close objects;
- slight preference is considered as it is in reality i.e. not transitive: when $a$ is slightly preferred to $b$, and $b$ to $c$, it is not certain that $a$ would be preferred to $c$;
- incomparable objects are declared incomparable, instead of being ranked arbitrarily.

The main stages of this method are:

DEFINITION OF CRITERIA
Definition of a list of criteria on which ranking is based, with their relative importance, or weight, assigned.

DEFINITION OF REFERENCE BUILDING
Definition of a reference building, either a standard building to national standards, a best practice example or the subject building before retrofit.

PERFORMANCE EVALUATION
Evaluation of the performances of the subject building against each individual criterion. These evaluations are made on physical scales, e.g. energy use will be evaluated in kWh/m².

COMPARISON *VS.* REFERENCE BUILDING
Comparison of the performance of the modified building with the reference building, giving for each criterion a 'concordance index' and a 'discordance index' to the statement, 'The building outranks the reference building'.

To define these indices, three variables are defined for each criterion: thresholds of preference $p$, indifference $q$ and veto $v$. The

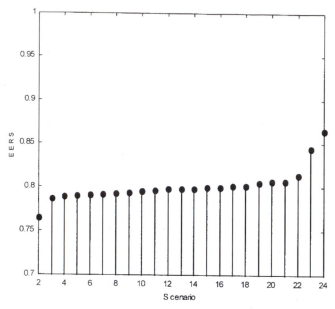

Figure 6.5 EERS values for all selected scenarios of the Norwegian case study building

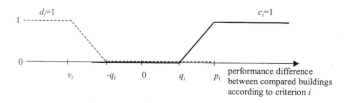

Figure 6.6 Definition of concordance and discordance indices ($c_i$ and $d_i$) using indifference, preference and veto thresholds ($\pm q_i$, $p_i$ and $v_i$, respectively)

threshold of preference, $p$, indicates the performance difference allowing a firm affirmation that '$a$ is preferred to $b$'. If a performance difference between modified building $m$ and reference building $r$ for criterion $i$ is in the range $m_i - r_i > p$, then $m$ outranks $r$ (or $m$ is preferred to $r$) with a concordance index $c_i = 1$. If the performance difference is between indifference threshold $q$ and $p$ then $0 < c_i < 1$. If the performance difference is between $-q$ and the veto threshold $v$, there is a discordance index $0 < d_i < 1$, and a difference higher than $v_i$ implies a discordance index $d_i = 1$ (i.e. strong opposition to the affirmation statement). These definitions are illustrated graphically in Figure 6.6.

GLOBAL OUTRANKING RELATION

Once individual concordance and discordance indices are calculated for each pair of compared buildings, a global outranking relation between buildings must be established. This outranking relation can be 'incomparable', 'preferred' or 'indifferent'.

The commercial ELECTRE III or ELECTRE IV software can help in this comparison and in ranking a series of buildings.

### 6.3.2 Criteria considered

In principle, multi-criteria analysis should consider an exhaustive and not redundant list of criteria. In order to be practical, the values for each criterion should be readily available and the list should not contain too many criteria. In this project, the criteria were limited to about ten, representing an acceptable compromise between detailed description and feasibility. Those criteria, listed in Table 6.1, were selected from a list of more than 24.

Table 6.1 Proposed criteria, together with their indifference, preference and veto thresholds and average weights. Thresholds for differences are either absolute or relative (in percent)

| Criterion | | Unit | Threshold levels | | | Weight |
|---|---|---|---|---|---|---|
| | | | $q_i$ | $p_i$ | $v_i$ | |
| **Energy criteria** Annual normalized energy use for: | | | | | | |
| heating | $E_h$ | kWh/m² | 10 | 50 | 100 | 10 |
| cooling | $E_c$ | kWh/m² | 3 | 10 | 20 | 10 |
| other appliances | $E_o$ | kWh/m² | 3 | 10 | 20 | 10 |
| Normalized cost of building | $C$ | ECU/m² | 3% | 50% | x2.5 | 10 |
| **Environmental criteria** Annual normalized carbon gas emission | $E\ CO_2$ | kg/m² | 3 | 10 | 50 | 5 |
| Annual normalized nuclear wastes emission | $E\ NW$ | Bq/m² | 30% | 50% | x10 | 5 |
| **Indoor Environmental Quality** Predicted percentage of dissatisfied | $PPD$ | % | 2 | 7 | 15 | 13 |
| Outdoor air flow rate per person | $Q_v$ | m³/(h.p) | 10% | 50% | <10 | 13 |
| Noise level at working place | $N_L$ | dB | 2 | 5 | 20 | 13 |

Table 6.2 Characteristics of case study buildings related to considered criteria (Criterion numbers refer to 'Ref' indicates reference buildings; 'Full' indicates retrofitted buildings)

| Criterion | Unit | CH-LS Ref | Full | CH-CW Ref | Full | DK Ref | Full | F Ref | Full | GR Ref | Full | D Ref | Full |
|---|---|---|---|---|---|---|---|---|---|---|---|---|---|
| $E_h$ | kWh/m² | 38 | 25 | 64 | 28 | 263 | 47 | 98 | 14 | 172 | 100 | 174 | 13 |
| $E_c$ | kWh/m² | 35 | 2 | 17 | 21 | 4 | 0 | 2 | 0 | 44 | 23 | 28 | 27 |
| $E_o$ | kWh/m² | 45 | 31 | 87 | 87 | 80 | 59 | 21 | 21 | 279 | 279 | 104 | 50 |
| C | ECUs/m² | - | 300 | - | 350 | - | 400 | - | 340 | - | 300 | - | 400 |
| E CO₂ | kg/m² | 50.8 | 34.3 | 102 | 83.2 | 212 | 64.9 | 74.0 | | 206 | 190 | 187 | 55.0 |
| E NW | kBq/m² | 568 | 383 | 1150 | 930 | 2373 | 725 | 828 | | 2284 | 2109 | 2093 | 616 |
| PPD | % | - | 0.1 | - | 3 | - | 20 | - | 0 | - | 57 | - | 0 |
| $Q_v$ | m³/(h·p) | 46 | 46 | 124 | 91 | 49 | 37 | 83 | 83 | 31 | 30 | 360 | 200 |

Annual energy uses, cost and pollutant emission are normalized to the gross heated floor area of the building in order to compare buildings of different size. They are calculated from simulations, preferably validated on the existing building. Pollutant emissions are calculated from the amount and type of energy fuel used, according to the database prepared by Suter et al.[2] Predicted percentage of dissatisfaction is either a design value (e.g. 10%) or calculated using the Fanger's theory.[3] Outdoor air flow rate per person and noise levels are either measured values, for the reference building, or design values for retrofit scenarios.

### 6.3.3 Checking the method

In order to ensure that ORME is practical and brings useful information, the method was checked on the case study buildings of this project. The effects of changing weights or threshold levels on the final judgement, the resulting ranking of buildings, were determined. It was found that the method, when applied to real buildings with realistic weights and threshold levels, is fairly robust – the ranking order was not dependent to any large extent on these parameters.

### 6.3.4 Example of application

The method was applied to six case study buildings, with the characteristics given in Table 6.2. Figure 6.7 shows ranking lists of the retrofitted buildings. It can be seen that these lists are slightly, but not dramatically, changed when threshold levels are modified.

Figure 6.7 also illustrates that the method sometimes will not distinguish between two buildings if they are judged too close to each other according to the adopted weights and threshold values.

### 6.4 CONCLUSIONS

The methodology includes two methods, which make it possible to rank or to rate buildings or retrofit scenarios according to more than one criteria.

The rating method, which can be applied easily using commercial statistical software, allows the rating of buildings according to their energy use and comfort conditions or against a more complete set of parameters involving environmental factors. An EERS can be defined, which is a measure of the potential of a retrofitting scenario.

Using the ELECTRE software, buildings or retrofit scenarios can be ranked according to several criteria and these can be weighted to represent the preferences of the user of the method. Application to several buildings has shown that the rank of a building in a series does not change significantly when the weights given to the various criteria or the threshold levels for veto, preference or indifference are changed within a realistic range.

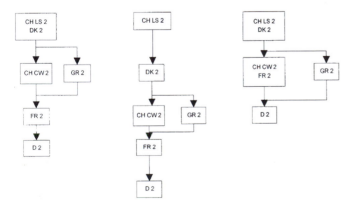

Figure 6.7 Most frequently encountered ranking lists of retrofitted buildings coming out of the sensitivity analysis to variations of threshold levels

The first method gives a calculated rating to any scenario and it has the advantage that the score is based on the most significant parameters. However, it allows for compensation of a poor rating according to one parameter by fair results on several other parameters. The second method does not allow this and does not allow a building showing too poor a value from one point of view to appear better than another building. This method requires the definition of weights, which allows the user to provide his own scale of values. Once this scale is set, the ranking is objectively obtained.

## REFERENCES

1   Roulet C-A, Flourentzos F, Santamouris M, *et al* (1999), *ORME – Office building rating methodology for Europe. OFFICE project report*, University of Athens.

2   Suter P, Frischknecht R, *et al*, (1996), *Oekoinventare für Energiesysteme*, Zurich.

3   Fanger PO, Melikov AK, Hansawa H, Ring J, Air turbulence and the sensation of draught, *Energy and Buildings*, **12**, 1988, 21–39.
or
Fanger PO, (1982), *Thermal Comfort*, Florida, USA, RE Krieger.

# Part II

# — Case Studies —

# Climatic Area 1 – Northern Europe

## — Introduction —

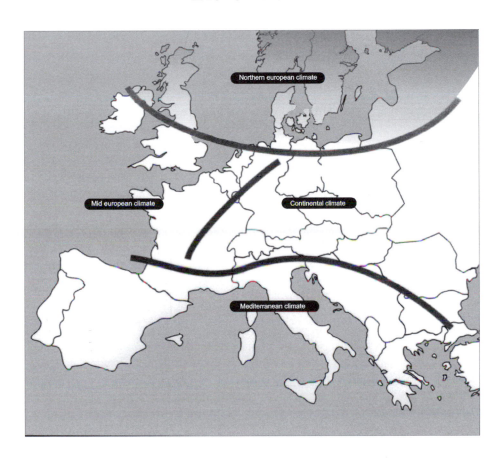

The zones included in the north European fringe are subject to the influence of air masses from the north, typically a relatively moderate Nordic climate, of the fresh coastal type. It is a somewhat wet climate with no dry season, particularly cold when the Baltic waters freeze, partially or totally. Summers are fresh and humid, without extremes of temperature. In spring, there are large diurnal temperature variations with rapid fluctuations. Autumn is long and mild, and has, with winter, the highest cloud cover and frequency of fog. Winds (south and south-west prevailing) reach high speeds especially in the west of the area. Humidity is relatively high, with considerable seasonal variation, while the cloud cover is considerable throughout the year.

The heating season runs from the beginning of autumn until the end of the spring. Average daily sunshine varies from 1–2 hours in winter to approximately eight hours in summer.

# Danfoss Headquarters, Nordborg, Denmark

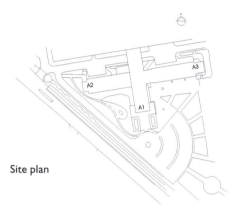

Site plan

Location: Nordborgvej, Nordborg
Owner: Private
Total size: 13,400 m²
Storeys: A1 12; A2 6
Year of construction: 1960–61
Degree of exposure: Exposed
Module: Cellular
Working hours: 08.00–17.00, Monday–Friday
Total energy consumption (1996): 256 kWh/m²
User system control: Mainly local
Heating system: Induction units heated by water
    from the central boiler system with district
    heating as source
Cooling system: Central refrigerant chillers cooling
    ventilation air
Lighting system: General – mainly standard
    fluorescent tubes with electromagnetic ballasts;
    Task lighting – mainly compact fluorescent tubes

The Danfoss Headquarters building is a high rise building complex situated in Nordborg on the island of Als in South Denmark. Nordborg is the home of Danfoss Inc., a worldwide company developing and producing a variety of components for heating, ventilation and lighting. The building complex consists of three parts: buildings A1 and A2 constructed in 1960–61 and building A3 constructed in 1991. It is only the oldest buildings, A1 and A2, which were considered in the OFFICE project. The complex is constructed around the tallest of the buildings, A1, which has main façades facing east and west. Buildings A2 and A3 are situated as perpendicular wings to the A1 main façades (see the Site Plan). The building is freestanding and situated in a low-density traffic area just outside Nordborg. Around 1000 people are working in buildings A1 and A2 during the normal office working period (08.00–17.00).

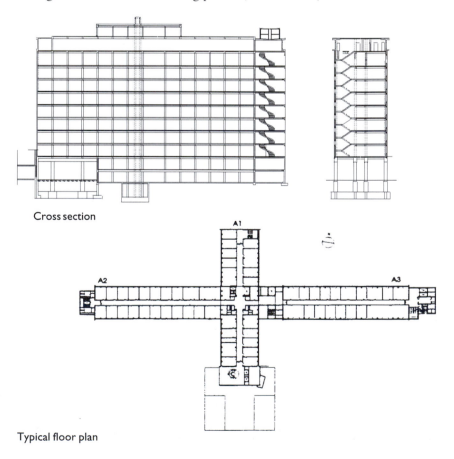

Cross section

Typical floor plan

View of the complex

# BUILDING CHARACTERISTICS

## Architectural description

Since the Danfoss Headquarters buildings date from the early 1960s, the exterior building structures are in general outdated in terms of insulation characteristics and airtightness. This is especially valid for the opaque structures such as the wall and the roof. The standard of insulation for the external wall was poor even compared to standards in force when the building was constructed in the early 1960s. Today the concrete elements in the external wall have decayed as a result of chemical processes in the concrete and they need to be changed. The external walls of A1 and A2 are different. In A1, the wall is almost massive concrete, while the external walls of A2 are made of low-density concrete with a thin concrete shield on the outside. In both cases there is a layer of plaster on the inside. In A1, a layer of cork is the only insulation, while an air cavity provides the insulation in the external walls of A2. Not surprisingly, the insulation values are poor in both cases (U 1.38/1.33 W/m²K, respectively) compared to the modern standard (U 0.3 W/m²K).

The windows are double-glazed (U 3.0 W/m²K) in timber frames. The windows are generally in fair condition in terms of the materials, but the connection between the frames and the surrounding wall is very leaky. In addition, the windows cannot be opened, which is considered unacceptable by the occupants.

The partition walls and the internal floor are classic in their make up, although today gypsum boards are mostly used instead of timber in partition walls. It is also rare for gypsum boards to be placed directly on the concrete element in the floor. Today suspended ceilings are often used. The roofs are flat and similar in construction to the internal floors, but with a thin layer of cork and plaster on the outside. The insulation levels are similar to those of the ground floor at around (U) 1.1 W/m²K.

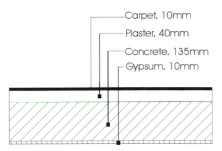

Floor detail

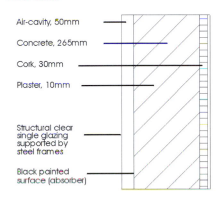

Wall detail – mass wall, building A1

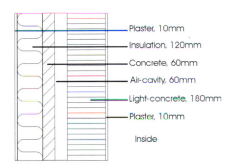

Wall detail – insulated internal wall, building A2

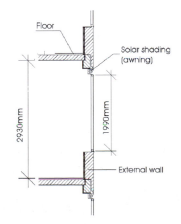

Vertical section – façade, building A1

| Material | Conductivity (W/m °C) | Density (kg/m³) | Specific heat (J/kg °C) | Solar assortment | Thickness (m) | U value (W/m² °C) |
|---|---|---|---|---|---|---|
| Characteristics of external wall, A1 | | | | | | |
| Plaster | 0.75 | 1700 | 800 | – | 0.01 | – |
| Cork | 0.08 | 500 | 2010 | – | 0.03 | – |
| Concrete | 1.6 | 2300 | 800 | – | 0.265 | – |
| TOTAL | – | – | – | – | 0.305 | 1.38 |
| Characteristics of external wall, A2 | | | | | | |
| Plaster | 0.75 | 1700 | 800 | – | 0.01 | – |
| Low-density concrete | 0.5 | 1400 | 1000 | – | 0.18 | – |
| Air cavity | – | – | – | – | 0.06 | 5.9 |
| Concrete | 1.6 | 2300 | 800 | – | 0.06 | – |
| TOTAL | – | – | – | – | 0.31 | 1.33 |
| Characteristics of partition wall | | | | | | |
| Insulation | 0.045 | 100 | 840 | – | 0.045 | – |
| Wood | 0.15 | 600 | 2500 | – | 0.013 | – |
| TOTAL | – | – | – | – | 0.058 | 0.7 |
| Characteristics of internal floor | | | | | | |
| Carpet | 0.1 | 500 | 1000 | – | 0.01 | – |
| Plaster | 1.1 | 2000 | 840 | – | 0.04 | – |
| Concrete | 1.6 | 2300 | 800 | – | 0.135 | – |
| Gypsum | 0.17 | 800 | 1006 | – | 0.01 | – |
| TOTAL | – | – | – | – | 0.195 | 1.85 |

## System characteristics

*HEATING PLANT*
System type: Central boiler heated by district heating
Units: 1
Nominal heating power (kW): 1200
Heated floor area (m²): 13,400
Distribution system: Induction units (700)
Hours of operation (h/year): 5000
Set-point temperature: 22°C
Maintenance state: Fair

*COOLING PLANT*
System type: Refrigerant chillers cooling the ventilation air
Units: 2
Nominal heating power (kW): 600
Heated floor area (m²): 7000
Distribution system: Ventilation system
Hours of operation (h/year): 2400
Set-point temperature: Supply air temperature 10–14°C
Maintenance state: Fair

*LIGHTING*
Fluorescent lamps: 4 per office
Incandescent lamps: 0–2 per office
Hours of operation (h/day): Office area: 0–9
    Common area: approx. 14
Maintenance state: Fair

*VENTILATION PLANT*
System type: Balanced CAV
Units: 6
Supply air flow rate [m³/s]: 5.2–6.2
Return air flow rate [m³/s]: 2.8–7.4
Supply air fan (kW): 3.2–4.0
Return air fan (kW): 1.5–4.3

*ELECTRICAL EQUIPMENT*
Computers (units): 1000
Hours of Operation (h/day): 8
Printer (units): 400
Hours of Operation (h/day): 10

## MECHANICAL AND ELECTRICAL EQUIPMENT

### Systems description

In Danfoss Headquarters, **heating** is provided by induction units situated along the perimeter of the building. The induction units are connected to the ventilation system so that ventilation air is supplied through the units. The room set-point of 22°C is regulated by occupant-controlled thermostats. There are no automatic reductions of heating temperature outside normal working hours. The induction units are essentially in fair condition, but the parts connected to the ventilation system (pressure regulators, etc.) need to be replaced. The two-pipe distribution system is fairly well insulated, but because the pipes are running along the poorly insulated façade, heat loss is substantial. Hot water for the heating system and the domestic hot water system comes from the district heating network.

**Cooling and ventilation** are combined in one mechanical system. This means that there is no localized cooling in the building only cooling of ventilation air in the central air handling units (AHUs). There are six AHUs in A1 and A2: one supply unit for each of the main façades in A1; one extract unit for the ten lowest floors of A1; one extract unit for the two top floors of A1 (roof A2); one supply unit for A2; and one extract unit for A2. There are separate cooling machines for A1 and A2 situated in the basements of the respective buildings. There are no heat recovery units.

Ventilation air is re-circulated outside working periods during winter. The ventilation air is taken in at ground level and, if necessary, pre-heated or cooled in the central AHUs. The air is transported through vertical ducts to the induction units along the perimeter of the building. The air is brought from the perimeter to the central corridor through door grilles, and further into the buildings through vertical ducts in an installation shaft in the gable end of A2 or in the middle zone of A1. Some air is also extracted from the toilets. The air-change rate in the perimeter rooms is approximately 2 h⁻¹ during the day and is slightly reduced during winter nights when air is also re-circulated. The ventilation air is usually cooled when the ambient temperature exceeds 14–15°C, but this varies as the system is manually controlled by the service staff.

**General lighting** is by standard fluorescent tubes controlled by the occupants. **Task lighting** is by compact fluorescent tubes, also controlled by the occupants. General lighting in common areas is usually turned on in the morning by the service staff and off at night by the security officers. In terms of **electrical/ computer equipment**, almost all occupants in the building have their own PC and there are four printers per ten people and one photocopier per 20 people.

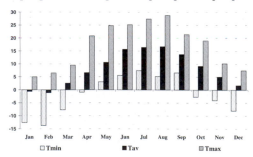

Monthly external temperatures °C

## BUILDING'S ENERGY PERFORMANCE

## General profile of energy use

Energy consumption for heating is very high in the Danfoss building compared to buildings built to modern standards. There are three reasons for this: the poor insulation of the building structures, the high infiltration rate arising from the leaky windows, and the fact that no heat recovery is included in the ventilation plant. The influence of the leaky windows is intensified by the fact that the Danfoss building is tall and exposed to the wind. Consequently, the energy demand for heating is more dependent on the local wind conditions than on the ambient temperature.

Mechanical cooling is not normally used in Danish office buildings, on account of the moderate climatic conditions in Denmark and also local tradition. For example, mechanical cooling is used more frequently in Sweden and Norway than in Denmark, although the climatic conditions are similar. Since the ventilation ducts are poorly insulated, the ventilation air needs to be cooled to 10–14°C to allow for the subsequent temperature rise.

Energy consumption for mechanical ventilation is normal for such an office building mainly thanks to the deliberately low air change rate (2 h⁻¹). It is not unusual for modern office buildings to be designed with air change rates of 2–3 h⁻¹. Still, the fan systems in the building are old and inefficient.

Energy consumption for lighting is normal for such a building. Even though the lighting system is a traditional, manually controlled system, the occupants do turn off the lighting quite often. The main reasons for this are the relatively large window area and the fact that the occupants are aware of the connection between room temperature and the lighting system.

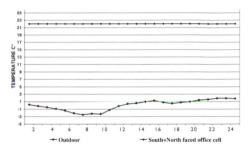

Air temperatures – Winter (12 January 1997)

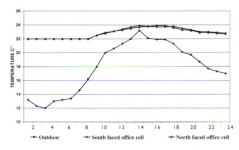

Air temperatures – Summer (19 July 1997)

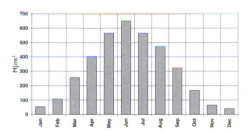

Global solar radiation – monthly average

Annual energy consumption breakdown by fuel type (1996)

| Energy | kWh/year | |
|---|---|---|
| District heating | 2,205,048 | for space heating and domestic hot water |
| Electricity | 1,231,410 | for other uses |
| TOTAL | 3,436,458 | |
| Average energy consumption per month | 286,372 | kWh |
| Average energy consumption per m² | 256 | kWh/year |

Distribution of energy consumption (1996)

| Energy | kWh/year | kWh/m²year |
|---|---|---|
| Space heating and domestic hot water | 2,205,048 | 165 |
| Ventilation (simulated) | 268,000 | 20 |
| Space cooling (simulated) | 53,600 | 4 |
| Lighting (simulated) | 227,800 | 17 |
| Equipment (simulated) | 294,800 | 22 |
| Other, pumps, lifts, etc. (estimated) | 387,210 | 28 |
| TOTAL | 3,436,458 | 256 |

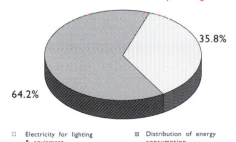

Annual energy consumption by fuel type

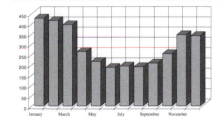

Total monthly energy consumption (MWh)

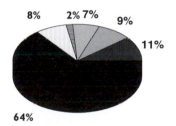

Distribution of energy consumption

# ENERGY RETROFITTING SCENARIOS

## Scenario 1 – Building improvements

### 1.1 INSTALLATION OF INTERPANE SUPER LOW-E WINDOWS

Replace the existing windows with normal double-glazing with Interpane super low-E windows. The low-E windows have a lower transmission coefficient (U value) and light/solar transmittance (t) than the existing windows. The key values for the super low-E window are:

Glass: U value 0.9 W/m$^2$K, t(light) = 0.76, t(solar) = 0.58
Frame: U value 1.6 W/m$^2$K.

Annual total energy consumption (kWh) – effect of replacement windows

|  | kWh/ year |
| --- | --- |
| Baseline | 4,427,360 |
| After window replacement | 3,833,606 |

### 1.2 IMPROVEMENT IN INSULATION OF ENVELOPE

The poorly insulated façade results in problems with heat loss and draughts. The façade is insulated with 120-mm mineral wool. This brings the U value down to 0.3 W/m$^2$K, the requirement in the Danish Building Regulation BR-95.

Annual total energy consumption (kWh) – effect of increased insulation of façade

|  | kWh/year |
| --- | --- |
| Baseline | 4,427,360 |
| After extra insulation | 3,950,320 |

### 1.3 USE OF HEAT RECOVERY OF VENTILATION AIR

The existing ventilation system does not include heat recovery. This means that all the ventilation air must be pre-heated from the ambient temperature to the required inlet temperature, a very energy consuming process. To reduce this demand, effective air–air heat recovery units are included in the ventilation plants (maximum temperature efficiency 80%). However, the extra pressure resistance induced will result in higher energy consumption for ventilation.

Annual total energy consumption (kWh) – effect of use of heat recovery

|  | kWh/ year |
| --- | --- |
| Baseline | 4,427,360 |
| With heat recovery | 3,643,326 |

## 1.4 REDUCTION OF VENTILATION RATE DURING WINTER

The ventilation rate in the office areas is currently 2 $h^{-1}$ summer and winter. This is higher than the recommended rate in terms of air quality (approximately 1.25 $h^{-1}$). Therefore there is potential for reducing the ventilation rate and thereby reducing the energy consumption for ventilation and space heating. This scenario modelled reducing the ventilation rate to 1.5 $h^{-1}$ during winter when the major proportion of savings on space heating can be achieved.

Annual total energy consumption (kWh) – effect of reducing the ventilation rate

|  | kWh/year |
| --- | --- |
| Baseline | 4,427,360 |
| After reducing ventilation rate | 4,082,310 |

## 1.5 SEAL LEAKY WINDOWS

The infiltration rate in the existing building is very high compared to a modern building, around 1.0 air change per hour. A reduction in the infiltration rate will result in substantial energy savings on space heating. This reduction can be achieved by sealing the existing leaky window frames. The infiltration rate is expected to be reduced to 0.25 $h^{-1}$, comparable to that in modern buildings. It should be noted that if the existing windows are replaced (Scenario 1.1, see above) the infiltration rate will be reduced, making additional sealing of window frames unnecessary in this case.

Annual total energy consumption (kWh) – effect of sealing leaky windows

|  | kWh/year |
| --- | --- |
| Baseline | 4,427,360 |
| After reducing infiltration | 3,520,046 |

## 1.6 REDUCTION IN HEATING SET-POINT DURING NIGHT AND WEEKENDS

The present heating set-point is 22°C (at all times). To reduce the energy consumption for space heating, the set-point is adjusted to 18°C during the night (18.00-7.00) and at weekends.

Annual total energy consumption (kWh) – effect of varying heating set-point

|  | kWh/year |
| --- | --- |
| Baseline | 4,427,360 |
| With heating set-point variation | 3,783,088 |

## Scenario 2 – Use of passive cooling techniques

## Scenario 2A

*2A.1 INSTALLATION OF MEDIUM-REFLECTIVE, LOW-E WINDOWS*

Replace the existing windows with normal double-glazing with medium-reflective, low-E windows. The low-E windows have a lower transmission coefficient (U value) and light/solar transmittance (t) than the existing windows. The key values for these windows are:

Glass: U value 1.5 W/m$^2$K, t(light) = 0.65, t(solar) = 0.46
Frame: U value 1.6 W/m$^2$K.

Annual total energy consumption (kWh) – effect of installation of medium- reflective windows

|  | kWh/ year |
|---|---|
| Baseline | 4,427,360 |
| After replacement windows | 4,100,936 |

*2A.2 REDUCTION OF VENTILATION RATE SUMMER AND WINTER*

The ventilation rate in the office areas is 2 h$^{-1}$, summer and winter. This is higher than the recommended rate in terms of air quality (approximately 1.25 h$^{-1}$). Therefore there is potential for reducing the ventilation rate and thereby reducing the energy consumption for ventilation, pre-heating and cooling of ventilation air. This scenario modelled reducing the ventilation rate to 1.5 h$^{-1}$ during summer and winter.

Annual total energy consumption (kWh) – effect of reducing the ventilation rate

|  | kWh/year |
|---|---|
| Baseline | 4,427,360 |
| After reducing ventilation rate | 3,994,674 |

*2A.3 USE OF EFFECTIVE SOLAR SHADING*

Excessive solar gains are causing both overheating and glare in the Danfoss building because the existing, old shading system is in poor condition. This scenario models the effect of installation of a modern BEMS-controlled external system (shading factor 0.2). This is considered an essential feature in office buildings with large window areas and no mechanical cooling. The solar shading is activated when solar radiation exceeds 125 W/m$^2$.

Annual total energy consumption (kWh) – effect of use of effective solar shading

|  | kWh/year |
|---|---|
| Baseline | 4,427,360 |
| With effective solar shading | 4,572,482 |

### 2A.4 USE OF EXPOSED THERMAL MASS

The concrete ceilings are exposed to reduce overheating in the office areas. The energy demand for cooling will not be influenced as there is no decentralized cooling in the building.

Annual total energy consumption (kWh) – effect of exposing thermal mass

|  | kWh/year |
|---|---|
| Baseline | 4,427,360 |
| After thermal mass exposed | 4,425,618 |

### 2A.5 USE OF NATURAL VENTILATION (VENTING) TO ASSIST MECHANICAL VENTILATION DURING SUMMER

In the existing building all ventilation is mechanical as none of the windows can be opened. This scenario models the effect of natural ventilation (venting) by opening windows. It is assumed that the windows will be manually opened by the occupants when the indoor temperature in the office cells exceeds 24°C.

Annual total energy consumption (kWh) – effect of additional, natural, ventilation

|  | kWh/year |
|---|---|
| Baseline | 4,427,360 |
| With natural ventilation | 4,436,472 |

## Scenario 2B

### 2B.1 INSTALLATION OF MEDIUM-REFLECTIVE, LOW-E WINDOWS

See Scenario 2A.1 above.

### 2B.2 DISCONTINUING USE OF MECHANICAL COOLING

Mechanical cooling is not often used in Danish office buildings as it is not considered necessary. This scenario investigated the effect of discontinuing use of mechanical cooling – the general temperature level in the building will rise.

Annual total energy consumption (kWh) – effect of *not* using mechanical cooling

|  | kWh/year |
|---|---|
| Baseline | 4,427,360 |
| Without mechanical cooling | 4,349,238 |

### 2B.3 USE OF EFFECTIVE SOLAR SHADING

See Scenario 2A.3 above.

### 2B.4 USE OF EXPOSED THERMAL MASS

See Scenario 2A.4 above.

### 2.5 USE OF NATURAL VENTILATION (VENTING) TO ASSIST MECHANICAL VENTILATION DURING SUMMER

See Scenario 2A.5 above.

## Scenario 3 – Electric lighting improvements

### Scenario 3A

*3A.1 USE OF DAYLIGHT SENSORS*

The energy consumption for artificial lighting can be reduced via an effective control. This scenario studies the use of daylight sensors to control the artificial lighting according to the daylight level in the office area (not corridors and other common areas).

Annual total energy consumption (kWh) effect of daylight sensor control of artificial lighting

|  | kWh/year |
| --- | --- |
| Baseline | 4,427,360 |
| With daylight sensors | 4,413,022 |

*3A.2 USE OF PRESENCE DETECTORS*

The energy consumption for artificial lighting can be reduced via an effective control. This scenario studies the use of presence detectors which switch off the artificial lighting in an office room when there have been no people in the room for 15 minutes.

Annual total energy consumption (kWh) effect of presence sensors for control of artificial lighting

|  | kWh/year |
| --- | --- |
| Baseline | 4,427,360 |
| With presence detectors | 4,424,010 |

*3A.3 INSTALLATION OF HIGH FREQUENCY (HF) BALLASTS*

The energy consumption for artificial lighting can also be reduced using high frequency (HF) ballasts instead of conventional electromagnetic ballasts. A saving of approximately 20% can be expected from this measure. This scenario studied the effect of installing such ballasts in office spaces and common areas.

Annual total energy consumption (kWh) effect of installing HF ballasts

|  | kWh/year |
| --- | --- |
| Baseline | 4,427,360 |
| With HF ballasts | 4,406,590 |

### Scenario 3B

*3B.1 USE OF DAYLIGHT SENSORS*
See Scenario 3A.1 above.

*3B.3 INSTALLATION OF HIGH FREQUENCY (HF) BALLASTS*
See Scenario 3A.3 above.

## Scenario 4 – HVAC system improvements

### 4.1 REDUCTION OF WINTER VENTILATION RATE

The ventilation rate in the office areas are 2 $h^{-1}$ summer and winter. This is higher than the recommended rate in terms of air quality (approximately 1.25 $h^{-1}$). Therefore there is potential for reducing energy consumption for ventilation and space heating by reducing the ventilation. This scenario models reduction of the ventilation rate to 1.5 $h^{-1}$ during the winter.

Annual total energy consumption (kWh) – effect of reducing winter ventilation rate

|  | kWh/year |
|---|---|
| Baseline | 4,427,360 |
| After ventilation rate reduction | 4,082,310 |

### 4.2 INSTALLATION OF MORE EFFICIENT FANS

The efficiency of the old fan systems (motor, fan, and fan drive) is as low as 50%. Replacement with modern fan systems will greatly reduce the energy consumption for ventilation. This scenario models replacement with modern systems with an efficiency of 75%.

Annual total energy consumption (kWh) – effect of more efficient fans

|  | kWh/year |
|---|---|
| Baseline | 4,427,360 |
| With more efficient fans | 4,297,112 |

### 4.3 USE OF PURE NATURAL VENTILATION (VENTING) DURING SUMMER

In the existing building all ventilation is mechanically provided as no windows are opening. This scenario studied the effect of using only natural ventilation during summer (i.e. no mechanical ventilation, only venting by opening windows).

Annual total energy consumption (kWh) – effect of use of venting only in summer

|  | kWh/year |
|---|---|
| Baseline | 4,427,360 |
| With only venting in summer | 4,286,124 |

### 4.4 USE OF NIGHT VENTILATION

In the existing building the ventilation system is operating for many hours every day including weekends. This scenario combines reduced running time for the ventilation system with a night-cooling control mode. The ventilation system is altered to run from 07.00 until 18.00 on working days (Monday to Friday) instead of 04.00–21.00 (although this can change from day to day, as determined by the service staff). The night ventilation control mode starts the system according to pre-set outside and indoor temperatures.

Annual total energy consumption (kWh) – effect of use of night ventilation

|  | kWh/year |
|---|---|
| Baseline | 4,427,360 |
| With night ventilation | 3,315,562 |

## Summaries

### SCENARIO 1 – BUILDINGS IMPROVEMENTS

**TOTAL VALUES**

Estimated energy savings: 3,044,480 kWh
Required capital cost: 1,795,600 ECU
Cost per unit of energy: 0.053 /.107 ECU/kWh
Financial gain per year: 168,840 ECU
Payback period: 10.7 years

### SCENARIO 2A – USE OF PASSIVE COOLING TECHNIQUES

**TOTAL VALUES**

Estimated energy savings: 777,200 kWh
Required capital cost: 1,335,980 ECU
Cost per unit of energy: 0.053 / .107 ECU/kWh
Financial gain per year: 70,380 ECU
Payback period: 19 years

### SCENARIO 2B – USE OF PASSIVE COOLING TECHNIQUES

**TOTAL VALUES**

Estimated energy savings: 400,660 kWh
Required capital cost: 1,393,600 ECU
Cost per unit of energy: 0.053 /.107 ECU/kWh
Financial gain per year: 48,450 ECU
Payback period: 28.8 years

### SCENARIO 3A – ELECTRIC LIGHTING IMPROVEMENTS

**TOTAL VALUES**

Estimated energy savings: 30,820 kWh
Required capital cost: 255,940 ECU
Cost per unit of energy: 0.053 /.107 ECU/kWh
Financial gain per year: 9,568 ECU
Payback period: 26.8 years

### SCENARIO 3B – ELECTRIC LIGHTING IMPROVEMENTS

**TOTAL VALUES**

Estimated energy savings: 30,820 kWh
Required capital cost: 209,040 ECU
Cost per unit of energy: 0.053 /.107 ECU/kWh
Financial gain per year: 9,568 ECU
Payback period: 21.8 years

## EVALUATION

Each scenario was evaluated with regard to energy , capital costs, financial and payback period.

It should be noted that an extra 12.5% is added to the calculated capital costs to cover consultancy fees. This is valid for all the calculated capital costs for the individual measures, the scenarios and the package.

## Scenario 1 – Building improvements

Measures resulting in a reduction in the energy consumption for space heating were examined:

- installation of Interpane super low-E windows;
- improvement in insulation of envelope;
- use of heat recovery of ventilation air;
- reduction of ventilation rate during winter;
- seal leaky windows;
- reduction in heating set-point during night and weekends.

The capital cost of scenario 1 is high due to the replacement of windows (35% of costs) and insulation of the envelope (32% of costs). The costs of reducing the infiltration rate are included in these two measures. There are no (or very small) extra costs resulting from reducing the ventilation rate and the heating set-point as these measures can be quickly completed by the service staff. Adding heat recovery to the ventilation system is also an expensive measure (20% of costs) as major changes need to be made to the ducting system. However the benefits of this scenario are also very high as 168,840 ECU would be saved each year on the energy bill (mainly for space heating and pre-heating of ventilation air). This results in a simple payback period of 10.7 years.

## Scenario 2 – Use of passive cooling techniques

In scenarios 2A and 2B, passive cooling measures are examined. Scenario 2A is the 'active' cooling scenario which involves mechanical cooling:

- installation of medium-reflective, low-E windows;
- reduction of ventilation rate summer and winter;
- use of effective solar shading;
- use of exposed thermal mass;
- use of natural ventilation (venting) to assist mechanical ventilation during summer.

Scenario 2B is the 'passive' cooling scenario, involving no mechanical cooling measures:

- installation of medium-reflective, low-E windows;
- no use of mechanical cooling;
- use of effective solar shading;
- use of exposed thermal mass;
- use of natural ventilation (venting) to assist mechanical ventilation during summer;

The important difference between scenarios 2A and 2B is that mechanical cooling is not included in the passive scenario. The ventilation rate is kept high to compensate for the lack of mechanical cooling.

The most expensive measure in scenarios 2A and 2B is the replacement of the existing non-opening windows with opening ones. The extra cost of using medium-reflective, low-E glazing instead of normal double-glazing is small. In total, the window solution accounts for 54% of the total costs of scenarios 2A and 2B, while solar shading accounts for 31%. Exposing the thermal mass in the ceiling accounts for approximately 4% of the costs.

The largest energy savings are obtained in scenario 2A (46,900 ECU/year vs. 24,120 ECU/year for 2B). The savings are mainly due to savings on space heating, arising from the low-E windows. The simple payback periods are 19 years for 2A and 28.8 years for 2B. These figures include savings for maintenance of the solar shading and the cooling plant (2A) and savings in the cost of window cleaning (the opening windows can be cleaned from inside).

## Scenario 3 – Electric lighting improvements

Scenarios 3A and 3B examine measures which affect the artificial lighting system. Scenario 3A includes the following measures:
- use of daylight sensors;
- use of presence detectors;
- installation of high frequency (HF) ballasts.

Scenario 3B combines two of the three measures from scenario 3A:
- use of daylight sensors;
- installation of high frequency (HF) ballasts.

The most expensive of the three measures examined in this scenario is introduction of automatic control via daylight sensors (only considered in office areas). In scenario 3A this measure accounts for 51% of the costs, while presence detector controls account for 16% and installation of HF-ballasts for 22% of the costs.

The total energy savings achieved in scenario 3A or 3B are not high. One of the reasons for this is that the saving potential is limited because the occupants already do turn off the lighting when they leave the offices and when there is sufficient daylight. Another reason is that reduced consumption of electricity for lighting results in an increase in the energy demand for space heating. Thus the simple payback periods are 35.8 years and 31.1 years for scenarios 2A and 2B, respectively. These figures include the savings obtained from the increased life of fluorescent tubes when they are used with HF-ballasts.

*SCENARIO 4 – HVAC SYSTEM IMPROVEMENTS*

TOTAL VALUES

Estimated energy savings: 1,569,140 kWh
Required capital cost: 639,180 ECU
Cost per unit of energy: 0.053/.107 ECU/kWh
Financial gain per year: 103,247 ECU
Payback period: 6.2 years

*PACKAGE P1*

TOTAL VALUES

Estimated energy savings: 3,155,700 kWh
Required capital cost: 2,399,940 ECU
Cost per unit of energy: 0.053/.107 ECU/kWh
Financial gain per year: 208,800 ECU
Payback period: 11.5 years

## Scenario 4 – HVAC system improvements

This scenario examines measures which influence the mechanical ventilation system:
* reduction of winter ventilation rate;
* installation of more efficient fans;
* use of pure natural ventilation (venting) during summer;
* use of night ventilation.

By combining a modern, effective fan system, a reduced ventilation system running period and natural ventilation during summer, the energy demand for ventilation is minimized. The energy demand for mechanical cooling is also reduced.

Again, the highest costs are incurred by the replacement of the existing non-opening windows with opening ones (85% of the total scenario cost). Installation of new, high efficiency fan systems only accounts for 3.5% of the cost, while a new control system for night ventilation accounts for just 0.5%. No costs are incurred by reducing ventilation rates. The resulting simple payback period is 6.9 years – a very profitable result. This includes savings for window cleaning (the opening windows can be cleaned from inside).

## Package 1

Package P1 includes the most promising combination of measures from the four scenarios:
* installation of Interpane super low-E windows;
* improvement in insulation of envelope;
* use of heat recovery of ventilation air;
* reduction of ventilation rate during summer and winter;
* improve fan efficiency in ventilation system;
* no use of mechanical cooling;
* use of effective solar shading;
* use of natural ventilation (venting) to assist mechanical ventilation during summer;
* automatic control of artificial lighting via daylight sensors;
* seal leaky windows (reduce infiltration rate);
* use of night ventilation;
* reduction in heating set-point during night and weekends.

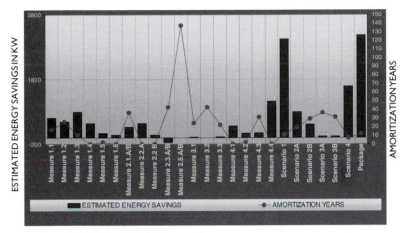

Estimated energy gains and payback periods

Installation of opening, super low-E windows accounts for 26% of the cost of this package, insulation of the envelope 24%, new ventilation plants 15% (with heat recovery, new effective fan system, new night ventilation mode and reduced ventilation rates), solar shading 18%, daylight control of lighting 5% and set back of heating set-point 0.05%.

In total, savings in energy consumption of 3,155,700 kWh, worth 180,900 ECU, can be made each year. As a result, the simple payback period for the package would be 11.7 years. This includes savings for maintenance of the solar shading and the cooling plant and savings for window cleaning (the opening windows can be cleaned from inside). The effect of the increased life of fluorescent tubes when used with HF-ballasts has also been taken into account.

# Sentralbygg 1, NTNU, Trondheim, Norway

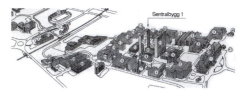

**Site plan**

Location: Alfred Getz vei 3
Owner: NTNU
Total size: 6500 m$^2$
Storeys: 13 + basement
Year of construction: 1961
Degree of exposure: Freestanding
Module: Cellular
Working hours: 08.00–17.00
Total energy consumption (1997): 290 kW/m$^2$
User system control: Central
Heating system: Central wet
Cooling system: None
Lighting system: Fluorescent tubes, electro-magnetic ballasts, incandescent

Sentralbygg 1 is situated on the campus of the Norwegian University of Science and Technology (NTNU). The first NTNU buildings were built for the opening of the University in 1910. After World War II, the University expanded and between 1958 and 1963 additional buildings with a total area of 15,000 m$^2$ were built. Sentralbygg 1 was finished in 1961.

The building has 13 floors above ground and one level below ground. The first two floors have shops and education rooms, and floors three to 13 have offices for the scientific staff and students. Storerooms and technical rooms are situated in the basement. The area of each floor is 460 m$^2$ and the total area including the basement is 6500 m$^2$.

View of the complex

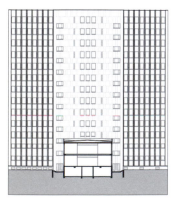

Sentralbygg 1, Trondheim
North elevation (1:400)

North elevation

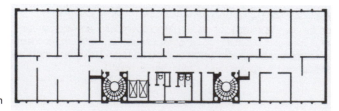

Typical floor plan

# BUILDING CHARACTERISTICS

## Architectural description

Sentralbygg 1 is one of two 13-storey buildings that are part of a large building complex (with a total floor area of 22,000 m²) on the NTNU campus in Trondheim. The whole building complex is north–south oriented with a corridor running through several freestanding buildings. Each building is east–west oriented. Sentralbygg 1 has large window façades facing north and south, and small gable façades facing east and west. The building has a concrete pillar-floor construction. The pillars are extruded on the north and south façades giving a vertical character to the building. This is further emphasized by the exterior colours: the pillars are painted grey while the prefabricated concrete walls under the windows are painted blue. There is one window between each pair of pillars on each floor. The double-glazed windows have wooden frames.

The building is not very well insulated according to the new Norwegian standard. The gable walls are insulated with 150mm Siporex and have a U value of 0.65 W/m²K. (The new requirement is 0.22 W/m²K.) North and south façades are insulated with mineral wool, 100mm under the windows and 25mm on the pillars. The middle U value for the wall is 0.50 W/m²K. The roof is insulated with 100mm mineral wool and 20mm mat and has a U value of 0.24 W/m²K. (The new requirement is 0.15 W/m²K.)

The first two floors of Sentralbygg 1 have shops and education rooms and floors three to thirteen have offices for the scientific staff and students. Storerooms and technical rooms are situated in the basement. Floors three to thirteen have a flexible floor plan and can be occupied by one or two institutes. A corridor zone with toilets, two lifts, and two stairways, is situated in the centre on the north side. Offices are located on each side of the corridor zone, on the north side and along a second inner corridor on the south side. The offices are cellular with insulated walls of gypsum board. The walls between the offices can easily be taken down and rebuilt between any two adjacent windows to increase or decrease the size of the offices. The window apertures are 1.54m high and 0.84m wide and give sufficient daylight to the offices. Windows over the doors allow daylight to reach the inner corridor. The windows are openable allowing for natural ventilation in addition to the mechanical ventilation. Since the building has no cooling system this extra ventilation is important on hot days. Shading is provided by internal venetian blinds on the south-facing windows. On hot days, the blinds are pulled down to prevent both overheating and glare problems. This results in reduced daylight and the electric lights are often used for the whole working day.

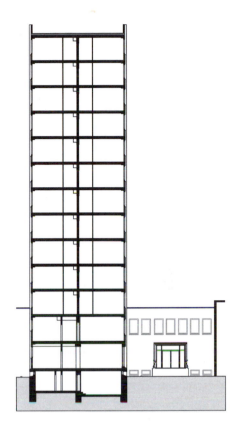

Vertical section

Characteristics of windows

| Material | Conductivity (W/m °C) | Density (kg/m³) | Specific heat (J/kg °C) | Solar assortment | Thickness (m) | U value (W/m² °C) |
|---|---|---|---|---|---|---|
| Glass | 0.8 | 2600 | – | – | 0.004 | – |
| Wood | 0.12 | 500 | 1400 | – | 0.08 | – |
| TOTAL | – | – | – | – | – | 2.8 |

Characteristics of external walls – east & west

| Material | Conductivity (W/m °C) | Density (kg/m³) | Specific heat (J/kg °C) | Solar assortment | Thickness (m) | U value (W/m² °C) |
|---|---|---|---|---|---|---|
| Siporex | 0.13 | 400 | 960 | – | 0.15 | – |
| Concrete | 1.7 | 2300 | 950 | – | 0.2 | – |
| TOTAL | – | – | – | – | – | 0.65 |

Characteristics of external walls – north & south

| Material | Conductivity (W/m °C) | Density (kg/m³) | Specific heat (J/kg °C) | Solar assortment | Thickness (m) | U value (W/m² °C) |
|---|---|---|---|---|---|---|
| Reinforced plaster | 1.2 | 2000 | – | – | – | – |
| Insulation | 0.04 | – | 760 | – | 0.1 | – |
| Gipsonit | – | – | – | – | 0.013 | – |
| TOTAL | – | – | – | – | – | 0.50 |

## System characteristics

### HEATING PLANT
System type: Central wet
Units: 1
Nominal heating power (kW/m$^2$): 0.15
Heated floor area (m$^2$): 6400
Distribution system: Radiators
Hours of operation: 2600
Set-point temperature (°C): 22
Maintenance state: Good

### VENTILATION PLANT
System type: Mechanical
Units: 3
Supply air flow rate (m$^3$/s): 7.9
Return air flow rate (m$^3$/s): 4.9
Supply air fan (kW): 36
Return air fan (kW): 36
Hours of operation: 06.00–18.00

### ELECTRICAL EQUIPMENT
Computers (unit): 125W
Hours of operation (h/day): 8
Printer (unit): 300W
Hours of operation (h/day): 8

### LIGHTING
Fluorescent lamps: 35W
Incandescent lamps: 60W
Hours of operation (h/day): 06.00–18.00
Maintenance state: Old

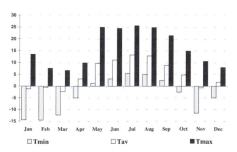

Monthly external temperatures °C

# MECHANICAL AND ELECTRICAL EQUIPMENT

## Systems description

**District heating** is used for heating of spaces, ventilation air and domestic hot water. The central **heating system** is located in the basement and the heat is distributed through pipes to radiators in the offices. One manually regulated radiator is placed under each window. The radiators do not have decentralized temperature control (i.e. thermostatic valves). The forward water temperature is centrally controlled according to the ambient temperature. There are two shunts: one for radiators in the basement and floors one to seven and one for radiators in floors eight to thirteen. In the summer, the system is turned off when the ambient temperature is higher than 15°C.

Sentralbygg 1 has a central mechanical **ventilation system** with a coil loop air-to-air heat recovery system on the main air handling unit (AHU). The maximum heat effectiveness is about 50%. The supply air is after-heated by district heating to reach a temperature of 15°C. Three AHUs are used. The main AHU is located on floor 2, on the roof of the building entrance. This unit handles supply and exhaust air for floors three to thirteen. Two smaller supply air units service the first and second floors and the basement, and the exhaust air from these floors is expelled via a fan on the second floor. Exhaust air from the toilets is extracted via a fan on the roof. The individual offices receive supply air through grills over the door and exhaust air is taken out to the corridor via an air gap under the door. Measurements show an air exchange rate of 3.5 ACH. Approximately one-third of the supply air comes from leakage through the windows. This is due to poor window sealing and air pressure which is high on such a tall building.

Sentralbygg 1 does not have a **cooling system**. Overheating is not usually a significant problem so far north. However, in this building the south-facing offices often overheat in summer.

The **electrical network** consists of delivery conduits running in an under-floor channel in the basement and through the central shaft to distribution boxes on each floor. Most wires are hidden in walls and ceilings, and in the offices wires are led through channels under the windows. This is a flexible solution that makes it easy to make alterations if the size of an office is changed.

For electric lighting, standard 35-watt fluorescent tubes with electromagnetic ballasts are used. Attached luminaires in the ceiling are placed in rows with one lamp for every window. The luminaires have diffusing plastic covers. Wall switches are placed both locally and centrally on each side of the inner corridor. In addition to the ceiling lights, task lighting is provided on every desk. The illumination level is quite low. The offices and corridor have a light level of 150 lux at desk level. A light level of 500 lux is achieved on the desktop directly beneath the 60-watt task lamp. On the floor of the central corridor, the light level is only 20 lux.

# BUILDING'S ENERGY PERFORMANCE

## General profile of energy use

Air temperatures shown in the graphs for a winter day and a summer day are measured temperatures for 1997. The global radiation figures are data from 1971, a typical year.

Electricity is used for lighting, equipment, ventilation fans, and for two elevators. The data for monthly electricity use shown in the graph are from 1990. The total electricity use in 1997 was 15% higher than for 1990 (monthly data for 1997 is not available), however the variation between the highest and lowest monthly electricity consumption is 35%. This can be explained by the decreased use of lighting during the summer season and less use of equipment during the students' long summer vacation.

District heating is used for heating of space, ventilation air and hot water. The monthly data shown in the graph are from 1997. The centrally controlled system for space heating is usually turned off in summer, but the ventilation air might be heated in the summer. Ventilation air is preheated first by an air-to-air heat exchanger and then by district heat if necessary. When ambient temperatures are higher than 15°C, the ventilation air is not heated. On days with high solar radiation giving rise to problems with daytime overheating, the preheating set-point is lowered to 13°C.

Annual energy consumption breakdown by fuel type

| Energy | kWh/year | |
|---|---|---|
| District heat consumption | 981,760 | for space heating |
| Electrical consumption | 768,000 | for other uses |
| TOTAL | 1,749,760 | |
| Average energy consumption per month | 145,813 | kWh |
| Average energy consumption per m² | 273 | kWh/year |

Distribution of energy consumption

| Energy | kWh/year | kWh/m²year |
|---|---|---|
| Space heating | 981,760 | 153 |
| Space cooling | 0 | 0 |
| Lighting | 307,200 | 48 |
| Equipment | 460,800 | 72 |
| TOTAL | 1,749,760 | 273 |

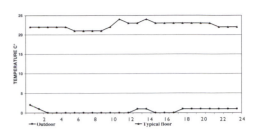

Air temperatures – Winter (6 November 1997)

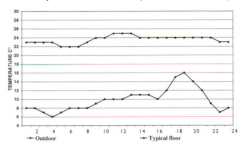

Air temperatures – Summer (8 August 1997)

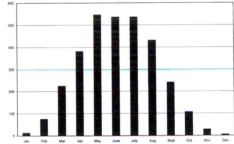

Global solar radiation – monthly averages MJ/m²

56.1%          43.9%

■ For other use kWh    ■ For space heating kWh

Annual energy consumption by fuel type

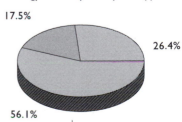

17.5%          26.4%

56.1%

■ Space Heating    ■ Lighting    ■ Equipment

Distribution of energy consumption

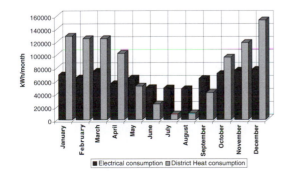

Total monthly energy consumption

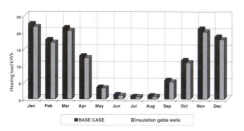

Effect of improved insulation of gable walls

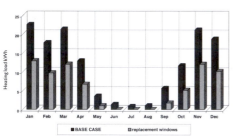

Effect of replacement windows

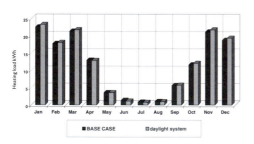

Effect of daylighting system

# ENERGY RETROFITTING SCENARIOS

## Scenario 1 – Building improvements

### 1.1 IMPROVED INSULATION ON EAST AND WEST GABLE WALLS

The gable walls are poorly insulated and temperatures in the offices located at the gables are too low on cold winter days. Increase insulation by addition of 100-mm mineral wool on the inside of the gable walls. This will improve the U value from 0.65 $W/m^2K$ to 0.3 $W/m^2K$. Energy consumption for heating will be reduced by 7 $kWh/m^2$.

Monthly total energy consumption ($kWh/m^2$) – effect of increased insulation of gable walls

|  | Jan | Feb | Mar | Apr | May | Jun | Jul | Aug | Sep | Oct | Nov | Dec |
|---|---|---|---|---|---|---|---|---|---|---|---|---|
| Baseline | 22.5 | 17.7 | 21.3 | 12.9 | 3.5 | 1.3 | 0.8 | 1.0 | 5.6 | 11.6 | 21.1 | 18.7 |
| After extra insulation | 21.6 | 16.9 | 20.4 | 12.3 | 3.3 | 1.1 | 0.7 | 0.8 | 5.1 | 10.9 | 20.2 | 17.9 |

### 1.2 REPLACEMENT OF WINDOWS

Replace the existing double-glazed windows with U value 2.8 $W/m^2K$ and TSET (total solar energy transmittance) of 0.75. On the south façade, triple-glazed windows with one LE-coating (U value 1.6; TSET 0.53) will be used. Shading devices will then be located between the two outer layers of the glazing. On the north façade, double-glazing with one LE-coating and argon gas (U value 1.6; TSET 0.59) will be used. Infiltration will then be reduced by 0.5 ACH, reducing the cold draught from the windows and improving comfort in winter. This measure will reduce energy consumption for heating by 50 %.

Monthly total energy consumption ($kW/m^2$) – effect of replacement windows

|  | Jan | Feb | Mar | Apr | May | Jun | Jul | Aug | Sep | Oct | Nov | Dec |
|---|---|---|---|---|---|---|---|---|---|---|---|---|
| Baseline | 22.5 | 17.7 | 21.3 | 12.9 | 3.5 | 1.3 | 0.8 | 1.0 | 5.6 | 11.6 | 21.1 | 18.7 |
| After window replacement | 12.9 | 9.7 | 12.0 | 6.7 | 1.0 | 0 | 0 | 0 | 1.7 | 5.1 | 12.0 | 10.1 |

### 1.3 INTEGRATION OF PASSIVE SOLAR AND DAYLIGHTING COMPONENTS

A daylighting system for south-facing windows will be used to reduce the need for electric lighting and increase the use of passive solar heating. The system will also result in improved comfort because of reduced glare. The reduction in internal heating gains from electric lighting is larger than the gains from solar radiation, although this will result in a small increase in energy used for heating. Energy consumption for electric lighting is reduced by 6 $kWh/m^2$ and energy consumption for heating is increased by 3 $kWh/m^2$.

The daylighting system is a simple system of venetian blinds. Each window has two blinds. The upper part of the window, 40% of the total aperture, has slats with reflective surfaces. The lower part has slatted blinds with diffusing surfaces. Calculations using RADIANCE were carried out for two sets of conditions (by Barbara Matusiak, NTNU): (1) Diffuse sky when both blinds are pulled up (Picture 1); (2) A sunny day when the lower blind is closed and the upper blind is placed in a position that reflects the light to the ceiling (Picture 2). The two situations are compared to a conventional solution with one venetian blind covering the whole window (Pictures 1b and 2b). The illuminance data given on the photographs are given in candela per m². In both cases the daylight level in the offices is sufficient as long as the ambient level is over 13,000 lux. In Trondheim, this is approximately 1100 working hours per annum, or 40% of working hours. (Skartveit A & Olseth JA, [1988], Meteorological Report Series, number 7, Bergen.)

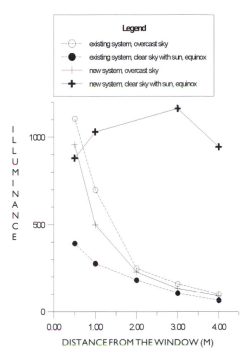

Illuminance on horizontal surface, 0.80 m above the floor. Calculations carried out using RADIANCE. (Barbara Matusiak, NTNU, 1998)

Picture 1: Diffuse sky; both blinds are pulled up. (Window with two blinds)

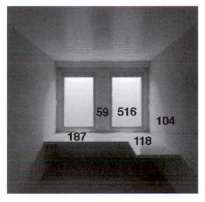

Picture 1b: Diffuse sky: blinds are pulled up. (Existing window)

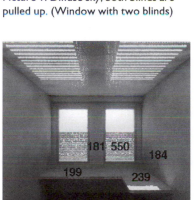

Picture 2: Sunny day; lower blinds are closed and upper blinds are positioned to reflect light to the ceiling

Picture 2b: Sunny day; lower blinds are closed. (Existing window)

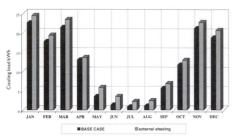

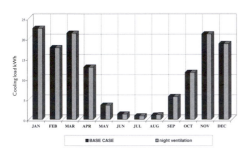

Effect of external shading devices

Effect of mechanical night ventilation

# Scenario 2 – Use of passive cooling techniques

The summers in Trondheim do not have many hot days and the need for cooling exists only for short periods. However, some high room temperatures have been recorded in Sentralbygg 1, so passive cooling techniques have been tested.

### 2.1 USE OF EXTERNAL SHADING DEVICES

Calculations show that the use of external shading devices will result in better temperatures for the warmest days, with a reduction of 2°C. External shading will reduce solar gain, and also resulted in a 14% increase in heating demand. Since the wind pressure factor is very large for this tall building, external blinds will be problematic and maintenance costs will be high.

If the windows are to be replaced, a triple-glazed window with blinds between the two outer glass sheets should be chosen. The shading provided will not be as good as external shading, but wind-related problems and maintenance costs will be smaller.

Monthly total energy load (kWh/m²) – effect of external shading devices

|  | Jan | Feb | Mar | Apr | May | Jun | Jul | Aug | Sep | Oct | Nov | Dec |
|---|---|---|---|---|---|---|---|---|---|---|---|---|
| Baseline | 22.5 | 17.7 | 21.3 | 12.9 | 3.5 | 1.3 | 0.8 | 1.0 | 5.6 | 11.6 | 21.1 | 18.7 |
| With shading devices | 24.4 | 19.3 | 23.4 | 13.5 | 5.8 | 3.5 | 2.2 | 2.4 | 6.8 | 12.8 | 22.7 | 20.6 |

### 2.2 USE OF MECHANICAL NIGHT VENTILATION

The use of night ventilation would result in reductions of 1-2°C in daytime temperatures. Night ventilation would only be used in warm periods and would thus not influence the heating demand. The only cost of this measure would be the cost of electricity for running the ventilation fans at night. Since Sentralbygg 1 has no cooling system the measure will not result in cost benefits, but the benefit of increased comfort will be important.

Monthly total energy load (kWh/m²) – effect of night ventilation

|  | Jan | Feb | Mar | Apr | May | Jun | Jul | Aug | Sep | Oct | Nov | Dec |
|---|---|---|---|---|---|---|---|---|---|---|---|---|
| Baseline | 22.5 | 17.7 | 21.3 | 12.9 | 3.5 | 1.3 | 0.8 | 1.0 | 5.6 | 11.6 | 21.1 | 18.7 |
| With night ventilation | 22.5 | 17.7 | 21.3 | 12.9 | 3.5 | 1.3 | 0.8 | 1.1 | 5.6 | 11.6 | 21.1 | 18.7 |

Night ventilation: indoor temperatures for the 'North' zone for five warm days in July

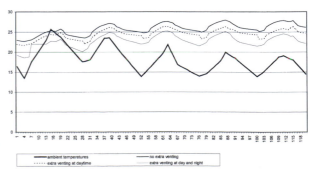

## Scenario 3 – Electric lighting improvements

### 3.1 USE OF DAYLIGHT COMPENSATION SYSTEM

Use of a daylight compensation system with dimming in the offices will reduce electricity consumption. Internal gains will also be reduced, although this will result in an increase in the energy demand for heating almost equal to the saving. Combining this scenario with building improvements that reduce the heat losses would be of greater interest. This measure should also be combined with new lighting features and ballasts because the 'on and off' systems that can be used with the existing luminaires with electronic ballasts are out of production. A dimming system for electromagnetic ballasts must therefore be used. These will also increase user comfort.

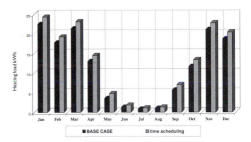

Effect of time scheduling

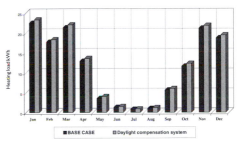

Effect of daylight compensation system

Monthly total energy load (kWh/m²) – effect of a daylight compensation scheme

|  | Jan | Feb | Mar | Apr | May | Jun | Jul | Aug | Sep | Oct | Nov | Dec |
|---|---|---|---|---|---|---|---|---|---|---|---|---|
| Baseline | 22.5 | 17.7 | 21.3 | 12.9 | 3.5 | 1.3 | 0.8 | 1.0 | 5.6 | 11.6 | 21.1 | 18.7 |
| With daylight compensation scheme | 23.3 | 18.3 | 22.0 | 13.6 | 4.0 | 1.5 | 0.9 | 1.2 | 6.0 | 12.3 | 21.8 | 19.4 |

### 3.2 USE OF TIME SCHEDULING

Time scheduling will be used for the whole floor. The savings would be largest for the corridor zone where electric lighting is usually on, both day and night. However the energy demand for heating would also increase in this scenario, as long as the building was not better insulated. Reduction in electricity consumption for lighting would be 20kWh/m², while the increase in heating demand would be 17kWh/m².

Monthly total energy load (kWh/m²) – effect of time scheduling

|  | Jan | Feb | Mar | Apr | May | Jun | Jul | Aug | Sep | Oct | Nov | Dec |
|---|---|---|---|---|---|---|---|---|---|---|---|---|
| Baseline | 22.5 | 17.7 | 21.3 | 12.9 | 3.5 | 1.3 | 0.8 | 1.0 | 5.6 | 11.6 | 21.1 | 18.7 |
| With time scheduling | 24.3 | 19.2 | 23.1 | 14.4 | 4.7 | 1.8 | 1.1 | 1.3 | 7.0 | 13.3 | 22.8 | 20.4 |

### 3.3 INSTALLATION OF NEW LUMINAIRES

Calculations of energy consumption for this scenario were not made on the basis of replacement of luminaires alone. This measure must be combined with the use of a daylight compensation system. The present electricity load for lighting is 10 W/m². This is acceptably low, but the resulting light level is inadequate. The light level is 20 lux in corridors (on the floor) and 150 lux in the offices (at the desktop). A sufficient light level of 500 lux is only achieved on those desks where task lighting is used. The luminaires should therefore be replaced with luminaires with high-lumen fluorescent tubes with electromagnetic ballasts, to increase the light level without increasing the electricity load.

## Summaries

*Scenario 1*

Buildings improvements:

- Improved insulation on east and west gable walls
- Replacement of windows
- Integration of passive solar and daylighting components

Total values

Estimated energy savings: 441,600 kWh
Required capital cost: 746,240 ECU
Cost per unit of energy: .050 ECU/kWh
Financial gain per year: 22 000ECU
Payback period: 34 years

## EVALUATION

## Introduction

Sentralbygg 1 was built in 1961. Retrofitting has recently been carried out on the exterior walls to improve both the concrete and the reinforcement. The HAVC system has also been refurbished. Apart from these major refurbishments, little has been done during the almost forty-year-life of the building. Even though the general state of the building is quite good, a larger, overall refurbishment is due. Expectations with regard to user comfort levels in offices have increased and the use of computers in every office has changed the way the offices are used. For example, to avoid reflections on the monitor screen, the computer is usually placed in front of the window. This often results in glare problems because of the large contrast between the screen and the window opening.

The calculated costs for this project are related to a baseline representing the present condition of the building. Few of the measures would be cost effective. However, the discussion here is based on the fact that the building will be retrofitted anyway so improvements with low capital costs might be recommended even if the payback period is large.

## Scenario 1 – Improvement of existing envelope

### 1.1 Improved insulation on east and west gable walls

Improved insulation on the east and west gable walls is recommended because the offices located next to these gable walls require this improvement to achieve desired comfort levels. The extent of this work is small compared to the overall size of the building.

- Energy savings for heating: 7 kWh/m$^2$
- Capital costs: 10.2 ECU/m$^2$
- Simple payback period: 30 years

### 1.2 Replacement of windows

Replacement of windows is recommended. The windows are in quite good condition even though they are nearly 40 years old. Only a few have been changed because of bad sealing. Nevertheless, the large heat loss and draught problems cause comfort problems, so the windows will soon have to be replaced anyway.

- Energy savings for heating: 67 kWh/m$^2$
- Capital costs: 106.4 ECU/m$^2$
- Simple payback period: 32 years

### 1.3 Integration of passive solar and daylighting components

The results below are given for the application of this scenario with the existing windows. Integration of passive solar and daylighting components is recommended only together with replacement of the windows. The extra cost of using double venetian blinds instead of conventional venetian blinds will then be relatively small.

- Energy savings for electricity: 6 kWh/m$^2$
- Capital costs: 9.8 ECU/m$^2$
- Energy increase for heating: 3 kWh/m$^2$
- Simple payback period: 61 years

## Scenario 2 – Use of passive cooling techniques

### 2.1 USE OF EXTERNAL SHADING DEVICES

External shading is not recommended because the cost is too high and the consequent increase in energy consumption for heating is too large. Improved shading will be achieved when venetian blinds are placed between the two outer sheets of triple-glazed windows as recommended for the new south-facing windows.

- Increased energy consumption for heating: 19 kWh/m$^2$
- Capital costs: 71.7 ECU/m$^2$
- Simple payback period: 77 years

### 2.2 USE OF MECHANICAL NIGHT VENTILATION

Use of night ventilation is recommended because it will result in a significant improvement in comfort for a low cost.

- Increased energy consumption for heating: 0.5 kWh/m$^2$
- Capital costs: 0 ECUs
- Simple payback period: 0 years

## Scenario 3 – Electric light improvements

### 3.1 USE OF DAYLIGHT COMPENSATION SYSTEM

Use of a daylight compensation system is recommended only in combination with replacement of luminaires. The increase in energy consumption for heating will be less if the building is better insulated. The results are given for a combined scenario of new luminaires with daylight compensation system on all lamps.

- Energy savings for electricity: 9 kWh/m$^2$
- Increased energy consumption for heating: 6 kWh/m$^2$
- Simple payback period: 129 years

### 3.2 USE OF TIME SCHEDULING

Time scheduling is recommended, especially in the corridors. This measure can be implemented with success with either the existing luminaires or new luminaires, and also in combination with a daylight compensation system. As noted for the use of daylight compensation scheme, the increase in energy consumption for

## Summaries

### SCENARIO 2
Use of passive cooling techniques:
- External shading
- Night ventilation

**TOTAL VALUES**
Estimated energy saving: 121,600 kWh
Capital cost: 458,880 ECU
Cost per unit energy: 0.05 ECU/kWh
Financial gain per year: 6 000 ECU
Payback period: 75 years

### SCENARIO 3
- Daylight compensation scheme
- Time scheduling
- New luminaires

**TOTAL VALUES**
Estimated energy saving: 57,600 kWh
Capital cost: 145,280 ECU
Cost per unit energy: .05 ECU/kWh
Financial gain per year: 2880 ECU
Payback period: 46 years

heating will be less if the building is better insulated. The results are given for the use of a timer on existing luminaires.

- Energy savings for electricity: 20 kWh/m$^2$
- Increased energy consumption for heating: 17 kWh/m$^2$
- Simple payback period: 6 years

### 3.3 INSTALLATION OF NEW LUMINAIRES

New luminaires are recommended because the existing ones give insufficient light levels. Energy savings will only be achieved if this measure is combined with a daylight compensation system or time scheduling.

## Scenario 4 – HVAC system improvements

No measures tested.

## Scenarios and packages – financial summaries

### SCENARIO 1 BUILDING IMPROVEMENTS

Improved insulation and new windows with daylighting components

- Present value of investment: -42.4 ECU/m$^2$
- Simple payback period: 32 years

### SCENARIO 2 USE OF PASSIVE COOLING TECHNIQUES

External shading and night ventilation

- Present value of investment: -91 ECU/m$^2$
- Simple payback period: -75 years

### SCENARIO 3 ELECTRIC LIGHTING IMPROVEMENTS

New luminaires with time scheduling and daylight compensation system

- Present value of investment: -13 ECU/m$^2$
- Simple payback period: 46 years

### PACKAGE 1

Scenarios 1, 2 and 3: improved insulation and new windows with daylighting components, external shading and night ventilation, new luminaires with time scheduling and daylight compensation system.

- Present value of investment: -13 ECU/m$^2$
- Simple payback period: 46 years

## PACKAGE 2

Scenarios 1, 2.2 & 3: improved insulation and new windows with daylighting components, night ventilation, new luminaires with time scheduling and daylight compensation system.

- Present value of investment: -48 ECU/$m^2$
- Simple payback period: 31 years

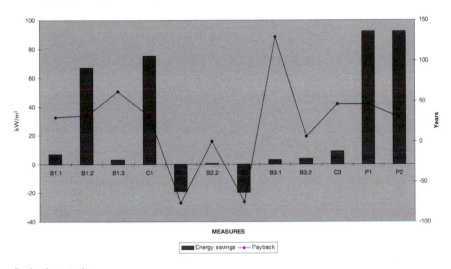

**Payback periods**

# Krokslatt 149, Gothenburg, Sweden

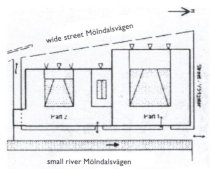

Site plan

Location: Mölndalsvägen 22-30C
Owner: Lundbergs Byggnads AB
Total size: 36,971 m² (gross area)
Storeys: 6
Year of construction: 1989, 1991
Degree of exposure: Exposed
Module: Mainly cellular
Working hours: 07.00–18.00
Total energy consumption (1997-98):
    159 kW/m²
User system control: BEMS
Heating system: District heating, 4-pipe induction
    units
Cooling system: Refrigerant water coolers, 4-pipe
    induction units
Lighting system: Suspended standard fluorescent
    tubes and task lighting

'Krokslatt 149' is a typical Swedish office building of the 1980s. It was built in two stages, a couple of years apart (1989 and 1991). The building consists of two sections, each of six floors, around two glazed atria. The atria are fully air-conditioned. Storage and parking areas are located underground. The building is owned by a large private property company and houses about 50 tenants. These are mainly technically oriented companies, ranging from small companies with five employees to large ones with about 200 employees. The offices are mainly cellular and are located towards the external and atrium walls. Krokslatt 149 was included in the OFFICE project mainly to study the opportunities for reduction of the building's rather high electricity consumption.

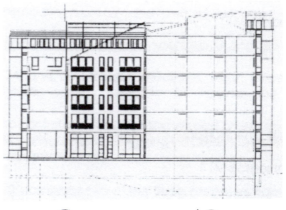

Longitudinal section

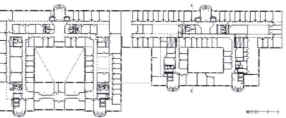

Typical floor plan

View of an atrium

Front view

## BUILDING CHARACTERISTICS

## Architectural description

The external walls of Krokslatt 149 are of wood-frame type and well insulated. The façade is mainly yellow brick, however some sections of the western façade have an external red granite stone cladding. The internal wall surface is painted gypsum board. The walls are insulated with mineral wool. All windows are typical Swedish three-pane wooden windows with no coating or gas filling. A few windows in the western façade have an outer pane of slightly solar-absorbing glass. Most of the windows have manually controlled venetian blinds between the two outer panes for solar shading. However, most façade windows on the upper floor have manually controlled external venetian blinds instead. All façade windows are openable.

The glazed parts of the atria, both walls and roofs, consist of three-pane clear insulation glass. There is no solar shading in the atria.

The walls towards the atria are nearly as well insulated as the external walls. The surfaces towards the atria are either of light coloured wooden panels or of white painted, sound absorbing panels. The windows towards the atria are also standard three-pane windows, however these are not easily openable in order to comply with fire regulations. Most of the windows towards the atria on the upper floors have manually controlled venetian blinds, either internal or between the two outer panes. The purpose of the blinds is mainly to reduce glare in summer, arising either directly from the sun or from reflections in windows on the opposite side of the atrium. The atria have no direct open communication with any other parts of the building, again in accordance with fire regulations.

All intermediate floors are made of pre-cast hollow concrete slabs with a thin top-casting and they usually have linoleum or plastic covering. The concrete slabs are usually exposed in the ceilings of the office areas, while corridors and some internal offices/meeting rooms have false ceilings.

The concrete floor in the walkable attic is very well insulated with mineral wool. Under the ground floor (300 mm concrete) there is 200 mm of cellular plastic insulation.

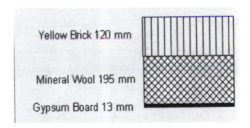

External Wall

#### Characteristics of external walls

| Material | Conductivity (W/m °C) | Density (kg/m³) | Specific heat (J/kg °C) | Solar assortment | Thickness (m) | U value (W/m² °C) |
|---|---|---|---|---|---|---|
| Yellow brick | 0.70 | 1700 | 800 | 0.7 | 0.120 | — |
| or Red granite | 3.5 | 2700 | 800 | 0.6 | 0.040 | — |
| Air gap (vented) | — | — | — | — | 0.040 | — |
| Mineral wool | 0.040 | 30 | 660 | — | 0.195 | — |
| Gypsum board | 0.16 | 800 | 1090 | 0.9 | 0.013 | — |
| TOTAL | — | — | — | — | 0.408 | 0.20 |

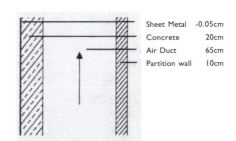

Sheet Metal -0.05cm
Concrete 20cm
Air Duct 65cm
Partition wall 10cm

Wall detail

## System characteristics

*HEATING PLANT*

System type: District heating
Units: 3
Nominal heating power (kW): 594
Heated floor area (m²): 29,889
Distribution system: Induction
Hours of operation (h/year): 8760
Set-point temperature: 22°C
Maintenance state: Good

*COOLING PLANT*

System type: Refrigerant water coolers
Units: 3
Nominal cooling power (kW): 960
Cooled floor area (m²): 29,889
Distribution system: Induction
Hours of operation (h/year): 8760
Set-point temperature: 24°C
Maintenance state: Good

*VENTILATION PLANT*

System type: CAV, 4-pipe induction units
Units: 7
Supply air-flow rate [m³/s]: 32
Return air-flow rate [m³/s]: 33
Supply air fan (kW): 56
Return air fan (kW): 51

### Characteristics of atrium walls

| Material | Conductivity (W/m °C) | Density (kg/m³) | Specific heat (J/kg °C) | Solar assortment | Thickness (m) | U value (W/m² °C) |
|---|---|---|---|---|---|---|
| Light panel | 0.15 | 700 | 1200 | 0.8 | 0.015 | – |
| Mineral wool | 0.040 | 30 | 660 | – | 0.170 | – |
| Gypsum board | 0.16 | 800 | 1090 | 0.9 | 0.013 | – |
| TOTAL | – | – | – | – | 0.198 | 0.25 |

### Characteristics of roof

| Material | Conductivity (W/m °C) | Density (kg/m³) | Specific heat (J/kg °C) | Solar assortment | Thickness (m) | U value (W/m² °C) |
|---|---|---|---|---|---|---|
| Grey sheet metal | 50 | 7800 | 460 | 0.6 | 0.001 | – |
| Wooden roof | 0.15 | 500 | 1630 | – | 0.015 | – |
| Walkable attic | – | – | – | – | 0–3 | – |
| Mineral wool | 0.040 | 30 | 660 | – | 0.300 | – |
| Pre-cast slab | 1.7 | 2300 | 920 | – | 0.250 | – |
| TOTAL | – | – | – | – | – | 0.13 |

### Characteristics of window and atria glazing

| Material | Conductivity (W/m °C) | Density (kg/m³) | Specific heat (J/kg °C) | Solar assortment | Thickness (m) | U value (W/m² °C) |
|---|---|---|---|---|---|---|
| Three-pane glass | – | – | – | 0.3 | – | – |
| TOTAL | – | – | – | – | – | 2.0 |

## MECHANICAL AND ELECTRICAL EQUIPMENT

### Systems description

The heating system in Krokslatt 149 consists mainly of four-pipe induction units below each window. The heating source is district heating, which in Gothenburg consists of about 70% waste heat (from oil refineries, waste incineration plants and large sewage water heat pumps). The district heating substation has three heat exchangers, two for the heating system and one for heating of service hot water. The heating system is designed for forward/return temperatures of 55°C/40°C down to external temperatures of -16°C. Heating is always available, but in the summer months it is only used for heating of service hot water. Each induction unit has a thermostatic valve for individual room temperature control. The atria have floor heating.

The **cooling system** is water-based with four-pipe induction units below each window and air-cooling coils in the air-handling units. In the core zones, meeting rooms, and a few open-plan offices, also have two-pipe induction units in the ceiling, and some open-plan offices have cooled ceilings. The cooled water is delivered by three refrigerant water coolers with reciprocating compressors. Since the building has a heat surplus almost all working days during the year, the coolers run throughout the year to keep the room temperature acceptably low. During the winter one cooler is sufficient; all three coolers are only used on very hot summer days. The condenser heat from one cooler is partly recovered to the heating system. However, most condenser heat is dumped to the outside air through fan-powered dry cooling coils on the roof.

The **ventilation system** consists of four main air-handling units with a constant air-flow rate, providing conditioned air (15–21°C) to the four-pipe induction units below each window. The air-handling units consist of filters, rotary air-to-air heat exchangers for heat recovery, heating and cooling coils, and centrifugal fans with backward-curved blades. The temperature efficiency of the air-to-air heat exchangers is about 70%. The supply air-flow rate (100% outdoor air) is about 8 l/s per person in the office areas.

## LIGHTING

Fluorescent lamps: (W/m²) 15–17
Incandescent lamps: Not known
Hours of operation (h/day): 11
Maintenance state: Good

## EQUIPMENT

Computers (units): 200
Hours of operation (h/day): 9
Printer (units): 30
Hours of operation (h/day): 9

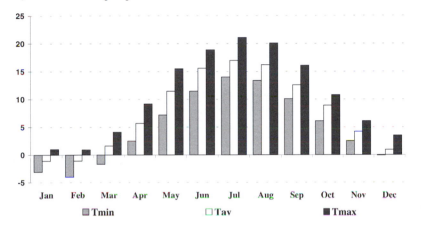

Monthly external temperatures °C

Each atrium is served by one air-handling unit that provides conditioned air (20°C) via displacement ventilation. In order to vent the atria in summer to avoid overheating, dampers are located in the base and below the roof of each atrium. Opening of the dampers is controlled by three temperature sensors in the upper part of each atrium.

The **lighting system** in the office areas mainly consists of suspended fixtures with standard fluorescent tubes and with electromagnetic ballasts. Most offices also have task lighting with high intensity discharge (HID) or standard incandescent bulbs. The installed lighting power in the offices is 15–17 W/m². The general lighting is individually controlled by wall switches in each office. The corridors are mainly lit by fixtures with compact fluorescent or HID lamps. The installed lighting power in the corridors is around 10 W/m².

On a typical floor, **electrical equipment** includes one PC at every workplace which use about 150 W each. There are about 20 PCs connected to each laser printer, which use 300–500 W each. There are also four copying machines, which use 1000–1500 W each. In addition, there are several faxes and plotters.

The heating, cooling and ventilation systems are controlled by a computer-based building energy management system (BEMS). External lighting and lighting in the atria are also controlled by the BEMS, as is the venting of the atria to avoid overheating in summer. The night-time ventilation is mainly controlled manually ('tomorrow will be a hot day') or by time setting. There is no optimized night ventilation strategy implemented via the BEMS.

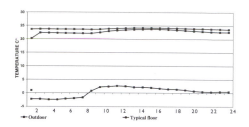

Air temperatures – Winter

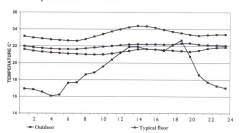

Air temperatures – Summer (28 July 1998)

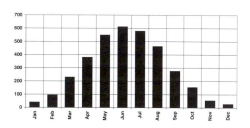

Global solar radiation – monthly average (MJ/m²)

Annual energy consumption by fuel type

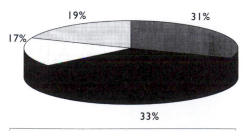

Distribution of energy consumption

# BUILDING'S ENERGY PERFORMANCE

## General profile of energy use

The energy data provided is from the monitoring year June 1997 to May 1998. This year included a record warm summer and a mild winter. This means that the electricity consumption in the summer months, particularly for August, is higher than for a typical year and the energy consumption for heating in the winter months, particularly for February, is lower. The energy consumption figures have not been normalized to a typical year.

The energy consumption of the building is very typical for a 1990s Swedish office building, about 50 kWh/year per m² for heating and about 100 kWh/year per m² of electricity. The electricity consumption is fairly even throughout the year, because of the water/air-based air-conditioning system, which means that the water coolers are running all year to provide an acceptably low indoor temperature. Of the heating energy only a small part is used for service hot water heating, about 7 kWh/year per m².

The main electrical energy end-uses are lighting and the equipment used by the tenants (46 kWh/year per m²). The next largest is the fans of the ventilation system (28 kWh/year per m²). Despite the fact that the refrigerant water coolers run throughout the year, they are not a dominating electrical energy end-use (18 kWh/year per m2). A significant amount of electricity is used for other purposes, e.g. lighting in stairwells and other non-tenant areas, as well as in the atria, external lighting, lifts, etc. (11 kWh/year per m²).

**Annual energy consumption breakdown by fuel type**

| Energy | kWh/year | |
|---|---|---|
| District heating | 1,348,400 | for space heating |
| Electricity | 3,413,600 | for other uses |
| TOTAL | 4,761,900 | |
| Average energy consumption per month | 396,800 | kWh |
| Average energy consumption per m² | 159 | kWh/year |

**Distribution of energy consumption**

| Energy | kWh/year | kWh/m²year |
|---|---|---|
| Space heating | 1,459,300 | 49 |
| Space cooling | 159,400 | 53 |
| Lighting | 802,100 | 27 |
| Equipment | 909,100 | 30 |
| TOTAL | 4,761,900 | 159 |

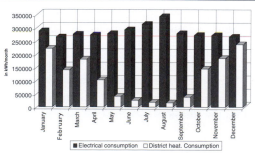

Total monthly energy consumption

## ENERGY RETROFITTING SCENARIOS

## Scenario 1 – Building improvements

As the building already has a very low annual energy consumption for heating, no measures involving improvement of the building envelope have been studied. The only measure of this kind studied was more efficient solar shading.

### 1.1 USE OF EFFICIENT SOLAR SHADING

The present means of solar shading is manually-controlled venetian blinds. These are mainly located between the outer two panes in the three-pane glass windows, but also externally on some of the east, south and west facing windows on the upper floor. This scenario investigated the effect of installing a BEMS-controlled external curtain system (solar shading factor 0.2) on all windows on the south, east and west external façades (not on the atria façades).

## Scenario 2 – Use of passive cooling techniques

### 2.1 USE OF FREE FLOATING TEMPERATURE IN THE ATRIA

Presently the atria are fully air-conditioned, heated in winter by floor heating and air from air-conditioning air handling units. In summer they are partly cooled by the air from air-conditioning air handling units. However, operating dampers in the bottom and the top of the atria carry out most of the summer venting. In this scenario, these venting facilities are kept, but all other mechanical systems in the atria, except artificial lighting, are taken away. In addition a BEMS-controlled internal solar shading system (horizontal curtains/sails) is added.

### 2.2 TEMPERATURE CONTROL OF NIGHT VENTILATION

Instead of operating the ventilation system by hand or by time controls at night and during weekends (if the building manager thinks night purging will be needed), a night ventilation control mode activates the ventilation system according to pre-set exterior and interior temperatures (active from 23.00–07.00).

### 2.3 USE OF RIVER WATER FOR FREE COOLING IN WINTER AND HEAT SINK IN SUMMER

A small river, the Mölndalsån, runs just next to the building property. This can provide free cooling of the cooling water from mid-October to April (six months per year) in place of the refrigerant water coolers. In the other (summer) months, the river water is used as heat sink, increasing the average summer Coefficient of Performance (COP) of the refrigerant water coolers from 2.5 to 4.5.

## Scenario 3 – Electric lighting improvements

### 3.1 USE OF HIGH FREQUENCY BALLASTS IN THE GENERAL LIGHTING SYSTEM

On the office floors (office areas, corridors and service areas), the existing ballasts are replaced with non-dimmable, high frequency (HF) ballasts. Use of HF ballasts gives a 20% saving in electricity consumption.

### 3.2 USE OF DAYLIGHT SENSORS

Daylight sensors, which control the artificial lighting system via dimmable HF ballasts, are installed in the office areas (only spaces facing the exterior or the atria).

### 3.3 USE OF PRESENCE DETECTORS

The artificial lighting in office areas (not meeting rooms, toilets, etc.) is controlled by presence detectors which switch off the lighting when no users are present.

## Scenario 4 – HVAC system improvements

### 4.1 REDUCTION OF HEATING SET-POINT

On office floors the present heating set-point of 22°C is reduced to 20°C during workdays and at weekends between 07.00 and 19.00. At night the set-point is reduced to 18°C. In the atria, the present heating set-point of 20°C remains unchanged during workdays and weekends from 17.00–19.00, but is reduced to 18°C at night.

### 4.2 INCREASE IN COOLING SET-POINT

The cooling set-point on the office floors is increased from 24°C to 26°C.

### 4.3 INSTALLATION OF MORE EFFICIENT FAN SYSTEM

The old fan system (fan, motor and motor-drive) with a specific fan power (SFP) of 3.2 kW/m³/s is replaced with a modern fan system in the main air-handling units (SFP of 2.5 kW/m³/s).

## EVALUATION

Each scenario was evaluated with regard to energy, capital costs, financial gains and payback period.

A number of the individual measures were combined into scenarios on the basis of their energy impact and profitability. These scenarios focused on reducing the energy consumption for each end-use: heating, cooling, lighting and ventilation. Finally, a total package was designed by combining the most profitable single measures. Essentially, this meant that the lighting measures were excluded.

## Scenario 1 – Building improvements

This scenario involves one measure:

- control of solar shading

## Scenario 2 – Cooling

This scenario involves five measures:

- use of efficient solar shading in atrium
- reduction of heating set-point in atrium
- increase in cooling set-point in atrium
- temperature control of night ventilation
- use of river water for free cooling in winter and heat sink in summer.

## Summaries

SCENARIO 1
Buildings improvements:

- Use of passive solar heating component

TOTAL VALUES
Estimated energy savings: -0.1 kWh
Required capital cost: 8.40 ECU/m$^2$
Cost per unit of energy: 84.00 ECU/kWh
Financial gain per year: -0.02 ECU
Payback period: -0

SCENARIO 2
Use of passive cooling techniques:

- efficient shading
- use of night ventilation
- reduction of heating
- reduction of cooling
- use of river water.

SCENARIO 3

Electric lighting improvements:

- Reduced indoor illumination level
- Use of task lighting
- Control of lighting equipment
- Use of efficient ballasts

TOTAL VALUES:

Estimated energy savings: 4.4 kWh
Required capital cost: 18.70 ECU
Cost per unit of energy: 0.09 ECU/kWh
Financial gain per year: 0.41 ECU
Payback period: 46 years

SCENARIO 4

HVAC system improvements:
- Improved control system
- Use of variable set-point temperature
- More efficient fan system

TOTAL VALUES

Estimated energy savings: 28.5 kWh
Required capital cost: 9.20 ECU
Cost per unit of energy: 0.05% ECU/kWh
Financial gain per year: 1.40 ECU
Payback period: 46 years

PACKAGE

TOTAL VALUES

Estimated energy saving: 31.1 kWh
Required capital cost: 2.15 ECU
Cost per unit of energy: 0.05 ECU/kWh
Financial gains per year: 1.55 ECU
Amortisation time: 1.4 years

## Scenario 3 – Lighting

This scenario involves three measures:

- use of high frequency ballasts in general lighting system
- use of daylight sensors
- use of presence detectors.

## Scenario 4 – Ventilation

This scenario involves two measures:

- temperature control of night ventilation
- installation of more efficient fan system.

## Package

The package involves the following measures:

- reduction of heating set-point
- increase in cooling set-point
- temperature control of night ventilation
- installation of more efficient fan system
- use of river water for free cooling in winter and heat sink in summer.

# Climatic Area 2 – Continental Europe

## — Introduction —

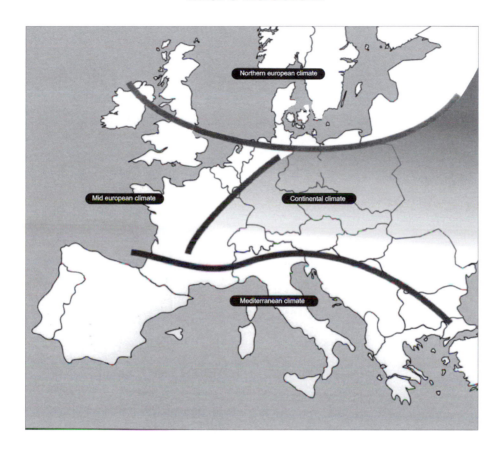

The Continental climate is characterized by low precipitation, with annual thermal swings becoming more pronounced as one moves further to the east.

Winters are severe (long and cold) and dry at the same time, with precipitation generally weak and irregular. The thaw begins quite late, and spring is particularly short, in some places non-existent. Summers are hot and vary in duration. The bulk of the annual precipitation falls in summer, as showers accompanied by thunderstorms. Autumn is often long and mild.

# Postbank Berlin, Berlin, Germany

**Site plan**

Location: Hallesches Ufer 60, Berlin
Owner: Private
Total size: 20,200 m$^2$
Storeys: 24
Construction year: 1971
Degree of exposure: Free-standing
Module: Open and cellular spaces
Working hours: 06:00–16:00
Total energy consumption (1997): 253 kWh/m$^2$
User system control: Central
Heating system: District heating
Cooling system: Refrigerant centrifugal, four-pipe induction
Lighting system: Fluorescent lamps

The Berlin headquarters of **Deutsche Postbank** consists of several large blocks of buildings in the centre of the city. The whole development was designed in the spirit of the 'late international' style by the construction department of **Deutsche Postbank**. The grouping of the development, balancing a tall block with lower buildings, represents a typical design scheme of this time. The high-rise office block, which was selected to be the case-study building, has a curtain wall façade constructed from steel and glass, with offices facing east and west. Within the building there are open-plan and cellular space offices. The building is fully air-conditioned.

Interior view – open-plan office

General view of the Postbank building

Interior view – office window

## BUILDING CHARACTERISTICS

### Architectural description

The Postbank building is composed of a three-storey-high base that is interconnected with the adjoining lower building blocks and a 21-storey free-standing core. The base and the upper-most four floors of the high-rise core are used for technical facilities and special purposes. The 16 floors in the middle of the building block are occupied by offices.

The building has a concrete skeleton construction with a sequence of columns adjacent to the east and west façades allowing a support-free central floor area. The clear span is 14.5 m with an interval between columns of 5.3 m. The dimensions of the square columns are approximately 1 x 1 m. Horizontal loads are supported by stiffened concrete walls in the elevator shafts. A fire wall divides each floor into a northern and a southern compartment. The southern compartment comprises the main floor space while most of the service rooms are located in the northern fire compartment. Compared with other office buildings of this type, the proportion of floor area used for service rooms in the Postbank building is relatively large. Compared to steel frame constructions of similar shape, the thermal mass is also relatively large.

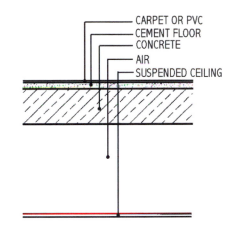

Floor detail

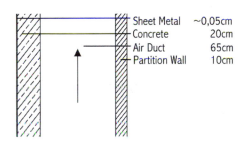

Wall detail (end wall)

| Material | Conductivity (W/m °C) | Density (kg/m³) | Specific heat (J/kg °C) | Solar assortment | Thickness (m) | U value (W/m² °C) |
|---|---|---|---|---|---|---|
| **Characteristics of parapet wall** | | | | | | |
| Concrete | 0.85 | 1800 | 1000 | 0.7 | 0.1 | – |
| Foam glass | 0.53 | 150 | 800 | 0.95 | 0.04 | – |
| Air layer | – | 1.3 | 100 | – | 0.02 | – |
| Sheet metal | 50 | 7800 | 400 | 0.9 | 0.0005 | – |
| TOTAL | – | – | – | – | 0.1605 | 0.9 |
| **Characteristics of windows** | | | | | | |
| Aluminium frame | 200 | 2700 | 880 | 0.35 | 0.1 | – |
| Glass | 0.8 | 2800 | 750 | 0.95 | 0.004 | – |
| Air layer | – | 1.3 | 100 | – | 0.012 | – |
| Glass | 0.8 | 2800 | 750 | 0.95 | 0.006 | – |
| TOTAL | – | – | – | – | 0.122 | 2.0 |
| **Characteristics of end wall** | | | | | | |
| Building board | 0.31 | 800 | 1000 | 0.9 | 0.015 | – |
| Mineral wool | 0.05 | 1000 | 840 | 0.9 | 0.05 | – |
| Building board | 0.31 | 800 | 1000 | 0.9 | 0.015 | – |
| Air layer | – | 1.3 | 100 | – | 0.665 | – |
| Concrete | 0.85 | 1800 | 1000 | 0.7 | 0.20 | – |
| Air layer | – | 1.3 | 100 | – | 0.02 | – |
| Sheet metal | 50 | 7800 | 400 | 0.9 | 0.0005 | – |
| TOTAL | – | – | – | – | 0.9655 | 0.75 |

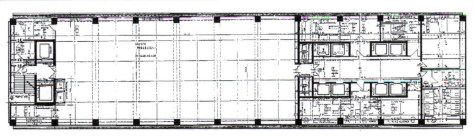

Typical floor plan

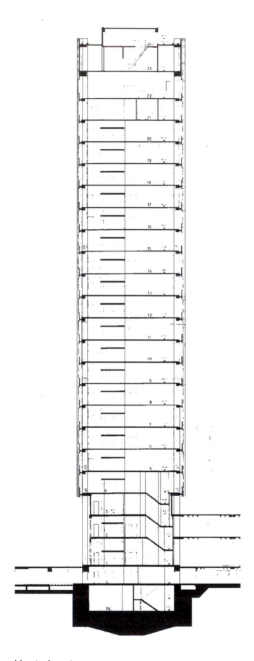

Vertical section

The offices have non-opening, continuous strip windows facing east and west; the northern and southern façades are windowless. Each glazed unit has dimensions of 1.45 m x 2.01 m; the corrected opening index of the interior façade is 63%. The windows are glazed with solar shading but have no exterior shading devices. On the inside, movable vertical lamellas protect the offices from glare; these lamellas are manually controlled.

The ventilation units are located below the windows in the parapet area. The parapet itself is made of concrete insulated with 4 cm of foam glass.

The northern and the southern end walls are made of concrete lined with sheet metal. Construction ventilation ducts are located on the interior side of these windowless walls. These walls are poorly insulated.

The intermediate floors of the Postbank building are made of concrete slabs supported by the principal girders. Over the slab a screed floor-covering with a linoleum finishing is exposed to the indoor environment. Ceilings made of perforated sheet metal are suspended from the floor above. Due to the wide span structure, the resulting void is relatively tall; the ducts for exhaust air are located in this space.

### Characteristics of intermediate floors

| Material | Conductivity (W/m °C) | Density (kg/m³) | Specific heat (J/kg °C) | Solar assortment | Thickness (m) | U value (W/m² °C) |
|---|---|---|---|---|---|---|
| Linoleum | 0.19 | 1200 | 140 | 0.9 | 0.005 | – |
| Screed flooring | 1.9 | 1800 | 1000 | 0.7 | 0.095 | – |
| Concrete | 0.85 | 1800 | 1000 | 0.7 | 0.18 | – |
| Air layer | 50 | 1.3 | 100 | – | 0.5 | – |
| Perforated metal | 50 | 7800 | 400 | 0.9 | 0.0005 | – |
| TOTAL | – | – | – | – | – | 1.7 |

# MECHANICAL AND ELECTRICAL EQUIPMENT

## Systems description

When the building was constructed the **heating system** was based on its own coal-fired district heating plant. New regulations for such boilers inclined the owner to abandon running their own boiler, which they did in 1994 since when heat has been acquired from another supplier of district heat. The district heat is used for space heating as well as for hot water. The air-conditioned floor area and rooms in the service zone of the building have different heating schedules. While the heat is distributed to the air-conditioned floor area with the supply air by the central air-handling units and by induction units in the offices, rooms in the service zone are equipped with conventional heaters.

The **cooling system** consists of three refrigerant centrifugal cooling engines situated in the basement of the building, providing the air-handling units with cold water. The cooling engines are themselves cooled by water from the nearby Landwehr Canal which is used to carry off the waste heat. The maximum temperature of the return water is fixed by local authorities. The temperature of the cold water distributed to the central air-handling units is 6°C; when the ambient temperature exceeds 24°C the induction units in the air-conditioned floor area are supplied with water at 13°C.

The **ventilation system** consists of two central air-handling units located in the third floor of the building. These units precondition the supply air before it is conducted to the induction units in the offices. One unit serves the east side of the building, the other the west side. Before entering the induction units in the offices the supply air has a temperature of 14–16°C (constant throughout the year). The set-point temperature in the offices is 23°C all year round, and occupants can adjust this temperature (±1.5°C). All supply air enters the office floors via the induction units in the air-conditioned zone; a portion of the air then flows from the air-conditioned floor space through the services area where the

## System characteristics

*HEATING PLANT*
System type: Central district heat
Nominal heating power (kW): 3100
Heated floor area (m²): 20,200
Distribution system: Individual units/heaters
Hours of operation (h/year): 2150
Set-point temperature: 22–24°C
Maintenance state: Adequate

*COOLING PLANT*
System type: Refrigerant centrifugal
Units: 3
Nominal cooling power (kW): 3500
Heated floor area (m²): 10,500
Distribution system: four-pipe
Hours of operation (h/year): 2500
Set-point temperature: 26°C
Maintenance state: Adequate

*VENTILATION PLANT*
System type: Mechanical
Units: 2 (plus independent unit on Floor 21)
Supply air-flow rate (m³/s): 46.6
Return air-flow rate (m³/s): 49.8
Supply air fan (kW): 182
Return air fan (kW): 164

foul air is extracted without heat recovery. The main reason for the relatively high air-change rate of 4/h is the re-use of the return air. When exterior temperatures are extreme (very high or low), the quantity of supply air is reduced. The basement is supplied with the exhaust air from the lower stories of the building. Meanwhile, the kitchen and restaurant on the top floor of the building have a separate air-handling unit located in floor 21 which operates on an independent schedule.

**Electrical network and equipment**: as in most office buildings, internal gains from office equipment, mostly computers, are high. The building was not originally designed for computer use. Instead of a computer network, a pneumatic tube installation system was provided. The floor-to-floor height of 3.63 m and the ducts in the parapet area offer good opportunities to lay all the wiring that is needed for modern electronic communication.

The whole building is equipped with **electric lighting** in the form of fluorescent tube lamps. In areas with computer workstations the lighting fixtures have been retrofitted; in service areas the original lighting fixtures are still in use. All lights have manual on/off controls. Both new and old lights have electromagnetic ballasts. The design illuminance is 500 lux within cellular office spaces and 750 lux within open-plan office spaces. The controls are generally located in the entrance area of the offices. In the open-plan office spaces a display shows which sections of the five rows of lights are actually switched on at any time. No task-lighting is used in the offices.

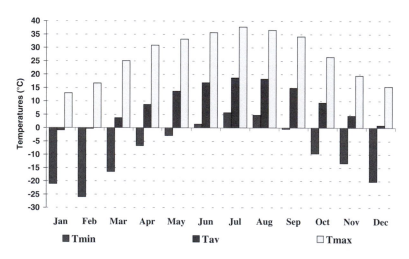

Monthly external temperatures °C

## BUILDING'S ENERGY PERFORMANCE

### General profile of energy use

The energy consumption per square metre of office area in the Postbank building is about 325 kWh/m² per year. The energy used for heating, including hot water, represents two-thirds of all energy consumption in the Postbank building, while electricity consumption, including electricity for cooling, represents about one-third of the total energy used. Approximately half of the heating energy is used to heat supply air in the central air-handling units; another 30% is distributed by the induction units. The rest of the heating energy is used for space heating in that floor area that is not air-conditioned.

Since the building was constructed, energy use has been monitored several times. Comparisons show that improvements to the HVAC system led to a reduction of about 25% in the annual heating energy use, while the cooling energy consumption remained more or less unchanged. The largest proportion of the electricity is used by the mechanical ventilation system, about 40% of the total electrical energy; almost 30% is used for lighting, about 10% for equipment, and about 20% for cooling.

The shape, as well as the HVAC system of the Postbank building, corresponds to typical design schemes of office buildings of the late 1960s. Accordingly, the energy consumption profile of the Postbank building also corresponds to these typical office buildings.

Annual energy consumption breakdown by fuel type

| Energy | kWh/year | |
|---|---|---|
| District heating | 1,259,703 | for space heating |
| Electricity | 1,207,500 | for other uses |
| TOTAL | 2,467,203 | |
| Average energy consumption per month | 205,600 | kWh |
| Average energy consumption per m² | 371 | kWh/year |

Distribution of energy consumption

| Energy | kWh/year | kWh/m²year |
|---|---|---|
| Space heating | 1,207,500 | 181 |
| Space cooling | 252,554 | 38 |
| Lighting | 582,957 | 88 |
| Other | 424,192 | 64 |
| TOTAL | 2,467,203 | 371 |

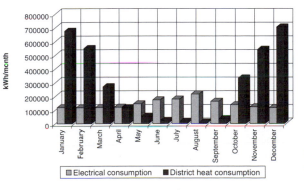

Monthly energy consumption

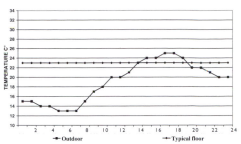

Air temperatures – Summer (7 August 1998)

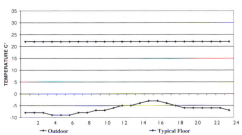

Air temperatures – Winter (1 February 1998)

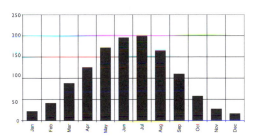

Global solar radiation – monthly average kWh/m²

Annual energy consumption by fuel type

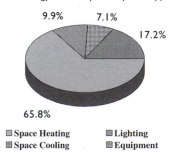

Distribution of energy consumption

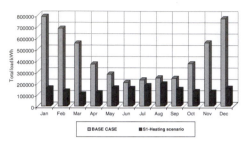

Monthly total energy consumption (kWh) – effect of Scenario 1, the heating scenario

# ENERGY RETROFITTING SCENARIOS

## Scenario 1 – Heating scenario

The heating scenario focuses on the improvement of the U value of the building envelope and on measures to enhance the efficiency of the HVAC system; both the setting of control parameters and the subsequent installation of heat recovery are considered.

### MEASURE 1: IMPROVEMENT OF U VALUE OF OPAQUE WALLS

The walls are quite poorly insulated with a U value of approximately 0.9 W/m²K. By adding 10 cm of mineral wool to the existing walls, the U value will reduce to 0.3 W/m²K. While this measure costs 59 ECU/m², the reduction in the annual heating energy demand is 35kWh/m². There is a positive effect on the heating demand (16% decrease), but a negative effect on the cooling demand (3% increase). The total annual energy cost is reduced by 1.7 ECU/m², giving a simple payback period of 35 years.

### MEASURE 3: INSTALLATION OF SUPER LOW-E GLAZING

The simulated glazing type is a super low-E-glazing with a U value of 0.9 W/m²K, and a transmission of 0.76/0.58. The simulation shows a decrease of 41 kWh/m²a (19%) in the heating demand and an increase of 7 kWh/m²a (30%) for cooling. The payback period is 27 years.

### MEASURE 4: REDUCTION OF HEATING SET-POINT TEMPERATURE DURING THE DAY

A reduction of the heating set-point temperature from 22.5°C to 21°C leads to a decrease in the heating energy consumption of 31 kWh/m²a without incurring any costs. Obviously changing set-point temperatures must be undertaken very carefully because it directly affects the indoor comfort levels.

### MEASURE 15: USE OF AN AIR-TO-AIR HEAT RECOVERY SYSTEM FOR VENTILATION AIR

Currently the ventilation system runs with 100% fresh air with no heat recovery. The use of an air-to-air heat recovery system reduces heating energy consumption by 104 kWh/m²a; however the electricity consumption of the ventilation system rises. The costs of this measure – 15.8 ECU/m² – are recovered within less than four years.

MEASURE 6: USE OF HEAT RECOVERY FROM THE COOLING PLANT'S CONDENSER COIL
Currently the waste heat of the cooling plant is lost to the Landwehr Canal. Recovering the heat from the condenser coil reduces the energy consumption for hot water by 2 kWh/m²a; the effect is so small because the energy demand for hot water within the office floors is itself insignificant. The payback period for the costs of 1.6 ECU/m²a is 15 years. If the restaurant on the top floor of the building, which has a considerable hot water consumption, is included in the model, the potential energy savings of this measure are higher.

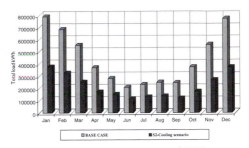

Monthly total energy consumption (kWh) — effect of Scenario 2, the cooling scenario

MEASURE 7: REDUCTION OF THE VENTILATION RATE DURING SUMMER AND WINTER
The current ventilation rate is 3–4 air changes per hour throughout the year. Reducing the air-change rate to 2.0/h causes a decrease in energy consumption for heating of 41 kWh/m²a and a reduction in the energy used for ventilation of 30 kWh/m²a. With no investment cost this measure reduces the running costs of the building by 5.7 ECU/m². However, the model does not take into account the fact that the exhaust air from the air-conditioned floor zone is used as supply air for other building zones. When applying this measure to the building, indoor comfort levels, especially within the non air-conditioned zones, must be carefully considered.

MEASURE 14: SEAL LEAKY WINDOWS
The present average infiltration rate is estimated to be 0.5 air changes per hour (ac/h) in the reference model. When assuming that the infiltration rate could be reduced by 50% to 0.25 ac/h by sealing leaky windows, a reduction in the heating energy demand of 22 kWh/m²a is achieved for the small cost of 1.6 ECU/m². The payback period would be less than two years. However, the infiltration rate has not actually been measured; the window frames were sealed all around with foil when the building was constructed.

## Scenario 2 – Cooling scenario

The cooling scenario includes M1 and M7, which are also part of the heating scenario. See Scenario 1 above for details.

MEASURE 2: INSTALLATION OF IMPROVED SOLAR GLAZING
The present glazing has a U value of 2.0 W/m²K and a transmission of 0.66/0.44 (light/solar); this is replaced with solar glazing with a U value of 1.3 W/m²K, and transmission 0.66/0.34. The colour of light is not affected. The simulation shows a decrease of 18 kWh/m²a (8%) in the heating demand and a decrease of 1 kWh/m²a in the cooling demand. While the investment costs are 31.7 ECU/m², the decrease in the annual energy costs is 1.1 ECU/m², giving a simple payback period of 29 years.

MEASURE 9: CONTROL STRATEGIES FOR MECHANICAL VENTILATION
Instead of running the ventilation system for some hours every night, a control strategy is implemented such that it operates between 06:00 and 17:00 on work

days, and an additional night ventilation control mode is included which starts the mechanical ventilation according to external and indoor temperatures. This measure leads to a significant reduction of the heating energy consumption; it decreases the energy use for ventilation as well. The effect on the cooling energy consumption is less significant. The overall reduction of energy use is 68 kWh/m$^2$ per year. As in the case of other measures that only consist of changing control parameters, there are no investment costs for this measure. One reason for the present operation schedule of the night ventilation is that an unpleasant odour is detectable in the morning if the ventilation system has not run during the previous night. Therefore the application of this measure would require associated measures to clear away this odour.

### MEASURE 11: USE OF EFFECTIVE INTERNAL SOLAR SHADING

This measure aims to reduce cooling loads, to enhance daylight penetration and to improve the working environment by installing new BEMS-controlled internal shading devices. The existing lamellas are manually controlled. Their main function is to protect the occupants from glare. The shading lamellas are adjusted from time to time to exclude harmful sunlight or to screen high sky luminances, however once adjusted they continue to reduce daylight penetration even when they are no longer needed.

A BEMS-controlled shading device will provide more visual comfort to the occupants and enhance daylight penetration. Nevertheless, the use of energy for electric lighting is only reduced significantly when this measure is combined with daylight responsive lighting controls (see measure 13 below). The daylight performance has not been modelled in the simulations discussed here. When modelled as a single measure, the reduction in energy consumption is less than 1 kWh/m$^2$ per year. The simple payback period is 260 years, while the lifetime of such elements is usually less than 20 years. On the other hand, the impact on the indoor environment is quite significant.

### MEASURE 13: DAYLIGHT RESPONSIVE CONTROL OF ARTIFICIAL LIGHTING

The energy-saving potential of daylight responsive lighting controls depends on the efficiency of the daylight strategy, therefore this measure should be combined with measures to improve the daylight performance of the building. When applied as a single measure, daylight responsive lighting controls reduce the electricity consumption by 14 kWh/m$^2$ per year, while heating energy consumption increases by 13 kWh/m$^2$. Because electric energy is more expensive than thermal energy, the payback period is 12 years with investment costs of 12 ECU/m$^2$.

### MEASURE 15: INSTALLATION OF HIGH FREQUENCY (HF) BALLASTS

The existing ballasts in all floor areas (offices, corridors, service rooms) are replaced by non-dimmable, high frequency (HF) ballasts. Use of HF ballasts gives a 20% energy saving. In energy terms, the 6 kWh/m$^2$ reduction in the energy consumption for electric lighting is completely offset by the 6 kWh/m$^2$ increase in the heating energy demand, however electric energy is more expensive than thermal energy, so the measure has a 31-year payback period.

## Scenario 3 – Electric lighting improvements

*ARTIFICIAL LIGHTING ENERGY SCENARIO*
This scenario includes the following measures:

*MEASURE 3: INSTALLATION OF SUPER LOW-E GLAZING*
See Scenario 1 (Heating scenario) above.

*MEASURE 13: DAYLIGHT RESPONSIVE CONTROL OF ARTIFICIAL LIGHTING*
See Scenario 2 (Cooling scenario) above.

*MEASURE 15: INSTALLATION OF HF BALLASTS*
See Scenario 2 (Cooling scenario) above.

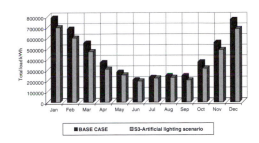

Monthly total energy consumption (kWh) –
effect of Scenario 3, the artificial lighting scenario

## Scenario 4 – HVAC system improvements

This scenario includes the following measures:

*MEASURE 7: REDUCTION OF THE VENTILATION RATE DURING SUMMER AND WINTER*
See Scenario 1 (Heating scenario) above.

*MEASURE 9: CONTROL STRATEGIES FOR MECHANICAL VENTILATION*
See Scenario 2 (Cooling scenario) above.

*MEASURE 8: INSTALLATION OF MORE EFFICIENT FANS*
The old fans with a total efficiency of 50% are replaced by a new fan system with an efficiency of 75%. This measure achieves savings in electricity consumption, but increases the energy consumption for heating. While the energy consumed for mechanical ventilation is reduced by 22% and the cooling energy use is reduced by 8%, the heating energy consumption increases by 3%. The overall energy savings are 6 kWh/m$^2$ per year, and the investment costs of 2.5 ECU/m$^2$ are covered within two years.

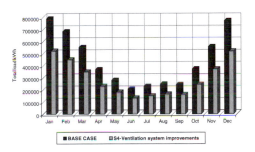

Monthly total energy consumption (kWh) –
effect of Scenario 4, the ventilation system improvements

## Scenario 5 – Other measures

## Scenario 5A Passive architectural scenario (without mechanical cooling)

The following measures which were described in the heating scenario (Scenario 1 above) are constituents of the passive architectural scenario:

- Measure 1: Improvement of U value of opaque walls
- Measure 3: Installation of super low-E glazing
- Measure 4: Reduction of heating set-point temperature during the day
- Measure 13: Use of daylight responsive artificial lighting controls (described in Scenario 2, the cooling scenario).

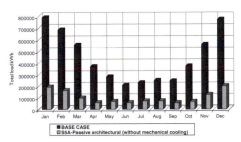

Monthly total energy consumption (kWh) –
effect of Scenario 5, the passive architectural scenario

Additional measures, which were not part of Scenarios 1–4 are also included in Scenario 5A. These measures are designed to be part of an integrated passive architectural scenario; their application only makes sense in combination with other measures, therefore the simulation results of these measures should not be overestimated.

### MEASURE 16: USE OF EXPOSED THERMAL MASS

To mediate indoor temperatures and save cooling energy, the suspended ceilings are removed in the office spaces and the concrete ceilings are exposed. This measure results in an increase of the energy consumption for heating for the total building of 6% and a 1% decrease of the cooling load. So if this measure is applied in isolation, the total energy consumption of the building will increase.

### MEASURE 18: USE OF NATURAL VENTILATION WITHOUT MECHANICAL COOLING

In this measure the mechanical ventilation system is decommissioned and existing windows are replaced with opening windows controlled by the BEMS. The new windows are divided into a lower, viewing window and an upper, daylighting window. Heating is provided by new water-heated radiators. The air-change rate is modelled to be 0.5/h during winter and 3–5/h in summer depending on wind and external temperature; natural night ventilation provides cooling during the summer.

### MEASURE 19: USE OF EFFECTIVE EXTERNAL SOLAR SHADING

To prevent overheating within a scenario of natural ventilation, BEMS-controlled, external Venetian blinds with a solar shading factor of 0.2 are added to the building. The decrease of 4 kWh/m$^2$ in electricity used for cooling corresponds to an increase of the same amount in thermal energy consumption for heating. So, when applied to the Postbank building as a single measure, external shading does not result in any energy savings.

## Scenario 5B – Passive architectural scenario (with mechanical cooling)

All measures in Scenario 5A are applied, except for measure 18 (Use of natural ventilation without mechanical cooling). Instead measure 17 is used:

### MEASURE 17: USE OF NATURAL VENTILATION IN CONJUNCTION WITH MECHANICAL COOLING

A chilled ceiling is installed which is active during the day (08:00–18:00), on weekdays and on weekends. The cooling energy used by this cooling system is 7 kWh/m$^2$ per year. This represents a 70% decrease in cooling energy use compared to the baseline.

## EVALUATION

Each scenario was evaluated with regard to energy, capital costs, financial gains and payback period.

### Scenario 1 – Improvement of existing envelope

- Improvement of U value of opaque walls
- Installation of super low-E glazing
- Reduction of heating set-point temperature during the day
- Use of an air-to-air heat recovery system for ventilation air
- Use of heat recovery from the cooling plant's condenser coil
- Reduction of the ventilation rate during summer and winter
- Seal leaky windows (reducing the infiltration rate)

A decrease of 95% in heating energy is the most significant result of the heating scenario; however, this is accompanied by an increase of 29% in electricity consumption for cooling. This is due to the higher transmittance of the new glazing and high internal electric lighting loads. A 17% reduction in the total electricity consumption is due to significant savings in electricity consumption for ventilation. The investment costs of 113 ECU/m² are recovered within less than ten years. The heating scenario shows the enormous potential for savings of energy for heating and ventilation when improvements to elements of the façade, alterations to the building's operation and some additional adjustments of the HVAC System are combined.

When the measures applied in Scenario 1 are analyzed as single measures, the most effective measures in terms of energy consumption are M5 (use of heat recovery on ventilation air) and M7 (reducing the ventilation rate during summer and winter) – both measures which focus on the ventilation system.

The measures with the shortest payback periods are M4 (reducing the heating set-point during the day), M5 (heat recovery), M7 (reducing the ventilation rate) and M14 (reducing the infiltration rate). These measures focus on both the heating and ventilation systems: while M4 (reducing the heating set-point) and M7 (reducing the ventilation rate) only involve altering the operation of the building, M5 (heat recovery) requires improvement of the HVAC system. M14 (reducing the infiltration rate) is the only measure of the four with short payback periods which affects the building envelope.

M1 (improvement of U value of opaque walls) and M3 (installation of super-low-E glazing), both focussing on the building envelope, are clearly the most costly measures and their effect on energy consumption when applied as single measures is less than half that of M5 (use of heat recovery) or M7(reducing the ventilation rate). Nevertheless, M1 (improving the U value of walls) and M3 (new glazing) are very significant elements within the heating scenario, because a well-insulated building envelope is a prerequisite to guarantee comfortable indoor conditions when operating the HVAC system under more severe parameters. Furthermore, the outstanding reduction in heating energy use of the overall scenario is only achieved when M1 and M3 are included.

## Summaries

The heating scenario shows that the application of a standard catalogue of measures to a typical sealed air-conditioned office building can successfully reduce the energy consumption within the boundaries of the initial design concept. The office design itself and the floor layout are not affected (e.g. not improved) by this scenario. Inside the air-conditioned floor area the temperature exceeds 24°C for 96 hours per year, and exceeds 25°C 21 hours per year; this might be considered acceptable. A crucial aspect of the heating scenario is that, despite the high investment costs (113 ECU/m²), the office design itself remains untouched, so this scenario is only successful in terms of energy savings – the working comfort is not significantly improved.

## Scenario 2 – Use of passive cooling techniques

- Improvement of U value of opaque walls
- Control strategies for mechanical ventilation (night ventilation)
- Reduction of the ventilation rate during summer and winter
- Installation of improved solar glazing
- Use of effective internal solar shading
- Daylight responsive control of artificial lighting
- Installation of high frequency (HF) ballasts

Measures M1 (additional insulation of façades), M2 (new glazing) and M7 (reducing the ventilation rate) not only affect heating energy use but also have an impact on energy consumption for ventilation and lighting. Therefore it is not surprising that relative savings in heating energy (51%), cooling energy (57%), electric lighting energy (55%) and in electrical energy consumption for mechanical ventilation (70%), are well balanced. The total annual savings achieved by the cooling scenario are 10 ECU/m², so the investment costs of about 120 ECU/m² are recovered within ten years.

Measures M10 (increasing the cooling set-point) and M12 (use of indirect evaporative cooling) are not included in the cooling scenario, mostly because of the increased overheating hours associated with these measures. Measure M11 (effective shading) improves the visual comfort in the offices when properly applied. A measure to redirect daylight was not included in the cooling scenario because the simulation of this measure was not feasible within the scope of this project. The simulation includes no overheating hours. Although the 52% reduction in total energy consumption is considerable, the building still consumes too much energy (164 kWh/m² per year) when the cooling scenario is applied. Therefore the measures of this scenario must be supplemented by other measures.

## Scenario 3 – Electric lighting improvements

- Installation of improved solar glazing
- Daylight responsive control of artificial lighting
- Installation of high frequency (HF) ballasts

The relative savings on energy consumption for electric lighting are 55%; there is potential for further savings when occupancy sensors and daylight redirecting devices are applied, however the simulation of such elements was not feasible within this project. The improved U value of the glazing leads to a 12% reduction in energy consumption for heating, while the cooling load increases by 19%. The increase in cooling load is due to the higher transmission of the new glazing resulting in larger solar gains. The reduction of internal lighting loads does not compensate for the increase of solar gains, so windows with higher radiation transmission should only be installed in the Postbank building along with exterior shading.

Scenario 3 saves 12% of the total energy consumption of the building. The annual savings in running costs are 2.7 ECU/m²; the investment costs are 58 ECU/m² giving a 21-year payback period. Artificial lighting is closely linked to the overall attractiveness of the working space. The strategy for retrofitting of the lighting should therefore be included in a refurbishment of the whole working environment; the benefits improving the quality of the office as a whole. If one only considers the impact on energy consumption, the artificial lighting measures are less efficient than other measures focussing on the building's thermal behaviour.

## Scenario 4 – HVAC system improvements

- Reduction of the ventilation rate during summer and winter
- Installation of more efficient fans
- Control strategies for mechanical ventilation (night ventilation)

The scenario simulating ventilation system improvements shows that changing the control parameters on the ventilation system and installing more efficient fans can decrease the energy consumption significantly. Total annual energy savings of 117 kWh/m², corresponding to 34% of the baseline consumption. This is realised with costs of 2.5 ECU/m² and a payback period of less than one year. The night ventilation measure (M9) is much more efficient when new fans are installed (M8). These two measures (M9 and M8) do not affect the indoor comfort, but a reduced ventilation rate (M7) has a negative effect. None of the measures included in the ventilation scenario improve the indoor comfort.

M7 (the reduction of the ventilation rate) is included in both the heating and cooling scenarios, where it was combined with measures to improve the thermal quality of the envelope of the building. In the ventilation scenario the ventilation rate is reduced without improvements to the building envelope.

This scenario is an efficient short-term investment, but as indoor comfort is not improved by this scenario it cannot be considered a comprehensive retrofitting strategy. Indoor air quality is actually an important issue within the Postbank building; the reason why the ventilation currently runs every night is that if it is not, an unpleasant odour is detectable in the morning. Therefore indoor air quality must be controlled carefully if there is to be any reduction in the ventilation rate.

## Summaries

TOTAL VALUES
Estimated energy savings: $267/260\,kWh/m^2$
Required capital cost: $147/252\,ECU/m^2$
Cost per unit of energy: $0.07\,ECU/kWh$
Financial gain per year : $19/17\,ECU/m^2$
Payback period: 10/15 years

PACKAGE P1

TOTAL VALUES
Estimated energy savings: $236kWh/m^2$
Required capital cost: $147\,ECU/m^2$
Cost per unit of energy: $0.075\,ECU/kWh$
Financial gain per year: $19\,ECU/m^2$
Payback period: 10 years

# Scenario 5 – Passive architectural scenarios

SCENARIO 5A – PASSIVE ARCHITECTURAL SCENARIO (WITHOUT MECHANICAL COOLING)
- Improvement of U value of opaque walls
- Installation of super low-E glazing
- Reduction of heating set-point temperature during the day
- Use of daylight responsive artificial lighting controls
- Use of exposed thermal mass
- Use of natural ventilation without mechanical cooling
- Use of effective external solar shading

This simulation shows a significant number of overheating hours, with the temperature exceeding 26°C in more than 50 hours and a peak temperature of 31.5°C during office hours. This result shows that the measures included in the scenario (5A) to prevent overheating are not sufficient to provide thermal comfort for the occupants. The 79% decrease in energy demand is impressive nevertheless. With the abandonment of mechanical ventilation and mechanical cooling within this scenario, no electricity is used for ventilation or cooling. The reduction in energy consumption for electric lighting is 48%, and the total saving in electrical energy consumption is 75%. There is also an 83% reduction in heating energy. Because this scenario not only includes improvements to the existent building elements but completely redefines the heating and ventilation strategy, the investment costs are high – $147\,ECU/m^2$. The payback period of ten years is acceptable, considering that the whole office concept is redefined by this scenario.

SCENARIO 5B – PASSIVE ARCHITECTURAL SCENARIO (WITH MECHANICAL COOLING)
The high number of overheating hours which arose in Scenario 5A lead to the scenario of supporting the passive architectural measures with a chilled ceiling system. Instead of M18 (use of natural ventilation without mechanical cooling) M17 (use of natural ventilation in conjunction with mechanical cooling) is applied. The cooling energy consumption with this cooling system is $7\,kWh/m^2$ per year; a 70% decrease in cooling energy use compared to the baseline. The energy consumption for other purposes is similar to scenario 5A. The total energy savings are 77% compared to the reference model, that is, only 2% higher savings than Scenario 5A. However with the chilled ceiling there are no overheating hours without affecting the outstanding energy performance of the scenario. This scenario encompasses the refurbishment of the whole office area, so the investment cost is high – $250\,ECU/m^2$. The payback period is 15 years.

# Package 1

Package P1 combines the most promising measures of Scenarios 1–4, but does not refer to the architectural measures of Scenario 5. All of the measures applied are described within the above-mentioned scenarios.

The combined application of the most promising measures of Scenarios 1–4 gives a saving of 74% in the total energy consumption of the Postbank building.

P1 is more efficient than any of the individual scenarios other than the architectural scenario S5. The package gives savings of 92% in heating energy, 67% in energy for mechanical ventilation and 48% in lighting energy. However there are no significant savings in cooling energy, nor is energy consumption for hot water or office equipment affected. While each of Scenarios 1–4 is highly efficient with regard to the energy use in the field it particularly addresses, none of these scenarios reduces the total energy consumption as successfully as package P1.

The investment costs of 147 ECU/m$^2$ are recovered within ten years. The total energy consumption post-retrofit of 89 kWh/m$^2$ is in the range of new constructions. Nevertheless, apart from the fact that no cooling energy is saved, this package has other weak points: it does not focus on the indoor environment or the office design concept. In other words, the only achievement of this package is to make savings in the energy bill, while the office environment will remain more or less as it was before retrofitting. Elements of the building are improved by the package but the building concept remains untouched. This means that the occupants would be obliged to work in their existing office environment for at least the payback period of ten years and the chance to upgrade the office environment would have been squandered.

## Conclusions

When compared to any of the other scenarios and to the package, the passive architectural scenario, Scenario 5 focuses far more on the office design concept as a whole. It aims to change the sealed building of the late 1960s into a naturally ventilated, up-to-date office building. Furthermore, the passive architectural scenario 5B is as efficient as the package P1 in terms of energy savings. The higher investment costs arise from the construction of a new façade and the installation of chilled ceilings. These higher costs are partially compensated through areas used for installation being retrieved for office use. But the main argument for spending more money on the refurbishment of the Postbank building is the resulting higher quality of the office environment. When windows can be opened the occupants' degree of perceived control over their working environment increases; this is a major factor within the appraisal of a working environment.

There are different degrees of retrofitting a building. Retrofitting activities range from single measures focussing on critical details of the existing building to comprehensive strategies to redesign an entire building. Energy consumption, the indoor environment, the adequacy of a floor layout and cost-effectiveness are among the factors considered in a retrofitting strategy. Both the present condition and the envisaged quality of the building determine which retrofitting strategy is most suitable in a particular case.

As the simulation of measures and scenarios shows, an energy-conscious selection of measures allows a significant reduction of energy use with very low investment costs and consequently short payback periods. In the case of the Postbank building, measures focussing on the ventilation system are among the most efficient in economic terms. These measures should be applied while the future use of the building is uncertain (meaning that the investment must be recovered within a short period).

When reduction of energy consumption is the only criterion used to select an appropriate retrofitting strategy the addition of measures that maximise energy savings, as in Package 1, is as efficient as a passive architectural scenario. The investment costs of the two strategies are similar. However Package 1 does not fundamentally improve the working environment, therefore this strategy should not be applied.

If the aim of the retrofitting strategy is to re-establish the Postbank building as an up-to-date office building, the passive architectural scenario, Scenario 5B, should be selected. Only a well-defined architectural strategy can convert existing, sealed, air-conditioned offices into contemporary, naturally- ventilated, high quality offices. Such an architectural strategy consists of more than measures related to energy use, so the total cost of a passive architectural retrofitting strategy will exceed the sum of costs of the above-listed measures. The benefit of a passive architectural scenario is the future quality of the Postbank office building as a whole. The offices in the refurbished building will conform to the standards of new constructions.

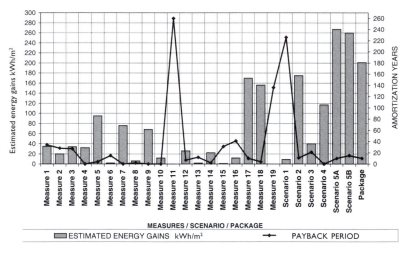

Estimated energy gains and payback periods

# City West Building, Bern, Switzerland

'City West' is an office tower located in the centre of Bern. It has two large areas at ground level mainly occupied by shops, 13 floors of offices and four underground levels occupied by parking lots, storage lots, shops and a restaurant. The building was erected between 1969 and 1971. Since then, neither the HVAC system nor the building structure have been changed. The owner, the Swiss state, is one of the pioneers in energy conservation in Switzerland. With the building's high energy loss and a decrease in visitor numbers in recent years, the government decided to retrofit the building. The plan was to concentrate on the retrofit on the façade of the tower, the ventilation system and part of the cooling system.

**Site plan**

Location: Effingerstrasse 20, Bern
Owner: Swiss Government
Total size: 25,000 m$^2$
Storeys: 17
Construction year: 1969–71
Degree of exposure: Exposed
Module: Cellular
Working hours: 07:00–18:00
Total energy consumption (1996; kWh/m$^2$): 224
   thermal / 113 electrical
User system control: Electric analogue
Heating system: District heating
Cooling system: Refrigerant centrifugal
Lighting system: Standard fluorescent

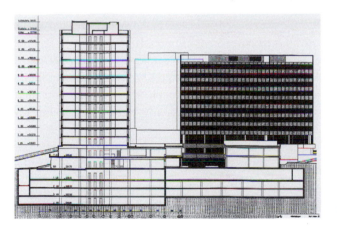

**Section view**

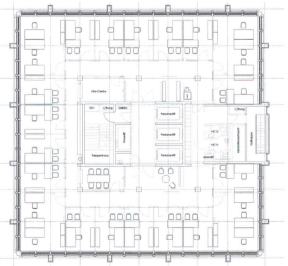

**Typical floor plan**

**Front view**

# BUILDING CHARACTERISTICS

## Architectural description

Although only 27 years old, various common weaknesses can be identified in the façade construction and some components have already reached their predicted lifespan and must be replaced. The roof and floors are secondary components in this multi-storied building. Their thermal losses are negligible compared to those from the façade. Therefore only the façade is described in detail here.

The walls consist of a concrete parapet with 2 cm mineral wool and an aluminium sheet. The aluminium sheet is weather-worn, but is still fully functional. A radiator is fastened at the inside of the parapet. This construction enables the inner wall temperature to reach 14°C when the external temperature is -10°C.

The window construction consists of an aluminium frame with side-opening windows. The double glazing has a k value of 3.1 W/m²K and a G value of 0.75. Both internal and external glass sealing are no longer tight. The sliding shutters are manually operated. The 'Storenkasten' is no longer tight against wind or against rainwater penetration. The high k value of the window construction is responsible for relatively low temperatures at the frame-to-glass junction. Thermal component analysis (with the program ISO2) showed an interior surface temperature of 6°C with an external temperature of -10°C.

The main pillars are constructed of concrete. They are arranged in a raster of 5.5 m, insulated with 3 cm mineral wool and protected with an aluminium sheet. The window frames are placed laterally to the main pillars. Thermal component analysis showed an interior wall temperature of only 11°C with an external temperature of -10°C.

The three parts of the façade described above – wall, window and concrete columns – together form a 'façade element'. The k value was calculated for the whole unit, including all thermal bridges. Most wall, floor and roof components of the two large ground-level areas are insulated with 2–4 cm mineral wool.

Characteristics of façade element

| Material | Conductivity (W/m °C) | Density (kg/m³) | Specific heat (J/kg °C) | Solar assortment | Thickness (m) | U value (W/m² °C) |
|---|---|---|---|---|---|---|
| Double glass | 0.81 | 2500 | 800 | – | 0.02 | – |
| Concrete parapet | 1.8 | 2400 | 1100 | – | 0.15 | – |
| Mineral wool | 0.04 | < 60 | 600 | – | 0.03 | – |
| Thermal bridges | – | – | – | – | – | – |
| TOTAL | – | – | – | – | 0.20 | 2.27 |

# MECHANICAL AND ELECTRICAL EQUIPMENT

## Systems description

The building's **heating system** relies on district heating. The transfer station sited in the third basement consists of two heat exchangers with a performance of 1200 kW each. The second heat exchanger is installed for excess capacity, the building complex requires a maximum of 1200 kW of heating power. A third heat exchanger with 75 kW heating power is used to heat service hot water.

The district heating temperature is set at 175°C/72°C, the distribution temperature is layed out for 90°C/70°C. The control of the twf/twr-temperature depends on external temperature. The heating distribution system consists of four areas: the restaurant, the tower, the annex, and the ventilation/air-conditioning. It is controlled by two-way regulating valves. The heating tubes leading to the offices are installed in the four corners of the tower behind an aluminium sheet. They are insulated with 4 cm mineral wool. Only a few of the heating tubes in the unheated spaces of the first basement are insulated. Heat emission is via radiators fastened to the parapet wall under the windows. Thermostatic valves limit heat emission if the ambient temperature exceeds 20–22°C. The heating season usually lasts from October to May, about 5400 hours per year.

The building's **cooling system** consists of a refrigerant centrifugal cooling plant with variable power output installed in the third basement. The nominal cooling power is 930 kW. The cooling requirement never exceeds 30% of the maximum power. The heat extraction system consists of an indirect air-cooled condensor with a nominal power of 970 kW sited on the roof of the multi-storied building. The cooling system is turned off at night. The cooling tubes distribute the energy into several ventilation stations with a constant twf/twr temperature of 6°C/12°C. The restaurant, all offices in the tower and annex and some of the shops are air-conditioned. The cooling period begins in May and usually ends in September, about 600 hours per year.

Various spaces with high thermal loads, such as the telephone exchange, server room, etc., are cooled separately with local split unit packages. The apartment on the 13th floor is also air-conditioned separately.

The **ventilation system** consists of over 20 separate ventilation units installed throughout the building complex. Many of them form small systems with air-flow rates of less than 1000 m³/h. Some of these units are no longer in use, or only used for a few hours during the year. The different ventilation units can be divided in two groups: units for parking areas, store rooms, etc., and air-conditioning units for the restaurant, shops and offices. The largest unit services the office tower. It is a CAV air-conditioning system. The mixing diffusers are placed in the ceiling as well as the exhaust air joints. The hourly air-change rate is five. The external air-flow rate is controlled according to the outside temperature. The supply air and return air fans are of low efficiency.

**Electrical network and equipment**: two 580 kVA transformers are installed in the first basement. There are two low-voltage distribution boards in

## System characteristics

*HEATING PLANT*
System type: District heating
Units: 2
Nominal heating power (kW): 2400
Heated floor area (m²): 11,152
Distribution system: Water based
Hours of operation (h/year): 5400
Set-point temperature: 20°C
Maintenance state: Good

*COOLING PLANT*
System type: Refrigerant centrifugal
Units: 1
Nominal cooling power (kW): 930
Cooled floor area (m²): 8030
Distribution system: Water based/air ducts
Hours of operation (h/year): 600
Set-point temperature: 24°C
Maintenance state: Fair

*VENTILATION PLANT*
System type: Mechanical CAV
Units: >20
Supply air-flow rate (m³/s): 25.8
Return air-flow rate (m³/s): 10.2
Supply air fan (kW): 45
Return air fan (kW): 15

*LIGHTING*
Fluorescent lamps: 1350
Incandescent lamps: <100
Hours of operation (h/day): 0–8
Maintenance state: Good

*ELECTRICAL EQUIPMENT*
Computers (units): 200
Hours of operation (h/day): 3
Printer (units): 50
Hours of operation (h/day): 5

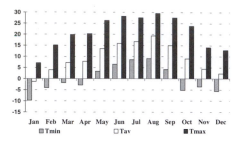

Monthly external temperatures °C

the second basement, one with 1000 A electrical power for the normal network, the other with 100 A electrical power for emergency power generation. The emergency power system is operated by a 90 kVA diesel engine. The server room has a separate, uninterruptable power supply (UPS). The lighting is mainly provided by standard fluorescent tubes. In 1991, the lighting in the offices was renovated.

Most workplaces in the offices have a computer. In the tower and annex, each floor has several printers and a photocopier.

## BUILDING'S ENERGY PERFORMANCE

The building was built in 1969–71. At that time no attention was paid to the building's likely heat loss. Consequently, the specific heat losses for the City West building are twice as high as today's local building code allows. The tower façade, with its uncoated double-glazing, is particularly poor in terms of energy loss. In addition, most other exterior surfaces (walls, lowest basement floor, etc.) should have a second layer of isolation.

Almost none of the ventilation units are equipped with heat recovery and many have a high air-change rate. This situation contributes to the high heat consumption.

The building's electricity consumption is also almost twice as high as the current average of similar buildings. Two factors must be emphasized.

The refrigerant centrifugal cooling plant is always run at less than 30% of its maximum power. With an average power loading of 20%, the compressor achieves a COP value of only 2.2. The oversized cooling pumps and heat extraction system are responsible for the system COP-value decrease to substantially under 2.0.

As mentioned above, almost all the ventilation units have high air change rates. This is due to strong fan drives, which result in higher than necessary electrical consumption.

The outdated, oversized circulation pumps in the heating system also contribute to the high electrical consumption.

Annual energy consumption breakdown by fuel type (1997–98)

| Energy | kWh/year | |
|---|---|---|
| District heating | 2,497,100 | for space heating |
| Electricity | 1,260,110 | for other uses |
| TOTAL | 3,757,210 | |
| Average energy consumption per month | 313,100 | kWh |
| Average energy consumption per m² | 28.1 | kWh/year |

Distribution of energy consumption (1997–98)

| Energy | kWh/year | kWh/m²year |
|---|---|---|
| Space heating | 1,907,000 | 171 |
| Space cooling | 80,000 | 10 |
| Lighting | 202,000 | 18 |
| Equipment | 198,000 | 17 |
| TOTAL | 2,387,000 | 216 |

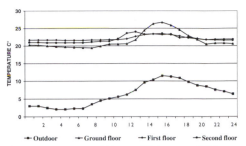

Air temperatures – Winter (19 January 1998)

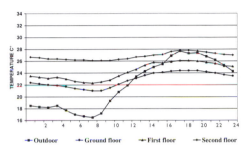

Air temperatures – Summer (5 August 1997)

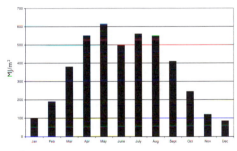

Global solar radiation – monthly averageMJ/m²

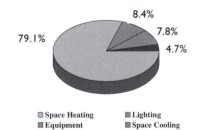

Annual energy consumption by fuel type

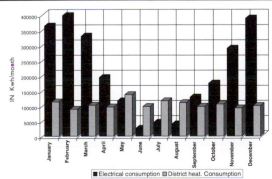

Monthly energy consumption

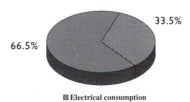

Distribution of energy consumption

## Summaries

# ENERGY RETROFITTING SCENARIOS

## Scenario 1 – Building improvements

*1.1 IMPROVEMENT OF THE BUILDING ENVELOPE*

The most extensive work is required to the lower façade. In addition, the insulation has to be improved on the tower roof and to the ground level of the building. On the tower façade, the following elements are improved:

- the double glazing with U value 3.1 $W/m^2K$ is replaced with low-E, heavy-gas double glazing with a U value 1.1 $W/m^2K$;
- new frame seals are fitted on all window frames. This decreases the infiltration rate from 0.5 to 0.1/h;
- extra mineral wool insulation is applied to: the concrete parapets, 7 cm: the wall by the staircase, 5 cm; and the concrete pillars, 3 cm. This reduces the U value of the main opaque envelope element from 2.22 to 1.22 $W/m^2K$;
- the aluminium sheets are removed, cleaned and reinstalled with an additional sheet;
- the existing manual shading devices are replaced by automatically and centrally controlled ones.

At the base area of the building and on the tower roof the following measures are undertaken:

- insulation thickness is increased on all flat roofs to 12–14 cm (main parts U value 0.22 $W/m^2K$);
- floors are also better insulated to a thickness of 6 cm;
- as far as possible, the U value of the walls will be decreased to <0.5 $W/m^2K$;
- the U value of the doors will be decreased to 2.0 $W/m^2K$.

Monthly total energy load (kWh) – effect of improving the building envelope

|  | Jan | Feb | Mar | Apr | May | Jun |
|---|---|---|---|---|---|---|
| Baseline | 243,000 | 197,000 | 187,000 | 129,000 | 91,000 | 47,000 |
| After improvement of envelope | 150,000 | 122,000 | 116,000 | 81,000 | 58,000 | 31,000 |

|  | Jul | Aug | Sep | Oct | Nov | Dec |
|---|---|---|---|---|---|---|
| Baseline | 29,000 | 41,000 | 65,000 | 120,000 | 177,000 | 238,000 |
| After improvement of envelope | 20,000 | 27,000 | 42,000 | 75,000 | 119,000 | 147,000 |

# Scenario 2 – Use of passive cooling techniques

Two scenarios were simulated for the City West office: the influence of the night cooling; and improvement of the interior climate through the use of automatically-operated shading devices.

For each simulation, the following assumptions were made about internal loads:

- occupants: area 15 m$^2$/person;
- energy consumption: 130 W/person;
- computers: 8 W/m$^2$;
- lighting: 10 W/m$^2$.

## 2.1 USE OF NIGHT COOLING

In the night cooling simulation, results can only be shown by the observed effects on internal temperature.

Monthly average daytime temperatures (°C) – effect of use of night cooling

|  | Jan | Feb | Mar | Apr | May | Jun | Jul | Aug | Sep | Oct | Nov | Dec |
|---|---|---|---|---|---|---|---|---|---|---|---|---|
| Baseline | 20.0 | 20.0 | 20.0 | 20.0 | 20.5 | 22.3 | 24.4 | 23.9 | 21.4 | 20.0 | 20.0 | 20.0 |
| With night cooling | 20.0 | 20.0 | 20.0 | 20.0 | 20.0 | 21.4 | 23.2 | 22.8 | 20.4 | 20.0 | 20.0 | 20.0 |

## 2.2 AUTOMATICALLY-OPERATED, MECHANICAL SHADING DEVICES

Currently the shading devices are operated manually. In addition to having an electric motor, the new ones are centrally controlled. This simulation was run 'with' and 'without' night cooling.

### WITH NIGHT COOLING

- Shading devices: controlled automatically; solar radiation dependent
- Light control: automatic; daylight dependent
- Ventilation air-flow rate constant: 5.0 h$^{-1}$
- Supply air temperature: 20°C
- Periods of operation: Monday to Friday, 06.00-19.00
- Night cooling: 5 days/wk, 01.00–06.00, 15 May to 15 September

Monthly total cooling load (kWh) – effect of use of automatic shading devices

|  | Jan | Feb | Mar | Apr | May | Jun | Jul | Aug | Sep | Oct | Nov | Dec |
|---|---|---|---|---|---|---|---|---|---|---|---|---|
| Baseline | 0 | 0 | 0 | 0 | 13,900 | 24,700 | 30,300 | 24,800 | 14,400 | 0 | 0 | 0 |
| With automatic shading devices | 0 | 0 | 0 | 0 | 99,00 | 18,100 | 27,400 | 22,600 | 10,300 | 0 | 0 | 0 |

## 4.2 NEW COOLING PLANT

TOTAL VALUES

Estimated energy savings: 53,000 kWh
Required capital cost: 133,000 ECU
Cost per unit of energy (mix): .062 ECU/kWh
Financial gain per year: 3300 ECU
Payback period: 40 years

## 4.3 IMPROVED HEATING AND COOLING DISTRIBUTION

TOTAL VALUES

Estimated energy savings: 120,700 kWh
Required capital cost: 23,100 ECU
Cost per unit of energy (mix): .055 ECU/kWh
Financial gain per year: 6900 ECU
Payback period: 3.4 years

WITHOUT NIGHT COOLING
- light control: automatic; daylight dependent
- ventilation air-flow rate constant: 5.0 h$^{-1}$
- supply air temperature: 18°C
- periods of operation: Monday to Friday, 06.00-19.00, May to September; manual control: 10.00–17.00; 5 days/wk; 24 hours/day, weekends July and August; automatic control: when external load, measured inside window >20 W/m$^2$
- cooling load: to hold temperature at 24°C.

**Monthly average daytime temperatures (°C) – effect of use of automatic shading devices**

|  | Jan | Feb | Mar | Apr | May | Jun | Jul | Aug | Sep | Oct | Nov | Dec |
|---|---|---|---|---|---|---|---|---|---|---|---|---|
| Baseline | 20.0 | 20.0 | 20.0 | 20.0 | 20.5 | 22.3 | 24.4 | 23.9 | 21.4 | 20.0 | 20.0 | 20.0 |
| With automatic shading devices | 20.0 | 20.0 | 20.0 | 20.0 | 20.0 | 21.4 | 23.2 | 22.8 | 20.4 | 20.0 | 20.0 | 20.0 |

# Scenario 4 – HVAC system improvements

The HVAC system improvements aim to decrease consumption of electricity and heat energy.

### 4.1 IMPROVED VENTILATION SYSTEMS

All main ventilation units will be renewed. The electricity consumption is reduced by use of more efficient fans with backwards-curved blades and using lower air-flow rates. The heating energy use will be reduced by renewing heat exchangers and using lower air-flow rates.

### 4.2 IMPROVED COOLING PLANT

The existing cooling plant is oversized. It runs at less than 20% of its nominal power. This leads to a low coefficient of performance (COP) of 2.2. Electricity consumption is reduced by replacing the existing cooling plant with a substantially smaller refrigerant reciprocating cooling plant, running at higher distribution temperatures (8°C/14°C instead of 6°C/12°C). Energy consumption for heating will also be reduced through the use of heat recovery in the cooling plant for heating the service hot water.

### 4.3 IMPROVED HEAT DISTRIBUTION NETWORK

The heat distribution network will be better insulated and run at a lower temperature. All water circulation pumps, now oversized, will be changed, further reducing the electricity consumption.

## EVALUATION

Each scenario was evaluated with regard to energy, capital costs, financial gains and payback period.

Night cooling and the automatically-operated shading devices cause a higher energy consumption. Nevertheless, these measures should be undertaken. They bring a much better thermal comfort level, which is part of the new ventilation concept (see below). The capital cost of the new shading devices is very high, but it can legitimately be seen as part of the façade retrofit. The Canton of Bern has included the application of heat recovery in its current local building code. This is the prime reason for a retrofit of the ventilation system even though the retrofit has a 27-year payback period which is barely worthwhile in financial terms. The new climate concept permits temperatures over 26°C, therefore lower air-change rates are possible.

The installed cooling power was far too generous. The power plant never exceeds 30% of its nominal power. However, for economic reasons, a refrigerant centrifugal power plant should work at a minimum of 60%, otherwise the COP is far too low. The owner of City West sets a high value on electricity savings, so they have decided to replace the power plant. The plan is to install a refrigerant reciprocating cooling plant with a higher COP value. The 40-year payback period is far too long, but the use of heat recovery (heat rejection) for service hot water heating ameliorates the payback period. After the retrofit of the façade the current pumps for heating and cooling distribution would be far too powerful. The new, smaller cooling and heating system (façade with lower U value) needs only a fraction of the old flow rate. This change is worthwhile – the payback period is less than four years.

## Package

The package, including all measures mentioned above, gives a saving of 120 kWh/m², that is more than half the baseline energy consumption. This package truly retrofits the building, since it will then fulfil the requirements of today's Swiss energy standards.

It will greatly improve the comfort of the occupants. The average internal temperature in July will be some 2.5°C lower and the highest internal temperature will be 4.5°C lower as a result of semi-passive solar measures including automatic shading devices and night cooling. It is interesting to see that night-cooling has a major effect on the average internal temperature (or on the cooling energy consumption) and automatic shading devices have a major effect on the peak temperatures (thermal comfort or cooling energy consumption). The overly-hot hours are completely suppressed.

The largest energy saving is a reduction in heating energy use, by nearly 60% (from 133 to 55 kWh/m²). This results from both the improvement of the building envelope and consequent reduction of infiltration, and from decreasing the ventilation air-flow rates from about 30,000 m³/h to a more reasonable 15,000 m³/h (which is still more air than necessary for 100 to 150 people).

Electrical energy saving is similar to heating energy saving in percentage terms at 50%, but it is smaller in absolute value (from 77 to 39 kWh/m$^2$). It is however larger when primary energy is considered; in Switzerland 2.5 kWh of primary energy is necessary to provide 1 kWh of electricity at the plug. Therefore, in terms of total energy, the electricity saving resulting from a better air-conditioning system is 95 kWh/m$^2$, a value close to the primary energy saving for heating.

The capital cost of the whole package is rather high and cannot be financed by the energy savings. It should however be pointed out that the building is in a poor physical state and shall be refurbished anyway. Most of the cost, say 90%, can then be attributed to refurbishment and only a small proportion to the retrofit measures, that is those measures taken exclusively to save energy.

## CONCLUSIONS

The largest cost is the improvement of the envelope, which cannot (and should not) be financed by energy savings. This measure is required by the poor condition of the curtain façade and is part of standard refurbishment of this building. It is interesting to see that night cooling has a major effect on the average internal temperature (or on the cooling energy consumption) and automatic shading devices have a major effect on the highest temperatures (thermal comfort levels or cooling power).

The retrofit study of this building started before the OFFICE project. Most of the decisions related to the retrofit were taken without detailed simulations. The extensive simulations performed for the OFFICE project confirmed these decisions, and were useful for the project.

# LESO Building, Lausanne, Switzerland

The LESO building is a passive solar experimental building. It was built to house the Solar Energy and Building Physics Research Laboratory of the EPFL, as well as to provide an experimental facility for measuring the characteristics of passive solar systems. Its southern section consists of nine 'calorimetric cells' arranged in three floors. Each cell is 7.2 m wide, 3.2 m high and 5.2 m deep. Each cell is thermally insulated from neighbouring cells, and closed, on its south wall, by the façade element to be tested. The façade elements can easily be changed within a week. Most cells are divided into two office rooms by a lightweight partition wall. The north section of the building includes services and staircase.

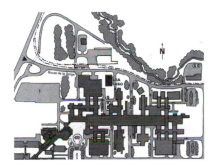

Site plan

Location: EPFL campus, Lausanne
Owner: Swiss Office of Federal Buildings
Total size: 670 m$^2$
Storeys: 3
Construction year: 1982
Degree of exposure: Sheltered
Module: Cellular
Working hours: 08:00–18:00
Total energy consumption (1996): 93 kWh/m$^2$
User system control: Manual
Heating system: Direct electric and district heating
Cooling system: None
Lighting system: Electric and daylight

Front view of the complex

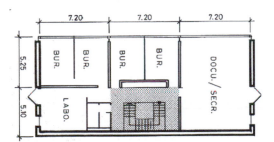

Typical floor plan

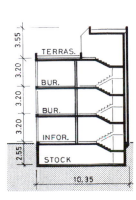

Cross section

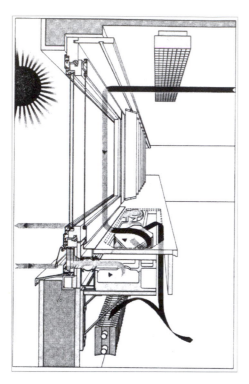

ISAL façade detail (integrated ventilation system including heat recovery)

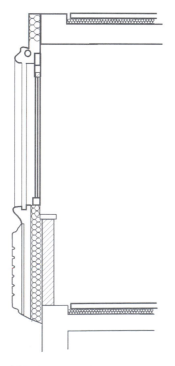

EPFL façade detail

# BUILDING CHARACTERISTICS

## Architectural description

The flat roof is a concrete deck with thick dual insulation: half of the thermal resistance is provided by polyurethane foam plates located between the deck and the roofing layer, while the other half is extruded polystyrene, lying over the roofing layer (inverted insulation), protected either by concrete plates or gravel. A 'sunspace' is built on this roof, at the top of the staircase.

The north, east and west walls are each made of two plain concrete block walls, with 18-cm glass wool sandwiched in between. There are small windows in the north wall to provide light to the staircase. The east and west walls, and the roof, have protruding elements made of steel–urea formaldehyde–steel sandwich panels. The south-east and south-west façades of these elements include windows. These elements are poorly insulated, since they are thin and present many thermal bridges. Office floors and partition walls between cells and between cells and staircases are also thermally insulated.

Characteristics of office floors

| Material | Conductivity (W/m °C) | Density (kg/m³) | Specific heat (J/kg °C) | Solar assortment | Thickness (m) | U value (W/m² °C) |
|---|---|---|---|---|---|---|
| PVC soil plates | 0.2 | 1380 | 1600 | – | 0.004 | – |
| Cement mortar | 1.4 | 2200 | 1300 | – | 0.06 | – |
| Expanded polystyrene | 0.036 | 30 | 1600 | – | 0.06 | – |
| Reinforced concrete | 1.8 | 2400 | 1300 | – | 0.25 | – |
| TOTAL | – | – | – | – | 0.374 | 0.51 |

Characteristics of external wall

| Material | Conductivity (W/m °C) | Density (kg/m³) | Specific heat (J/kg °C) | Solar assortment | Thickness (m) | U value (W/m² °C) |
|---|---|---|---|---|---|---|
| Cement brick | 1.1 | 2000 | 1300 | – | 0.18 | – |
| Glass fibre panel | 0.04 | 40 | 710 | – | 0.18 | – |
| Air layer, ventilated | variable | 1.2 | 1600 | – | 0.02 | – |
| Cement brick | 1.1 | 2000 | 1300 | – | 0.15 | – |
| TOTAL | – | – | – | – | 0.53 | 0.2 |

The EPFL façade

The southern façade consists of nine different façade elements, each enclosing a cell of two office rooms. These façade elements include, among others, a high insulation technique (HIT) façade, a '**parietodynamic**' façade, a double skin, etc. Glazing is at least double insulated. Several windows have low-E coated glazing or films. Since it was built, in 1982, about 16 façade elements have been measured and tested on this building. This means that most elements have been changed at least once. Tested elements, no longer present on the building, include sunspaces attached to one or two floors, Trombe walls, and semi-transparent air-solar collectors with underground heat storage.

Characteristics of roof covering

| Material | Conductivity (W/m °C) | Density (kg/m³) | Specific heat (J/kg °C) | Solar assortment | Thickness (m) | U value (W/m² °C) |
|---|---|---|---|---|---|---|
| Sand and gravel | 0.7 | 1 900 | 920 | – | 0.05 | – |
| Extruded polystyrene | 0.036 | 25 | 1600 | – | 0.08 | – |
| Roofing | 0.2 | 1380 | 1600 | – | 0.02 | – |
| Polyurethane PUR | 0.03 | 55 | 1600 | – | 0.08 | – |
| Vapour barrier | 0.2 | 1200 | 1900 | – | 0.002 | – |
| Cement mortar to give slope | 1.4 | 2200 | 1300 | – | 0.1 | – |
| Reinforced concrete | 1.8 | 2400 | 1300 | – | 0.25 | – |
| TOTAL | – | – | – | – | 0.58 | 0.18 |

Left: good solar protection – the awnings are well ventilated;
Right: poor solar protection – a layer of hot air is formed between the awning and the window

## System characteristics

### HEATING PLANT (PER OFFICE ROOM)

System type: Direct electric heater
Units: 1
Nominal heating power (kW): 1.5
Heated floor area (m²): 18.9
Distribution system: None
Hours of operation (h/year): 700 @ full power, 200 @ 'standby'
Set-point temperature: 20°C
Maintenance State: Good

### LIGHTING

Fluorescent lamps: 6
Incandescent lamps: 1
Hours of operation (h/day): 0–4 (depending on season, weather conditions, etc.)
Maintenance state: Good

### ELECTRICAL EQUIPMENT

Computers (units): 2
Hours of operation (h/day): 8
Printer (unit): 0.4
Hours of operation (h/day): 8

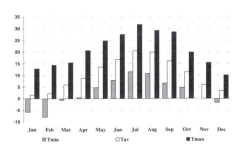

Monthly external temperatures °C

# MECHANICAL AND ELECTRICAL EQUIPMENT

## Systems description

Both active and passive **cooling systems** are employed in the LESO building. Climate control in summer is based on passive free cooling. During the day, the ventilation rate is kept at a minimum. Windows and doors are closed, to avoid external warm air entering the building. External solar protection (projection fabric blinds) are kept down, to keep solar gain to a minimum. Before leaving the building at the end of the working day, the occupants open doors and windows located at the building entrance and at the top of the building. These openings are protected against driving rain and intruders. Most office doors are also kept open at night. The massive structure of the building is thus slowly cooled during the night by the air-flow rate generated by the stack effect. In the morning, the building is ready to cope with the limited thermal gains of the next day.

An active cooling system is used in the workshop located on the ground floor, just above the underground rock bed. Small fans, of the type used in electronic devices, blow cool air through the rock bed during the night, cooling it. The next day, this rock bed stores the heat flowing through the floor, thus cooling the floor and the workshop.

**Ventilation** is mostly natural, either through windows or by exchange through office doors with the staircase, which is ventilated by the stack effect. Only the lavatories have extraction fans, switched on during office hours by a clock. One façade element, the '**parietodynamic**' one, includes a ventilation system located below the windows. The external air is filtered, then passes through a plate heat exchanger and an electric heater before being blown into the room. Extracted air passes along the glazing, between the external, double, low-E-coated glazing and an internal, single glass pane. This ensures active thermal insulation of the window. The air then passes through the heat exchanger before being expelled.

**Electrical network and equipment**: this experimental building includes many facilities for monitoring its thermal behaviour. Each cell is heated independently by an electric heater connected to a meter. Lighting and other electrical appliances (one or two desktop computers per room) are connected to another meter. Thus the electricity consumption of each individual cell can be measured.

A cable network connects each office room to the EPFL network, itself directly connected to an electronic highway. This includes telephone, telefax, and Internet (though optical fibre) connections.

The data collection in the LESO building is fully automated. A central data logger collects the data provided by ten peripherals, each of which can be connected to up to 50 sensors. A peripheral is located in each cell, and one is dedicated to the meteorological station. The central data logger is also connected to the computer network, thus making the collected data available to everybody at any time.

## BUILDING'S ENERGY PERFORMANCE

### General profile of energy use

The overall energy use of this experimental building is rather low – 93 kWh/m², only half of which being used for space heating. This results from well-insulated construction, passive solar design, and energy conscious occupants. The passive solar design significantly shortens the heating season, which in this building begins in November and ends mid-March. Standard buildings in the area need heating from October to mid-May.

The building was designed in 1982 not only to provide an experimental facility, but also as a demonstration building showing that passive solar design can be cheap (this building has proved the cheapest, per unit floor area, of the campus) and efficient. Nevertheless, it is possible to do better now, and some weaknesses were found in the building envelope. Therefore, the building was to be refurbished in 1998 to bring it up to the current best standards. It is expected that energy use for heating and lighting will significantly decrease with the improved envelope.

Office rooms are electrically heated, despite the high cost of electricity, to facilitate the individual measurement of heating energy in each cell for scientific experiments.

Passive cooling provides an excellent summer comfort level on the first two floors and an acceptable temperature on the third floor, without any artificial cooling.

Annual energy consumption breakdown by fuel type (1997)

| Energy | kWh/year | |
|---|---|---|
| District heating | 30,800 | for space heating |
| Electricity | 31,500 | for other uses |
| TOTAL | 62,300 | |
| Average energy consumption per month | 5200 kWh | |
| Average energy consumption per m² | 93 kWh/year | |

Distribution of energy consumption (1997)

| Energy | kWh/year | kWh/m²year |
|---|---|---|
| Space heating | 30,800 | 46 |
| Space cooling | 0 | 0 |
| Lighting and equipment | 31,500 | 47 |
| TOTAL | 62,300 | 93 |

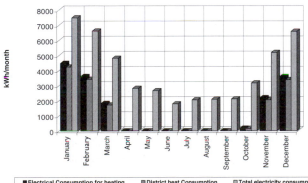

Monthly energy consumption

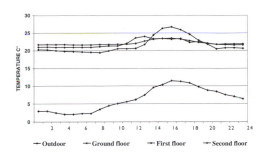

Air temperatures – Winter (17 February 1997)

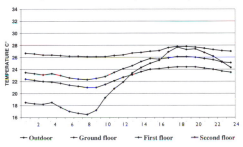

Air temperatures – Summer (8 August 1997)

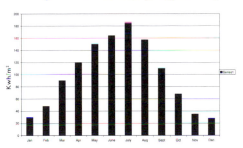

Global solar radiation – monthly average kWh/m²

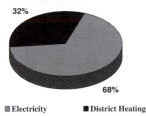

Annual energy consumption by fuel type

Distribution of energy consumption

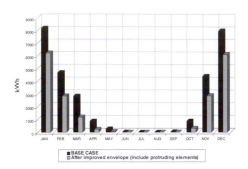

Calculated total heating load - envelope improvements

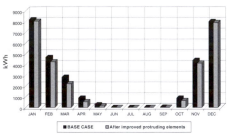

Calculated total heating load - improvements to protruding elements

# ENERGY RETROFITTING SCENARIOS

## Scenario 1 – Building improvements

### 1.1 IMPROVEMENT OF PROTRUDING ELEMENTS

Some façade elements, in particular an ironwork prismatic element protruding on the roof and façades, present poor thermal properties. These are replaced by a new bow-window and skylights, improving thermal comfort and daylighting in connecting rooms as well as avoiding energy waste.

Monthly energy consumption for heating (kW) – effect of envelope improvements

|  | Jan | Feb | Mar | Apr | May | Jun | Jul | Aug | Sep | Oct | Nov | Dec |
|---|---|---|---|---|---|---|---|---|---|---|---|---|
| Baseline | 8180 | 4670 | 2820 | 880 | 260 | 10 | 0 | 0 | 40 | 870 | 4390 | 8000 |
| After envelope improvements | 6220 | 2830 | 1180 | 230 | 50 | 0 | 0 | 0 | 10 | 300 | 2860 | 6120 |

Monthly energy consumption for heating (kW) – effect of improvements to protruding elements

|  | Jan | Feb | Mar | Apr | May | Jun | Jul | Aug | Sep | Oct | Nov | Dec |
|---|---|---|---|---|---|---|---|---|---|---|---|---|
| Baseline | 8180 | 4670 | 2820 | 880 | 260 | 10 | 0 | 0 | 40 | 870 | 4390 | 8000 |
| After protruding elements improvements | 8040 | 4260 | 2220 | 540 | 130 | 0 | 0 | 0 | 20 | 650 | 4130 | 7910 |

### 1.2 IMPROVEMENT OF SUNSPACE

The sunspace located at the top of the staircase is changed to a new one, with better frames and high performance, low-E-coated double-glazing.

### 1.3 IMPROVEMENT OF SOUTHERN FAÇADE

All the various experimental elements on the southern façade are changed to a new, up-to-date façade. This includes very good insulation, high performance commercial glazing, and an optimised light shelf. Materials are chosen according to sustainable development criteria.

## Scenario 2 – Use of passive cooling techniques

### 2.1 INSTALLATION OF CEILING FANS

Ceiling fans are installed to improve comfort at high temperatures. This measure was tested on two office types: EPFL and ISAL. These two offices have different southern façades. Note that no mechanical cooling system is installed in the LESO building. However, a cooling requirement was simulated. The baseline temperature is controlled between 20°C and 26°C. With ceiling fans, the temperature is allowed to rise to 28°C.

Monthly energy consumption for cooling (kW) – effect of ceiling fans

|  | Jan | Feb | Mar | Apr | May | Jun | Jul | Aug | Sep | Oct | Nov | Dec |
|---|---|---|---|---|---|---|---|---|---|---|---|---|
| Baseline | 0 | 0 | 0 | 0 | -8.7 | -69.1 | -142 | -115 | -38.5 | -6.87 | 0 | 0 |
| With ceiling fans | – | – | – | – | – | 2 | 45 | 20 | 4 | – | – | – |

### 2.2 USE OF PASSIVE NIGHT VENTILATION

During the warm season, the office rooms are well protected against overheating during the day by the use of solar protection and a minimum ventilation rate. They are passively cooled during the night by natural ventilation through large openings that are protected from wind, rain and other possible intrusions. This technique is well adapted to heavy, well-insulated buildings in climates with night temperatures below the comfort level. This measure was also tested on two office types: EPFL and ISAL.

Monthly energy consumption for cooling (kW) – effect of passive night ventilation

|  | Jan | Feb | Mar | Apr | May | Jun | Jul | Aug | Sep | Oct | Nov | Dec |
|---|---|---|---|---|---|---|---|---|---|---|---|---|
| Baseline | 0 | 0 | 0 | 0 | -8.7 | -69.1 | -142 | -115 | -38.5 | -6.87 | 0 | 0 |
| With night ventilation | – | – | – | – | – | – | 21 | 10 | 3 | – | – | – |

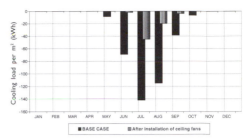

calculated total cooling load - installation of ceiling fans

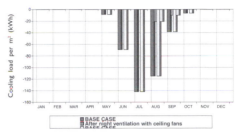

calculated total cooling load - night cooling and ceiling fans

Controlled opening connecting an office room to the adjacent staircase – for passive cooling

Ceiling fans give acceptable comfort levels up to temperatures as high as 28°C

Controlled opening at the top of a staircase to allow exit of warm air during passive cooling

Air entry for passive cooling located in the entrance lock. The grid ensures security and the entry can be completely closed in cold weather

## Scenario 3 – Daylighting improvements

### 3.1 INSTALLATION OF IMPROVED LIGHTING SYSTEM (*DELTA* SYSTEM)

Manual control of solar protection and artificial lighting is replaced by fuzzy logic control of shadings and luminaries. This system was developed within the DELTA project.* The baseline is manual control of solar protection, by an energy conscious user, and manual light switching to obtain a light level of at least 500 lux on the work surface. Temperature is maintained between 20 and 24 °C by simulated heating and cooling systems with on/off thermostats having 0.5 K tolerances. The first improvement was the installation of a commercial automated control of artificial lighting – the LUXMATE system from Zumtobel. This system maintains, when 'on', a 500-lux light level at a reference location on the work surface. The second improvement modelled was the installation of an automatic control for the solar protection. Two control algorithms were selected – the L&G and DELTA algorithms. Both tend to minimise energy consumption. In addition, when a user is present, they also optimise visual comfort. They can also take account of the user's wishes and include safety rules. The L&G algorithm is a classical artificial intelligence algorithm, based on a decision tree. The DELTA algorithm uses fuzzy logic to treat the same set of rules. (Reference heated floor area: 670 m$^2$.)

---

* DELTA: A blind controller using fuzzy logic. OFEN project 50943, final report. LESO-EPFL, 1996.

# EVALUATION

Each scenario was evaluated with regard to energy, capital costs, financial gains and payback period.

## Scenario 1 – Building improvements

- Improvement of protruding elements
- Improvement of sunspace
- Improvement of south façade

Improvement of existing envelope should result in the total energy consumption of the building decreasing by 40%, that is from 53 to 32 kWh/m². Included in this energy total are 12 kWh/m² for lighting, unchanged in this scenario, and 4.5 kWh/m² theoretical demand for simulated cooling. Energy demand for heating is reduced by 54%. Comfort is increased. With this improvement only, the uncontrolled temperature always remains between 16 and 30°C, and between 18 and 27°C for 80% of the time. The energy content of the southern façade is reduced from about 500 kWh per square metre of façade area to less than 200 kWh/m².

## Scenario 2 – Use of passive cooling techniques

- Installation of ceiling fans
- Use of passive night ventilation

This scenario has shown that when passive cooling is well used no mechanical cooling is necessary in this building. Summer comfort is greatly improved since the number of hours when the internal temperature rises above 26°C are reduced from 1300 to 440, while the 440 hours at temperatures above 27°C found in the reference case completely disappear. This corresponds to the experience of the occupants. The cost of such measures is close to zero.

## Scenario 3 – Improved daylighting

- Installation of improved lighting system (DELTA system)

Simulations show dramatic energy savings can be made through improvements in daylighting: 44% saving in heating energy, by a better use of passive solar; 78% saving in theoretical cooling energy, because of better solar protection; and 61% reduction in the energy used for lighting. These savings partially result from the new improved façade, which includes the **anidolic** system. This scenario is now combined with the first one.

# Summaries

*SCENARIO 1 – BUILDINGS IMPROVEMENTS:*

**TOTAL VALUES**
Estimated energy savings: 40.6 kWh
Required capital cost: 60 ECU
Cost per unit of energy: 0.1 ECU/kWh
Financial gain per year: 4.1 ECU
Payback period: 15 years

*SCENARIO 2 – USE OF PASSIVE COOLING TECHNIQUES*

**TOTAL VALUES**
Estimated energy savings: 18.9 kWh
Required capital cost: 0 ECU
Cost per unit of energy: 0.1 ECU/kWh
Financial gain per year: 1.9 ECU
Payback period: 0 years

*SCENARIO 3 – LIGHTING IMPROVEMENTS*

**TOTAL VALUES**
Estimated energy savings: 40.3 kWh
Required capital cost: 75 ECU
Cost per unit of energy: 0.1 ECU/kWh
Financial gain per year: 4 ECU
Payback period: 19 years

*PACKAGE*

**TOTAL VALUES**
Estimated energy savings: 51.2 kWh
Required capital cost: 75 ECU
Cost per unit of energy: 0.1 ECU/kWh
Financial gain per year: 5.1 ECU
Payback period: 15 years

## Package

Simulations show that, even on this low energy building, a package combining all three scenarios results in 60% heating energy savings, completely suppresses the need for mechanical cooling, and reduces the energy used for lighting by 64%. In this special case, the refurbishment also provides 5% additional office area.

# Le Recamier, Lyon, France

'Le Recamier' is an office building located close to a major road axis in the centre of Lyon and is surrounded by narrow, one-way streets. The building is an independent part of a larger triangular-shaped building situated in an administrative and business ward.

The building hosts three companies, most notably CERTU, a technical service of the French Ministry of Public Works which has been there for the last three years. The offices of CERTU operate 12 hours a day with 165 permanent employees and a few visitors per day. The offices of CERTU occupy about 44% of the total area of Le Recamier.

The north façade is separated from neighbouring buildings of the same height by a ten metre wide street. Solar access for east and south-east façades and for lower floors is not hindered by trees or the three-storey neighbouring buildings except when the sun is at low altitude angles.

The latitude of the site is 45°43' N and the longitude 04°57' E. It is 201 metres above sea level.

**Site plan**

Location: Rue Juliette Recamier 5
Owner: Private
Total size: 4371 m²
Storeys: 7
Year of construction: 1987
Degree of exposure: Sheltered
Module: Cellular
Working hours: 12 h / working day
Total energy consumption (1996): 95 kWh/m²yr
User system control: Central temperature control
Heating system: Electric
Cooling system: Refrigerant centrifugal in meeting
    room
Lighting system: Standard fluorescent tubes with
    electromagnetic ballasts

**Front view**

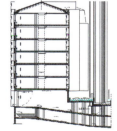

**Vertical section**

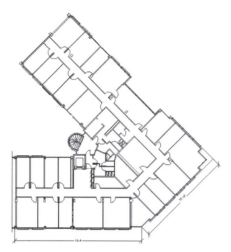

Typical floor plan

Wall detail

Vertical section – interior view

# BUILDING CHARACTERISTICS

## Architectural description

Le Recamier was built in 1987 and is typical of the office buildings constructed in Lyon during this period. The building described here is the east part of a triangular-shaped building occupied by CERTU.

Le Recamier is composed of two wings which form a corner of the whole building. The first wing has its north façade facing other buildings of the same height, separated by a street; the south side looks onto the interior courtyard of the triangular whole. The south-east and east façades of the second wing are rather distant from neighbouring buildings.

The ground floor is composed partly of meeting rooms and offices and partly of open spaces – library, reception room, open corridor. The library has large glazed surfaces to the north and east sides. Technical spaces are located in the inner part of the corner.

Other floors are organized with more or less the same scheme: a blind corridor provides access to office rooms which look out to the different façades. On each floor, meeting rooms, computer or office appliance spaces are located beside the technical spaces. These spaces are blind spaces.

All the external walls of the building are made of reinforced concrete. Some are curtain walls including aluminium. The internal face of the walls support an industrial insulation element made of rockwool and plastering.

The pitched roof has a 35% incline and is constituted of wood, aluminium and curved tiles.

All windows are double-glazed casements including a layer of tinted glass. They are all equipped with awnings for shading.

The building includes a 1000 m² underground parking area. Moreover, the ground floor and the six upper floors are equipped with false ceilings.

Characteristics of external wall

| Material | Conductivity (W/m °C) | Density (Kg/m³) | Specific heat (J/kg °C) | Solar assortment | Thickness (m) | U value (W/m² °C) |
|---|---|---|---|---|---|---|
| Concrete | – | – | – | – | – | 0.42 |
| Rockwool | – | – | – | – | – | – |
| Plaster | – | – | – | – | – | – |
| TOTAL | – | – | – | – | – | 0.42 |

Vertical section

## MECHANICAL AND ELECTRICAL EQUIPMENT

### Systems description

The **heating system** is composed of electric resistances inserted in every floor, with extra electric heaters in each office. The individual power of each local heater is 1.5 kW. The total power of the floor heating is 600 kW. The control system normally allows the floor heating only to operate during night-time in order to store heat within the floor concrete during the low electricity tariff period. During the day, the floors are not supplied with electric power and extra heating is produced as required by the local heaters. In reality, this scheme is out of order, resulting in a nearly constant set-point temperature of 20°C.

The **ventilation system** is independent. Only the air extraction is mechanically controlled by a fan. The air-handling units (AHU) are located on the roof in a technical room. The total return air flow rate is $1.67 \, \text{m}^3/\text{s}$ for the first AHU (ventilation of the offices) and $2.78 \, \text{m}^3/\text{s}$ for the second AHU (meeting rooms). Fresh air is supplied naturally through air inlets located inside the window frames, which is quite common in France. Extraction is effected through air outlets on the opposite wall to the façade with a mean air flow rate of $20 \, \text{m}^3/\text{h}$ (which is the hygienic ventilation rate for one person).

There is no **cooling system** in the offices and occupants are complaining about thermal comfort in some of them. To avoid excessive overheating they open the windows and draw the existing blinds. This has some disadvantages: the blinds prevent air from entering the offices, and without them, excessive air speed can occur which is incompatible with office work. Only the meeting rooms (about 800 m²) can be cooled if necessary, using an 18 kW refrigerant centrifugal cooling unit.

### System characteristics

*HEATING PLANT*

System type: Electric heating with mechanical ventilation
Units: Individual
Nominal heating power (kW): 153
Heated floor area (m²): 4371
Distribution system: Central electric heating and local electric heaters
Hours of operation:
    Heated floor: 22.00 – 6.00
    Local heating: 08.00 – 11.00
Set-point temperature (°C): 19
Maintenance state: Heated floor out of order in some zones

*COOLING PLANT*

System type: Refrigerant centrifugal in meeting rooms
Units: 1
Nominal cooling power (kW): 18
Cooled floor area (m²): 800
Distribution system: Air
Hours of operation (h/year): Depending on room use
Set-point temperature (°C): 22
Maintenance state: Normal use

*LIGHTING*

Fluorescent lamps:
    Standard fluorescent tubes with electro-magnetic ballasts in office rooms
Incandescent lamps: In stairways
Hours of operation: 07.00 – 20.00
Maintenance state: Normal use

*VENTILATION PLANT*

System type: Mechanical ventilation (simple extraction)
Units: 2
Supply air flow rate (m³/s): 2.78
Return air flow rate (m³/s): 4.45

Monthly external temperatures

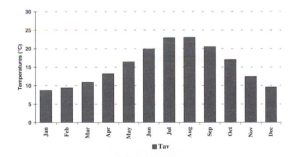

Interior view

Interior view

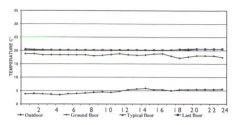

Air temperatures – Winter (4 December 1997)

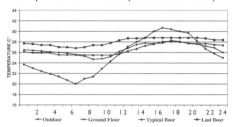

Air temperatures – Summer (8 August 1997)

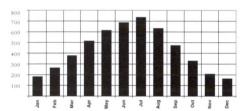

Global horizontal solar radiation – monthly average (MJ/m²)

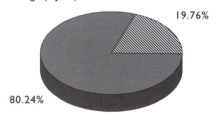

19.76%

80.24%

▨ For other use    ■ For space heating

Annual energy consumption – breakdown according to the fuel type

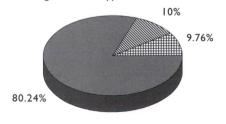

10%

9.76%

80.24%

■ Space Heating  ▨ Lighting  ▨ Equipment

Annual energy consumption – breakdown by end use

## BUILDING'S ENERGY PERFORMANCE

### General profile of energy use

The figures given in the graphs and tables have been calculated from a simulation exercise after calibration of the building model (both in free floating conditions corresponding to summer and in controlled conditions representing winter). The space heating consumption was calculated for a 20 °C set-point temperature. The cooling energy use has also been calculated for this building for a 26 °C set-point temperature. The lighting consumption was calculated from the power of the lamps within the building and a time schedule taking into account the daylighting potential in the existing building.

It can be seen that calculated consumed electricity is 97.8 kWh/m² p.a. for space heating alone, which is within the normal range of office building consumption (80-190 kWh/m² p.a. for heating and DHW demand). Cooling energy requirements are very low for the simulation climate, only 1.8 kWh/m². In the retrofitting exercise it is interesting to see if this cooling consumption can be avoided through passive cooling techniques for an equivalent thermal comfort. A reduction in the heating consumption should also be possible by dealing with the poor sealing of the envelope and through better management of the heating system. Lighting consumption is already very low and no retrofitting measures were investigated in this regard.

Distribution of energy consumption

| ENERGY | kWh/year | kWh/m²year |
|---|---|---|
| Space Heating | 427,484 | 97.8 |
| Space Cooling | 7866 | 1.8 |
| Lighting | 43,273 | 9.9 |
| Other | 123,699 | 28.3 |
| TOTAL | 602,322 | 137.8 |

Annual energy consumption breakdown by fuel type

| ENERGY | kWh/year | |
|---|---|---|
| Electricity | 435,350 | for space heating and cooling |
|  | 166,972 | for lighting and equipment |
| Total | 602,322 | |
| Average energy consumption per month | 50,193 | kWh/month |
| Average energy consumption per m² | 137.8 | kWh/m²year |

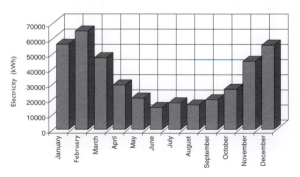

Overall electrical consumption

# ENERGY RETROFITTING SCENARIOS

## Scenario 1 – Building improvements

### 1A.1 REPLACEMENT OF WINDOW FRAMES

Replacement of the existing aluminium window casement by PVC casements with lower U-value (3 W/m²K instead of 4 Wm²K).

Monthly total energy consumption (kWh) – effect of replacement of window frames

|  | Jan | Feb | Mar | Apr | May | Jun | Jul | Aug | Sep | Oct | Nov | Dec |
|---|---|---|---|---|---|---|---|---|---|---|---|---|
| Baseline | 12137 | 9925 | 9892 | 4275 | 1671 | 643 | 1028 | 1258 | 943 | 4243 | 8720 | 12700 |
| After replacement | 11375 | 9274 | 9114 | 3804 | 1424 | 538 | 1020 | 1316 | 789 | 3865 | 8126 | 11930 |

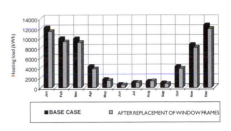

Effect of window frame replacement

### 1A.2 INSULATION OF OUTSIDE WALLS

Increase the level of insulation of the outside walls by addition of 4 cm of glass wool.

Monthly total energy consumption (kWh) – effect of increased insulation of outside walls

|  | Jan | Feb | Mar | Apr | May | Jun | Jul | Aug | Sep | Oct | Nov | Dec |
|---|---|---|---|---|---|---|---|---|---|---|---|---|
| Baseline | 12137 | 9925 | 9892 | 4275 | 1671 | 643 | 1028 | 1258 | 943 | 4243 | 8720 | 12700 |
| After extra insulation | 11908 | 9735 | 9703 | 4183 | 1628 | 626 | 1020 | 1259 | 916 | 4149 | 8551 | 12461 |

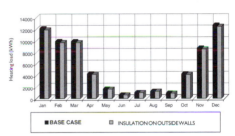

Effect of reduction of air infiltration

### 1A.3 REDUCTION OF AIR INFILTRATION

Reduce air infiltration through the façades (by sealing at the window frame level) and via the vertical lift shafts.

Total monthly energy consumption (kWh) – effect of reduction of air infiltration

|  | Jan | Feb | Mar | Apr | May | Jun | Jul | Aug | Sep | Oct | Nov | Dec |
|---|---|---|---|---|---|---|---|---|---|---|---|---|
| Baseline | 12137 | 9925 | 9892 | 4275 | 1671 | 643 | 1028 | 1258 | 943 | 4243 | 8720 | 12700 |
| After reduction | 7287 | 5780 | 5450 | 1720 | 454 | 387 | 1383 | 1798 | 430 | 1890 | 4990 | 7673 |

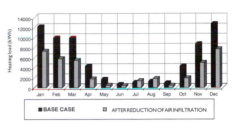

Effect of increased insulation

### 1A.4 INCREASE INDOOR THERMAL STORAGE

Increase the indoor thermal mass (by removing the carpet on floors and adding heavier partition walls) to reduce the thermal load due to solar gains in summer.

Monthly total energy consumption (kWh) – effect of increasing indoor thermal storage

|  | Jan | Feb | Mar | Apr | May | Jun | Jul | Aug | Sep | Oct | Nov | Dec |
|---|---|---|---|---|---|---|---|---|---|---|---|---|
| Baseline | 12137 | 9925 | 9892 | 4275 | 1671 | 643 | 1028 | 1258 | 943 | 4243 | 8720 | 12700 |
| After increase | 12186 | 9976 | 9985 | 4318 | 1638 | 577 | 866 | 1101 | 862 | 4284 | 8753 | 12718 |

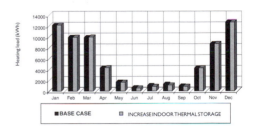

Effect of increased indoor thermal storage

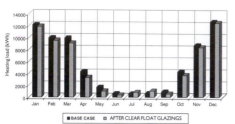

Effect of clear float glazing

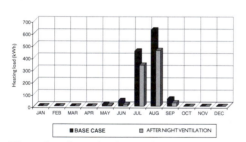

Effect of adding glazed double skin

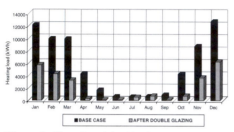

Effect of mechanical night ventilation

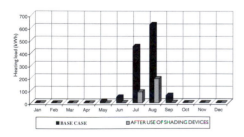

Effect of ceiling fans

### 1B.5 CLEAR FLOAT GLAZING

Replacement of the bronze anti-sun glazing of the façade by clear float glazing to increase passive solar gain.

Monthly total energy consumption (kWh) – effect of clear float glazing

|  | Jan | Feb | Mar | Apr | May | Jun | Jul | Aug | Sep | Oct | Nov | Dec |
|---|---|---|---|---|---|---|---|---|---|---|---|---|
| Baseline | 12137 | 9925 | 9892 | 4275 | 1671 | 643 | 1028 | 1258 | 943 | 4243 | 8720 | 12700 |
| After reglazing | 11847 | 9493 | 9048 | 3295 | 1030 | 369 | 829 | 1040 | 557 | 3681 | 8369 | 12494 |

### 1B.6 GLAZED DOUBLE SKIN

Use of a glazed double skin on each façade to increase insulation and to pre-heat ventilation air in winter. In summer, fresh air is taken directly from the outside. This system requires that supplied and extracted air are mechanically controlled.

Monthly total energy consumption (kWh) – effect of glazed double skin

|  | Jan | Feb | Mar | Apr | May | Jun | Jul | Aug | Sep | Oct | Nov | Dec |
|---|---|---|---|---|---|---|---|---|---|---|---|---|
| Baseline | 12137 | 9925 | 9892 | 4275 | 1671 | 643 | 1028 | 1258 | 943 | 4243 | 8720 | 12700 |
| After add'n of dble skin | 5697 | 4302 | 3261 | 307 | 96 | 91 | 529 | 722 | 120 | 726 | 3651 | 6230 |

## Scenario 2 – Use of passive cooling techniques

### 2.1 USE OF MECHANICAL NIGHT VENTILATION

Night ventilation by a mechanical ventilation system. Equivalent 3 ACH of fresh air is imposed by the mechanical ventilation system from 8.00 pm to 7.00 am to pre-cool spaces.

Monthly cooling load (kWh) – effect of mechanical night ventilation

|  | Jan | Feb | Mar | Apr | May | Jun | Jul | Aug | Sep | Oct | Nov | Dec |
|---|---|---|---|---|---|---|---|---|---|---|---|---|
| Baseline | 0 | 0 | 0 | 0 | 16 | 47 | 453 | 627 | 60 | 0 | 0 | 0 |
| With night ventilation | 0 | 0 | 0 | 0 | 7 | 14 | 336 | 457 | 28 | 0 | 0 | 0 |

### 2.2 USE OF CEILING FANS

Ceiling fans increase the air speed around the human body which improves thermal comfort. Previous studies have shown that the comfort temperature limit is increased by as much as 3° C, allowing a cooling set point of 28°C.

Monthly cooling load (kWh) – effect of ceiling fans

|  | Jan | Feb | Mar | Apr | May | Jun | Jul | Aug | Sep | Oct | Nov | Dec |
|---|---|---|---|---|---|---|---|---|---|---|---|---|
| Baseline | 0 | 0 | 0 | 0 | 16 | 47 | 453 | 627 | 60 | 0 | 0 | 0 |
| With ceiling fans | 0 | 0 | 0 | 0 | 0 | 0 | 87 | 194 | 2 | 0 | 0 | 0 |

### 2.3 USE OF AN INDIRECT EVAPORATION SYSTEM

Outdoor air is cooled by an evaporative cooler and circulated into a heat exchanger where fresh air for the ventilation system is brought in. A global efficiency for the evaporator and exchanger of 0.68 has been assumed.

Monthly cooling load (kWh) – effect of an indirect evaporator

|  | Jan | Feb | Mar | Apr | May | Jun | Jul | Aug | Sep | Oct | Nov | Dec |
|---|---|---|---|---|---|---|---|---|---|---|---|---|
| Baseline | 0 | 0 | 0 | 0 | 16 | 47 | 453 | 627 | 60 | 0 | 0 | 0 |
| With indirect evaporator | 0 | 0 | 0 | 0 | 8 | 30 | 382 | 524 | 45 | 0 | 0 | 0 |

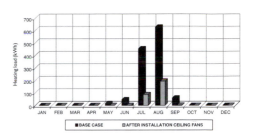

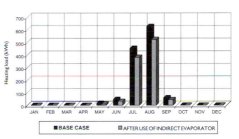

Effect of indirect evaporator/ventilation system economizer cycle

### 2.4 USE OF EXTERNAL SHADING DEVICES

Shading devices installed on all windows – outside roller tissue blinds with heat gain factor 0.2.

Monthly cooling load (kWh) – effect of external shading devices

|  | Jan | Feb | Mar | Apr | May | Jun | Jul | Aug | Sep | Oct | Nov | Dec |
|---|---|---|---|---|---|---|---|---|---|---|---|---|
| Baseline | 0 | 0 | 0 | 0 | 16 | 47 | 453 | 627 | 60 | 0 | 0 | 0 |
| With shading devices | 0 | 0 | 0 | 0 | 0 | 1 | 87 | 194 | 2 | 0 | 0 | 0 |

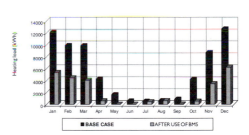

Effect of external shading devices

## Scenario 3 – Electrical lighting improvements

Flourescent lamps replacing inefficient discharge lamps; task lighting in offices; photo control of general lighting and timers in meeting rooms.

## Scenario 4 – HVAC system improvements

### 4.1 USE OF A BUILDING MANAGEMENT SYSTEM

Use of a building management system (BMS) to fix scheduled variable set points and air change rates depending on requirements. The assumed scenario is: in winter, 19°C with 0.5 ACH during working hours, 16°C with 0.1 ACH outside working hours; in summer, the set point is 26°C during working hours with no cooling outside working hours and the same ACHs as in winter.

Monthly total energy consumption (kWh) – effect of a BMS

|  | Jan | Feb | Mar | Apr | May | Jun | Jul | Aug | Sep | Oct | Nov | Dec |
|---|---|---|---|---|---|---|---|---|---|---|---|---|
| Baseline | 12137 | 9925 | 9892 | 4275 | 1655 | 596 | 573 | 632 | 884 | 4243 | 8720 | 12700 |
| With BMS | 5378 | 4484 | 4063 | 608 | 50 | 47 | 461 | 635 | 65 | 561 | 3476 | 6240 |

Calculated total energy load – measure 4.1

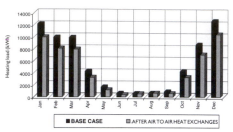

Calculated total energy load – measure 4.2

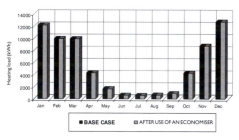

Calculated total energy load – measure 4.3

### 4.2 USE OF AIR-TO-AIR HEAT RECOVERY SYSTEM

Use of an air-to-air heat exchanger with efficiency set to 0.7. This system requires that both supplied and extracted air are mechanically controlled.

Monthly total energy consumption (kWh) - effect of an air-to-air heat recovery system

|  | Jan | Feb | Mar | Apr | May | Jun | Jul | Aug | Sep | Oct | Nov | Dec |
|---|---|---|---|---|---|---|---|---|---|---|---|---|
| Baseline | 12137 | 9925 | 9892 | 4275 | 1655 | 596 | 573 | 632 | 884 | 4243 | 8720 | 12700 |
| With a/a heat exchanger | 9963 | 8093 | 7929 | 3242 | 1164 | 378 | 520 | 643 | 579 | 3265 | 7068 | 10461 |

### 4.3 USE OF AN ECONOMIZER CYCLE ON THE VENTILATION SYSTEM

The adopted principle is to reduce the supply of fresh air when the ambient temperature is higher than the temperature of extracted air (that is, the mean indoor temperature).

Monthly total energy consumption (kWh) - effect of a ventilation system economizer cycle

|  | Jan | Feb | Mar | Apr | May | Jun | Jul | Aug | Sep | Oct | Nov | Dec |
|---|---|---|---|---|---|---|---|---|---|---|---|---|
| Baseline | 12137 | 9925 | 9892 | 4275 | 1655 | 596 | 573 | 632 | 884 | 4243 | 8720 | 12700 |
| With economizer | 12137 | 9926 | 9894 | 4276 | 1655 | 595 | 556 | 607 | 882 | 4244 | 8721 | 12700 |

# EVALUATION

Each scenario was evaluated with regard to energy gains, capital costs, financial gains and payback period.

## Scenario 1A – Improvement of existing envelope

Improvement of existing envelope with replacement of window casements, sealing of air infiltration locations, increase of façade insulation (up to 12cm of glass wool). A 55% reduction in energy consumption for heating can be obtained. However, there is a consequent increase of thermal discomfort during summer (the highest internal temperature is increased by 2°C), mostly due to a reduction in the air change rate (from 1 ACH to 0.5 ACH). With a cooled building, energy consumption would be doubled using such a configuration.

The cost associated with this scenario is also very high, because of the window treatments, and it has a simple payback period of 56 years.

## Scenario 1B – Improvement of existing envelope

Improvement of existing envelope with the addition of a glazed double skin attached to all façades and replacement of existing anti-sun bronze glazing with clear float glazing to increase solar gain. This scenario results in a 63% reduction in energy consumption for heating, but also brings a large increase in energy requirements for cooling in summer (+183%) even when assuming that the double skin is well ventilated in summer. If not, excessive temperatures of up to 40°C would be reached inside the building. The cost of such a retrofit would also be excessive.

## Scenario 2 – Use of passive cooling techniques

Passive cooling techniques include the use of efficient shading devices, night ventilation, ceiling fans and indirect evaporative cooling. When applied together these techniques provide thermal comfort conditions in summer. No additional cooling measures are required. The temperature of 28°C is exceeded for only a few hours in the day, which is comfortable if air speed is high enough, which it would be thanks to ceiling fans.

However, such a scenario is very expensive (especially installation of efficient shading devices) for a relatively small reduction in total energy consumption, resulting in negligible payback. Night ventilation alone carries no investment cost and leads to 30% reduction of energy use for cooling, but the fans increase electricity consumption leading to higher overall running costs

## Scenario 3 – Electric lighting improvements

Improvement of the artificial lighting network using fluo-compact lamps in the corridors instead of the existing high-intensity discharge ones which are not very

## Summaries

*SCENARIO 1A*
Buildings improvements:

* Replace window frames
* Increase outside wall insulation
* Reduce air infiltration
* Increase indoor thermal storage

*TOTAL VALUES:*
Estimated energy saving: 34,462 kWh
Capital cost: 192,850 ECU
Cost per unit energy: 0.1 ECU/kWh
Financial gain per year: 3445 ECU
Payback period: 56 years

*SCENARIO 2*
Use of passive cooling techniques:

* Night ventilation
* Shading devices on all windows
* Ceiling fans
* Indirect evaporator

*TOTAL VALUES:*
Estimated energy saving: 1195 kWh
Capital cost: 36,575 ECU
Cost per unit energy: 0.1 ECU/kWh
Financial gain per year: 120 ECU
Payback period: 305 years

SCENARIO 3
Electric lighting improvements:

• Use of fluo-compact lamps

SCENARIO 4
HVAC System Improvements:

• BMS
• Air-to-air heat exchanger
• Economizer

TOTAL VALUES
Estimated energy saving: 41,125 kWh
Capital cost: 38,570 ECU
Cost per unit energy: 0.1 ECU/kWh
Financial gain per year: 4,116 ECU
Payback period: 10 years

PACKAGE P1
Scenarios 1, 2 & 3

TOTAL VALUES
Estimated energy saving: 56,882 kWh
Capital cost: 226,100 ECU
Cost per unit energy: 0.1 ECU/kWh
Financial gain per year: 5,688 ECU
Payback period: 194 years

efficient; task-lighting for the offices with photo-cell controls to switch off electric lighting when daylight is sufficient; and a timer control for the meeting room and the copy room. Together, these meaures should lead to a 64% saving in electricity consumption for lighting (down to 6.1 kWh/m² annual consumption).

Electronic ballasts were also considered. They would save an additional 25% of electricity consumption in offices, decreasing annual consumption for lighting to 4.6 kWh/m².

## Scenario 4 – HVAC system improvements

Improvement of the heating, ventilation and cooling unit using an air-to-air heat recovery system and a building management system with winter heating set point of 19°C, reduced to 16°C at night, and a set point of 26°C during summer. These measures give better control of the heating system combined with heat recovery, greatly reducing energy requirements – by 62%. Increasing the set point in summer does not have a significant effect on the energy required for cooling. The calculated simple payback period for this scenario is ten years.

## Package P1

If scenarios 1, 2 and 3 are combined in a package, the result is a building with a very low energy requirement – only 13 kWh/m² per annum. No cooling is needed and thermal discomfort is reduced to only a few hours (maximum 19 hours in the hottest zone). However, this result is achieved at a high cost in a retrofitting case, with a simple payback period of 194 years.

## General conclusions

The most cost-effective measures should be selected, i.e. BMS, heat recovery system, sealing of air cracks, and night-time mechanical ventilation in summer. The last leads to higher consumption of electricity for fans but should prevent the installation of an air cooling unit. It is also necessary to educate the users to respect some schedule for operating their windows, the existing blinds and the lighting. More efficient shading devices and a better choice of windows and casements at the design stage would have considerably reduced the energy needs of this building. It is now difficult to retrofit because of high costs.

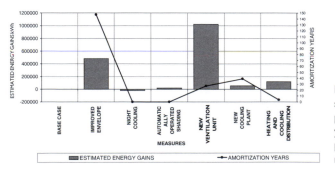

Estimated energy savings (kWh) and payback periods (in years) of various possible retrofit measures

# Climatic Area 3 – Mid-European

## — Introduction —

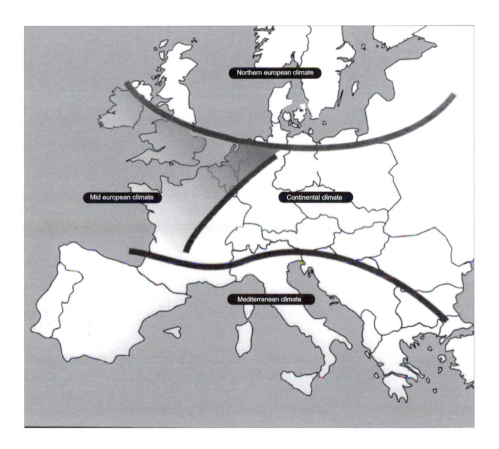

The zones included in the mid-European fringe are characterized by an oceanic climate throughout, with slight variation between the north and south and between the east and west coasts. The main characteristic of this climate is the lack of extremes due to the maritime influence and the instability of the weather.

The seasonal thermal swings are not great. Summer rarely sees high temperatures and winter is never really severe. The most extreme months tend to be February and August, due in part to the delaying effect of the ocean. The daily variations are also relatively small. The almost constant influence of humid maritime air and the high degree of cloud cover tend to temper considerably the diurnal extremes, while the wind and cloud strongly reduce the intensity of nocturnal radiation.

Rain is often severe and lasting, humidity is constant and mist is frequent but not persistent. The abundant rainfall is accompanied by a considerable degree of cloud cover which influences the amount of sunshine. Autumn and winter are the wettest seasons, while summer is relatively dry. Furthermore, frost is not very persistent and snow rare.

# Central and West Houses, London, UK

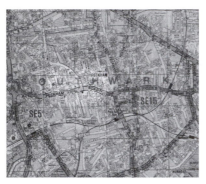

Site plan

Central and West Houses are adjacent buildings set back 15 metres from the busy Peckham High Street with front façades oriented south and trees screening them from the road. The buildings are separate, joined only by a corridor at ground level, but they share utility meters. They were probably constructed around 1870, originally as housing. They have been converted to cellular offices front and back with a central spine corridor and end staircases. It is difficult to be certain of the construction details. Roofs were insulated in past refurbishments but double-thickness, uninsulated brick walls with a rubble fill are typical for that time. The offices are naturally ventilated, heated, and have no air conditioning.

Location: 32-33 Peckham High Street
Owner: London Borough of Southwark
Total size: 1530 m$^2$
Storeys: 5
Year of construction: c. 1870
Degree of exposure: Urban
Module: Cellular
Working hours: 09.00–18.00
Total energy consumption (1997/8): 572704 kWh
User system control: Manual
Heating system: Gas boilers, room radiators with TRVs
Cooling system: None
Lighting system: Standard flourescent tubes attached to ceiling; room switches

General View

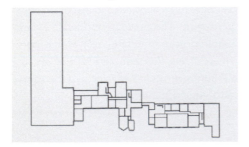

Typical floor plan

Front view

## BUILDING CHARACTERISTICS

## Architectural description

Central and West Houses are two adjoining, connected buildings standing on the busy Peckham High Street in the South London Borough of Southwark. While an exact construction date is not known, the buildings appear to have been constructed in the late nineteenth century, probably around 1870, judging from the style of construction. Peckham High Street runs almost exactly east–west, so the roadside façade of the building is oriented almost due south. Trees screen the building from the pavement and the main road. These provide some shading for the offices on the lower floors in summer. Both buildings have part-buried basements with cutaway windows at the rear. West House also has the same cutaway basement windows at the front of the building.

Internally, West House has ground, first and second floors containing offices, with a central staircase and a second staircase at the east end of the building. Central House has additional office space in attic rooms within its more steeply sloping roof space and has staircases at either end of the floor plate. Hence, the buildings have north- and south-facing offices on each of the lower floors. One top floor office in West House and the attic offices in Central House extend the width of the building.

The walls are probably double-thickness brick with a rubble-filled cavity – the solid wall construction favoured at the estimated time of construction. There are also solid cross walls, giving the structure of the buildings a good potential for thermal mass. Corridor walls and some office walls are lightweight partitions. Internally, the walls are plastered and painted.

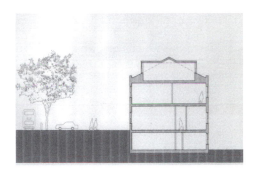

Vertical section

Characteristics of external wall

| Material | Conductivity (W/m °C) | Density (Kg/m³) | Specific heat (J/Kg °C) | Solar assortment | Thickness (m) | U value (W/m² °C) |
|---|---|---|---|---|---|---|
| Facing brick | 0.830 | 2175.0 | 920.0 | 0.725 | 0.110 | |
| Rubble fill | 0.790 | 1840.0 | 1054.0 | – | 0.075 | |
| Brick | 0.880 | 2050.0 | 920.0 | – | 0.110 | |
| Heavy plaster | 1.180 | 1778.0 | 1000.0 | 0.400 | 0.015 | |
| TOTAL | | | | | | 1.863 |

Interior view – office with south-facing windows

Interior view – corridor

Characteristics of solid internal walls

| Material | Conductivity (W/m °C) | Density (Kg/m³) | Specific heat (J/Kg °C) | Solar assortment | Thickness (m) | U value (W/m² °C) |
|---|---|---|---|---|---|---|
| Heavy plaster | 1.180 | 1778.0 | 1000.0 | – | 0.015 | |
| Brick | 0.650 | 1530.0 | 920.0 | – | 0.650 | |
| Heavy plaster | 1.180 | 1778.0 | 1000.0 | – | 0.015 | |
| TOTAL | – | – | – | – | – | 2.727 |

Floor constructions varied widely at the likely time of construction. Timber joists may be in-filled with a variety of materials. However, any thermal mass present is insulated from the office space by the carpets on the floors and the lightweight plaster on the ceilings.

The roofs of the buildings have undergone refurbishment. The roof of West House appears to have been replaced more recently and is in good condition. A refurbishment is currently planned for the roof of Central House. Neither roof is likely to be insulated to modern standards at present.

Characteristics of roof coverings

| Material | Conductivity (W/m °C) | Density (Kg/m³) | Specific heat (J/Kg °C) | Solar assortment | Thickness (m) | U value (W/m² °C) |
|---|---|---|---|---|---|---|
| Facing slate | 1.900 | 2700.0 | 770.0 | 0.900 | 0.004 | |
| Wooden joists | – | – | – | – | – | |
| Air gap | – | – | – | – | 0.050 | |
| Mineral fibre | 0.039 | 1510.0 | 840.0 | – | 0.030 | |
| Wool felt underlay | 0.040 | 160.0 | 1360.0 | – | 0.0025 | |
| TOTAL | – | – | – | – | – | 0.85 |

Windows to the north are reasonably large and frequent along the façade. There are more and larger windows on the south façade, with full-height windows on the first floor of West House. The windows throughout are of the vertical sliding, sash window type, typical of the time, and the windows and frames are probably original. They are single-glazed and often fit or close poorly. A large proportion of the south-facing windows have secondary glazing. This, and stops on the window frames, restrict window opening significantly. White plastic, horizontal venetian blinds are fitted internally to all south-facing windows for glare and sunlight control.

Characteristics of secondary glazed windows with blinds

| Material | Conductivity (W/m °C) | Density (Kg/m³) | Specific heat (J/Kg °C) | Solar assortment | Thickness (m) | U value (W/m² °C) |
|---|---|---|---|---|---|---|
| 6mm float glass | 1.000 | – | – | 0.267 | 0.006 | |
| Air gap | – | – | – | – | 0.010 | |
| 6mm float glass | 1.000 | – | – | 0.351 | 0.006 | |
| Light blind | – | – | – | – | – | |
| TOTAL | – | – | – | – | – | 2.39 |

# MECHANICAL AND ELECTRICAL EQUIPMENT

## Systems description

**Heating system:** The buildings have very basic services, with only space heating and provision of domestic hot water. There are no mechanical ventilation or air-conditioning systems installed. The simple heating system consists of two central boilers serving wall-mounted radiators in rooms and circulation areas. Each boiler has a nominal rating of 45kW and provides hot water for space heating and for hot water via a calorifier. The boilers and hot water calorifiers are housed in separate boiler rooms in the basements of each of the buildings.

**Electrical network and equipment:** The boiler controls are equally basic. There are timed on-off controls for each boiler, which currently bring the boilers on at 6 am during the heating season. There is an advanced start on Monday mornings to preheat the building after the weekend during which the boilers are switched off. The heating system has frost protection controlled by an external thermostat. All of the controls are manually operated, with no form of building management system or electronic controls. The heating system is switched off over the summer, but the boilers remain in operation to provide hot water.

Electricity requirements include the demands of lighting, office equipment, central telephone and computer services. The current **lighting system** consists of ceiling-mounted, frosted plastic luminaires with fluorescent tubes, standard ballasts operating at mains frequency and wall-mounted switches at office entrances. While the lighting load is low, at around 10 W/m$^2$, the quality of the artificial lighting provided is not up to the standard of new office buildings.

**Office equipment** loads are typical for a modern office, with one PC per person, one printer between two users and other equipment, mainly fax machines and photocopiers. Electricity also serves some catering uses: one vending machine, kettles, fridges, toasters and a few microwave ovens. In summer, there is widespread use of desktop fans, typically of around 250W capacity, and in winter there is some tacitly accepted use of electric fan heaters or similar by office occupants.

There is an emergency telephone switchboard, which operates 24 hours a day throughout the year. Since August 1997, there has also been a local area network (LAN) server located in Central House.

## System characteristics

### HEATING PLANT

System Type: Boilers and radiators
Units: 2
Nominal heating power (kW): 45
Heated floor area (m$^2$): 1530
Distribution system: Hydronic
Hours of operation (h/year): 2250
Set-point temperature: Not known
Maintenance state: Fair

### COOLING PLANT

System type: None
Units: n/a
Nominal cooling power (kW): n/a
Cooled floor area (m$^2$): n/a
Distribution system: n/a
Hours of operation (h/year): n/a
Set-point temperature (°C): n/a
Maintenance state: n/a

### LIGHTING

Fluorescent lamps: 230
Incandescent lamps: None
Hours of operation (h/day): 11
Maintenance state: Fair

### EQUIPMENT

Computers (units): 70
Hours of Operation (h/day): 9
Printer (units): 53
Hours of operation (h/day): 9

### VENTILATION PLANT

System type: None
Units: n/a
Supply air flow rate (m$^3$/s): n/a
Return air flow rate (m$^3$/s): n/a
Supply air fan (kW): n/a
Return air fan (kW): n/a

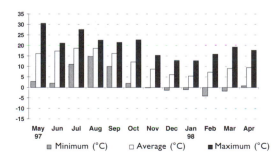

Monthly external temperatures

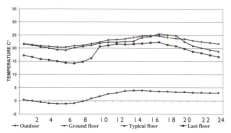

Air temperatures – Winter (23 January 1998)

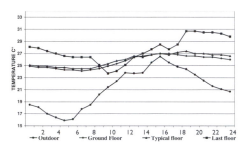

Air temperatures – Summer (22 July 1997)

**GLOBAL SOLAR RADIATION MONTHLY AVERAGE**

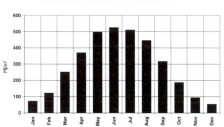

Global solar radiation – monthly average MJ/m²

Historic Electricity Consumption Data for 1994-96

West House (nominally 16% of floor area and energy consumption)

| | 1994 | | | 1995 | | | 1996 | | |
|---|---|---|---|---|---|---|---|---|---|
| | day | night | total | day | night | total | day | night | total |
| jan | 0 | 0 | 0 | 5357 | 1106 | 6463 | 6523 | 1464 | 7987 |
| feb | 0 | 0 | 0 | 5016 | 949 | 5965 | 5878 | 1406 | 7284 |
| mar | 0 | 0 | 0 | 4917 | 1019 | 5936 | 6149 | 1487 | 7636 |
| apr | 0 | 0 | 0 | 4817 | 1088 | 5906 | 6087 | 1643 | 7730 |
| may | 0 | 0 | 0 | 5391 | 1264 | 6655 | 6280 | 1728 | 8008 |
| jun | 0 | 0 | 0 | 5488 | 1295 | 6783 | 6484 | 1668 | 8151 |
| jul | 4415 | 1104 | 5519 | 6517 | 1581 | 8099 | 7039 | 1712 | 8752 |
| aug | 4415 | 1104 | 5519 | 6751 | 1698 | 8449 | 6733 | 1728 | 8461 |
| sep | 4415 | 1104 | 5519 | 5980 | 1572 | 7552 | 6512 | 1602 | 8114 |
| oct | 4415 | 1104 | 5519 | 6353 | 1631 | 7984 | 6636 | 1656 | 8292 |
| nov | 4415 | 1104 | 5519 | 6311 | 1425 | 7736 | 6380 | 1438 | 7818 |
| dec | 1111 | 190 | 1300 | 6169 | 1473 | 7643 | 5740 | 1398 | 7139 |
| | | | 28895 | | | 85169 | | | 95370 |

Historic Electricity Consumption Data for 1994-96

Central House (nominally 14% of floor area and energy consumption)

| | 1994 | | | 1995 | | | 1996 | | |
|---|---|---|---|---|---|---|---|---|---|
| | day | night | total | day | night | total | day | night | total |
| jan | 0 | 0 | 0 | 4687 | 968 | 5655 | 5708 | 1281 | 6989 |
| feb | 0 | 0 | 0 | 4389 | 831 | 5220 | 5143 | 1230 | 6373 |
| mar | 0 | 0 | 0 | 4302 | 891 | 5194 | 5380 | 1301 | 6681 |
| apr | 0 | 0 | 0 | 4215 | 952 | 5167 | 5326 | 1438 | 6764 |
| may | 0 | 0 | 0 | 4717 | 1106 | 5823 | 5495 | 1512 | 7007 |
| jun | 0 | 0 | 0 | 4802 | 1133 | 5935 | 5673 | 1459 | 7132 |
| jul | 3863 | 966 | 4829 | 5703 | 1384 | 7087 | 6159 | 1498 | 7658 |
| aug | 3863 | 966 | 4829 | 5907 | 1485 | 7393 | 5891 | 1512 | 7403 |
| sep | 3863 | 966 | 4829 | 5233 | 1376 | 6608 | 5698 | 1402 | 7100 |
| oct | 3863 | 966 | 4829 | 5559 | 1427 | 6986 | 5807 | 1449 | 7256 |
| nov | 3863 | 966 | 4829 | 5522 | 1247 | 6769 | 5582 | 1258 | 6840 |
| dec | 972 | 166 | 1138 | 5398 | 1289 | 6687 | 5023 | 1223 | 6246 |
| | | | 25283 | | | 74523 | | | 83449 |
| | | | 54178 | | | 159692.7 | | | 178820 |

All figures are electricity consumption in kWh

# BUILDING'S ENERGY PERFORMANCE

## General profile of energy use

Historic data shows that energy consumption in these buildings is extremely high. Summer monitoring shows very high daily energy consumption. As the heating system is switched off in the summer, this energy is being used solely to meet the hot water demand. This demonstrates the inefficiency of using the central boilers to supply hot water.

Annual energy consumption breakdown by fuel type

| Energy/fuel type | kWh/year | |
|---|---|---|
| Electricity consumption | 124,988 | |
| Gas consumption | 447,716 | |
| TOTAL | 572,704 | |
| Average energy consumption per month | 48,568 | kWh/month |
| Average energy consumption per m² | 375 | kWh/m²year |

Long-term monitoring – gas and electricity meter readings and consumption figures

| | | Month | Month days | Gas consumption (kWh) | Daily Gas consumption (kWh) | Daily Gas consumption (Wh/m²) | Electricity consumption (kWh) | Daily Elec. consumption (kWh) | Daily Elec. consumption (kWh/m²) |
|---|---|---|---|---|---|---|---|---|---|
| 1 | 1997 | May | 31 | 23282 | 751 | 491 | 8972 | 289 | 189 |
| 2 | | Jun | 30 | 13435 | 448 | 293 | 9070 | 302 | 198 |
| 3 | | Jul | 31 | 5930 | 191 | 125 | 10104 | 326 | 213 |
| 4 | | Aug | 31 | 6424 | 207 | 135 | 9728 | 314 | 205 |
| 5 | | Sep | 30 | 14526 | 484 | 316 | 10821 | 361 | 236 |
| 6 | | Oct | 31 | 38082 | 1228 | 803 | 10630 | 343 | 224 |
| 7 | | Nov | 30 | 61482 | 2049 | 1339 | 10634 | 354 | 232 |
| 8 | | Dec | 31 | 63871 | 2060 | 1347 | 11288 | 364 | 238 |
| 9 | 1998 | Jan | 31 | 68960 | 2225 | 1454 | 11783 | 380 | 248 |
| 10 | | Feb | 29 | 57443 | 1981 | 1295 | 10776 | 372 | 243 |
| 11 | | Mar | 31 | 56492 | 1822 | 1191 | 10881 | 351 | 229 |
| 12 | | Apr | 30 | 37791 | 1260 | 823 | 10302 | 343 | 224 |
| 13 | | May | 31 | 24915 | 804 | 525 | 10028 | 323 | 211 |
| 14 | | Jun | 30 | 16445 | 548 | 358 | 10690 | 356 | 233 |
| 15 | | Jul | 31 | | | | | | |
| | | | | 489075 | | | 145707 | | |
| Total | | | | 447716 | | | 124988 | | |
| Means | | | | | 1147 | 750 | | 341 | 223 |

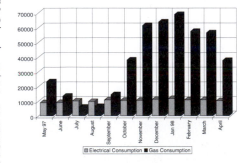

Electrical energy and gas consumtion

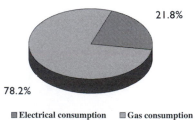

21.8%

78.2%

■ Electrical consumption     ■ Gas consumption

# ENERGY RETROFITTING SCENARIOS

## Scenario 1 – Building improvements

### 1.1 INSULATION OF OUTSIDE WALLS

Apply 25mm of expanded polystyrene internally to building's external walls.

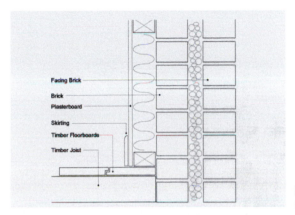

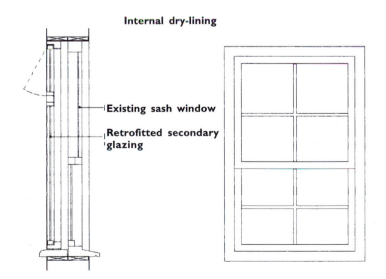

Combined effect of improvements to the building envelope

Section through external wall with internal dry-lining

### 1.2 INCREASE ROOF INSULATION

Increase insulation in the roof to achieve a U value of $0.45 \ W/m^2K$.

### 1.3 SECONDARY GLAZING

Add secondary glazing to all windows.

**Internal dry-lining**

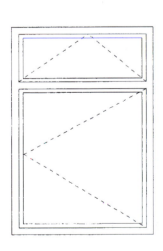

Existing sash window

Retrofitted secondary glazing

Elevation of aluminium window

Section through windows with secondary glazing

Elevation of sash window

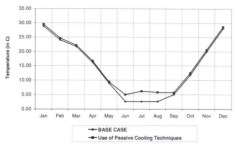

Combined effect of passive cooling techniques

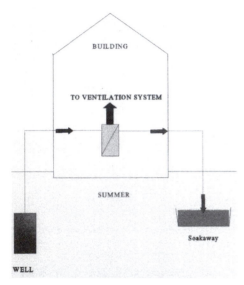

Schematic of the groundwater system

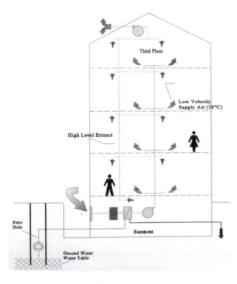

Schematic of groundwater cooling and displacement ventilation

# Scenario 2 – Use of passive cooling techniques

### 2.1 INTERPANE SHADING

Install interpane shading between existing outer glazing and secondary panes on the south façade only.

### 2.2 USE OF NIGHT VENTILATION

Night ventilation using existing openings.

### 2.3 USE OF CEILING FANS

Install ceiling fans to increase summertime comfort temperature.

### 2.4 USE OF CHIMNEY EXTRACTION FANS

Install extraction fans in existing chimneys to improve winter ventilation and to supplement summer ventilation and night cooling.

### 2.5 USE OF GROUNDWATER COOLING

Install a displacement ventilation comfort cooling system using groundwater cooling.

# Scenario 3 – Electric lighting improvements

### 3.1 USE OF TASK LIGHTING

Reduce the background lighting level (and lighting load) by one-third through delamping and provide individual tasklights for all occupants.

### 3.2 USE OF OCCUPANCY DETECTION CONTROLS

Add occupancy detection controls to the existing lighting system.

### 3.3 USE OF PHOTOCELL DIMMING CONTROLS

Install photocells for daylight-linked dimming control on a new lighting system. HF ballasts are required to implement daylight-linked dimming. It is assumed that this measure is implemented along with the replacement of the existing lighting system. The cost of this replacement was not included in the economic analysis. The analysis includes only the cost of the photocells and controls.

### 3.4 INSTALLATION OF HF BALLASTS

Replace the existing lighting system with flourescent lamps with HF ballasts.

### 3.5 INSTALLATION OF LG 3 CATEGORY 2 LUMINAIRES

Replace existing luminaires with CIBSE Lighting Guide 3 Category 2 luminaires, suitable for offices where visual display units (VDUs) are in use.

### 3.6 INSTALLATION OF HIGH-LUMEN LAMPS

Carry out one-in-three delamping and install high luminous efficiency lamps to maintain target lux levels.

## Scenario 4 – HVAS system Improvements

### 4.1 INSTALLATION OF BOILER OPTIMUM START CONTROLS

Replace fixed and advanced start controls on existing boilers with optimum start controls.

### 4.2 TRV UPDATING

Replace existing TRVs and other space temperature controls with new, correctly installed TRVs throughout. Issue instructions to occupants on correct use of these controls.

### 4.3 INSTALLATION OF CONDENSING BOILERS

Replace existing boilers with new condensing boilers.

### 4.4 INSTALL LOCAL INSTANTANEOUS DHW HEATERS

Remove existing calorifiers and provide domestic hot water using local, electric instantaneous water heaters.

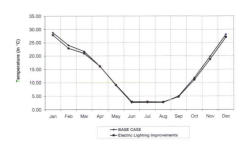

Combined effect of electric lighting improvements

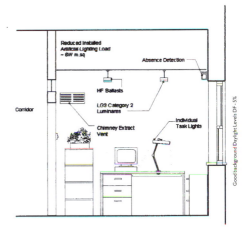

Schematic of internal lighting system elements

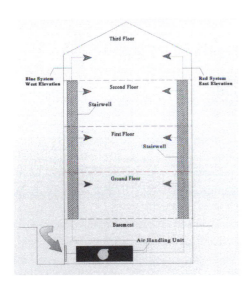

Schematic of the proposed HVAC system

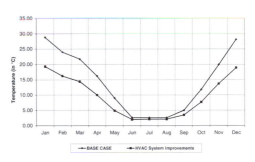

Combined effect of HVAC system improvements

## Summaries

*SCENARIO 1*

Buildings improvements:

- Increase wall insulation
- Increase roof insulation
- Install secondary glazing

### TOTAL VALUES

Estimated energy savings: 74.01 kWh
Required capital cost: 172.50 ECU
Cost per unit of energy: 0.018 ECU/kWh
Financial gain per year: 1.31 ECU
Payback period: 74 years

*SCENARIO 2*

Use of passive cooling techniques:

- Install interpane shading in the secondary glazed, south-facing windows
- Night ventilation using existing openings
- Install ceiling fans
- Install ventilation fans in chimneys
- Ground cooling

### TOTAL VALUES

Estimated energy saving: -8.10 kWh
Required capital cost: 141.68 ECU
Cost per unit of energy: -0.1 ECU/kWh
Financial gain per year: -0.89 ECU
Payback period: n/a

## EVALUATION

Each scenario was evaluated with regard to energy gains, capital costs, financial gains and payback period.

### Scenario 1 – Improvement of existing envelope

Addition of internal dry-lining insulation, roof insulation to achieve a U value of 0.45 W/m$^2$K, and secondary glazing to all windows.

Insulation of the external solid walls by internal dry-lining can reduce the heat loss by 45% with a similar effect on the heating fuel consumption. However, this is an expensive measure requiring much detailed work around the windows, mouldings, etc., with an estimated payback period of around 120 years. Extra roof insulation has only a marginal effect on energy consumption, as does the additional secondary glazing (existing on the south façade, added only to the north façade), but the combination of these two measures will have an impact on local heat loss, radiant surface temperatures and hence on comfort. Due to cost and disruption, loss of space and loss of accessible internal thermal mass, wall insulation is not a recommended option when compared with improvements to the heating supply system.

### Scenario 2A – Use of passive cooling techniques

Installation of interpane shading in secondary glazed, south-facing windows, use of night cooling utilizing existing openings, and installation of chimney fans.

### Scenario 2B – Use of passive cooling techniques

Installation of interpane shading in secondary glazed, south-facing windows, use of night cooling utilizing existing openings, installation of chimney fans and a groundwater cooling system with displacement ventilation.

Monitoring of the building in summer showed that internal temperatures were higher than desirable and current options to reduce temperatures were not satisfactory.

Solar shading on the south side of the buildings (option 2.1) using a venetian blind between the external pane and the secondary glazing, with natural ventilation of the hot air from between the panes, gave reductions in hours of overheating of between 13% (hours over 25°C) and 75% (hours over 29°C), but still left the temperature over 25°C for 20% of the time and over 27°C for 10% of the time.

Night ventilation of the buildings (option 2.2), by leaving appropriate (burglar proof) windows open to remove the daytime heat build-up, produced very similar results. The program predicted a reduction in peak daytime temperature of only 0.7°C (although we believe that this could be improved by employing appropriate controls to allow longer ventilation times in hot periods).

Installation and use of ceiling 'Punka' fans (option 2.3) was estimated to reduce effective temperatures by 1°C, resulting in overheating hours only slightly worse than achieved with the shading or night cooling options alone.

Installation and use of extraction fans in the chimneys (option 2.4) offered very small overall improvements in comfort but their effect is likely to have been swamped by the average air change rates used in the program. We believe that by giving a minimum air change rate of 0.5 ACH at all times, greater comfort will be achieved in times when wind-driven ventilation is minimal.

Obtaining cooled water from the water table beneath the building is one way of lowering temperatures in summer without employing traditional air-conditioning using electric chillers (ground sourced cooling – option 2.5). The analysis and proposals by Ove Arup and Partners show that temperatures within the building could be maintained within the comfort criteria by a displacement ventilation system using air cooled via a heat exchanger from a ground water borehole. The cost of the system is estimated at £55,000 and the installation of the displacement ventilation system would cause some disruption in the building. The energy consumption of the fans of the displacement ventilation system is quite high at 11.5 kWh/m$^2$, but this figure is calculated on the basis of the fans to operate all year round to control temperatures and provide ventilation.

The recommended package of shading, night cooling and extraction fans is quite effective in reducing overheating, giving 13% of time over 25°C, 3–4% over 27°C and no time over 29°C, although this is worse than the commonly adopted standard of 5% over 25°C and 2.5% over 27°C. Punka fans would improve the situation but were not felt to be applicable to all rooms on account of low ceiling heights. Electricity consumption by the extraction fans is low, estimated at 1.5 kWh/m$^2$ per year, less than the existing desktop fans (1.9 kWh/m$^2$) which they are assumed to replace. Punka fans at 1.8 kWh/m$^2$ per year also use slightly less than the desktop fans they would replace.

Since the buildings currently have no 'active' cooling there is no financial payback to be discussed. Costs of the measures are difficult to define and night cooling requires some manual operation (to avoid overcooling resulting in low temperatures at the start of occupation) or automatic operation and control. The extraction fans in the chimneys could possibly be used to greater effect for the night ventilation, by increasing their capacity with temperature control.

## Scenario 3 – Electric lighting improvements

Lighting system replaced, occupancy detection controls installed, reduced background lighting load, task lighting provided, high frequency (HF) ballasts used with high luminous efficiency lamps and LG3 Category 2 luminaires suitable for VDU use.

Installed artificial lighting loads are currently low (*c.* 12 W/m$^2$), but still account for an annual consumption of around 18 kWh/m$^2$, which lies somewhere between 'typical' and 'good' when compared to the stock of UK office buildings.

Reducing the general illumination levels and providing task lighting would reduce energy consumption by 20%, and installing occupant (absence) detection

### Scenario 3
Electric lighting improvements:

- Delamping with installation of task lighting
- Occupancy detection controls
- Install HF ballasts
- Install LG3 Category 2 luminaires
- Install high luminous efficiency lamps

**Total values:**
Estimated energy gains: 11.29 kWh
Required capital cost: 82.79 ECU
Cost per unit of energy: 0.1 ECU/kWh
Financial gain per year: 1.25 ECU
Payback period: 66 years

### Scenario 4
HVAC System Improvements:

- Optimum start controls for boilers
- Fit thermostatic radiator valves
- Install new condensing boilers
- Install local, instantaneous electric DHW system

**Total values**
Estimated energy gains: 64.06 kWh
Required capital cost: 8.97 ECU
Cost per unit of energy: 0.018 ECU/kWh
Financial gain per year: 1.13 ECU
Payback period: 8 years

is estimated to decrease consumption by 40%. These are both low cost measures with payback periods of four and six years, respectively.

Photocell dimming is also sometimes thought to be less acceptable to occupants. We would not generally recommend photocell dimming for cellular offices with good daylighting where absence detection offers energy savings with no perceptible loss of occupant control.

More major lighting changes such as installing HF ballasts and high illuminance luminaires reduce consumption by 20 and 30%, respectively, but such measures are seen to be expensive if the total replacement costs are considered. If implemented as components of a new lighting installation they give reasonable payback periods with the added advantage, in the case of HF ballasts, of improved comfort due to reduced lamp flicker.

The recommended package for lighting energy consumption improvement is task lighting and occupant detection giving a payback period of five years and a resultant energy consumption for lighting of less than 9 kWh/m². Again this compares very favourably with the 'good practice' figure of 14 kWh/m².

## Scenario 4 – HVAC system improvements

Installation of new, condensing boiler, replacement of all TRVs in the building for improved occupant control, instantaneous electric DHW substituted for calorifier fed from main boiler.

Heating supply system improvements, as a package, reduce energy consumption by 41% with a payback period of about eight years. Recommended measures are a new condensing gas boiler, improved controls including optimum start and weather compensation, thermostatic radiator valves and a separate, instantaneous electric domestic hot water system. A separate hot water system is estimated to give around 90% of the (delivered) energy saving over the current system.

With these heating supply system improvements, the annual energy consumption for space heating is estimated at 76 kWh/m², which compares very favourably with the 'good practice' figure of 79 kWh/m² for space heating and hot water. The estimated figure for hot water consumption is around 3 kWh/m² of primary energy. As indicated above, wall insulation could reduce the heating energy consumption still further, by around 45%, giving an extremely low overall figure.

### WINTER TEMPERATURES

It was noted during monitoring that temperatures were sometimes maintained above the modelled temperature of 23°C and there were still some complaints that occupants were cold. The most likely causes of this are draughts, cold surfaces and poor temperature control. The TRVs will help with the control and the double glazing on the north windows will reduce cold radiation and could reduce draughts with carefully designed opening arrangements.

## Package P1

Lighting system replaced, occupancy detection controls installed, reduced background lighting load, task lighting provided, HF ballasts used with high luminous efficiency lamps and LG3 Category 2 luminaires suitable for VDU use.

## Package P2

As for P1 (lighting system replaced, occupancy detection controls installed, reduced background lighting load, task lighting provided, HF ballasts used with high luminous efficiency lamps and LG3 Category 2 luminaires suitable for VDU use) *plus* installation of ground cooling system with displacement ventilation.

## General conclusions

The recommended package of improvements to the heating system, lighting and summer comfort reduces the energy consumption (excluding electricity use by office equipment) by nearly 50% whilst improving both summer and winter comfort, at a total cost of around £30,000. This places the refurbished offices clearly in the category of 'good practice' as defined in the BRECSU Energy Use in Offices Consumption Guide.

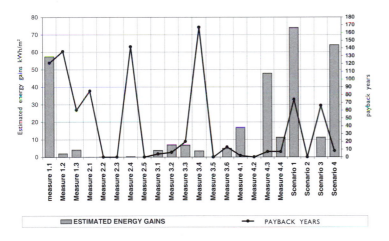

Estimated energy savings (kWh) and payback periods (in years) of various possible retrofit measures

# Climatic Area 4 – Mediterranean

# Introduction

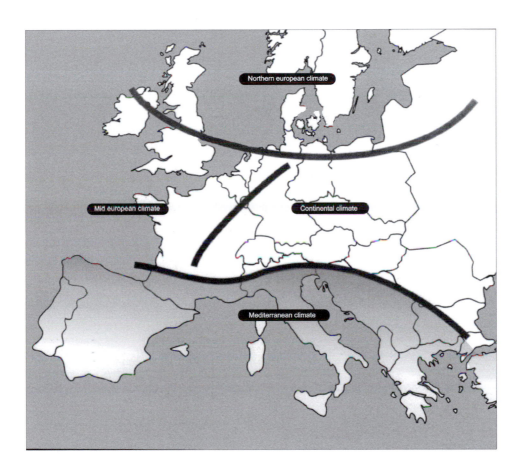

The area's climate, which is representative of the entire Mediterranean fringe, is characterized by hot, dry summers, mild winters with long days, predominantly clear skies, and a great deal of sunshine. Local variations may occur depending on proximity of the sea, topographic relief and winds. The coastal areas are often fresher, benefiting from the many winds blowing in the Mediterranean area.

The town/country nature of the local environment can have an effect on the air movement experienced at a particular site. Wind flow is also influenced by topography; the terrain of an area can cause medium or large-scale variations in wind flow on a particular site. For example, topographical features can provide protection or over-expose. They can also modify the direction of the prevailing winds over considerable areas. Air in contact with surface warmed by solar radiation tends to rise, while air in contact with cold surfaces tends to sink. The resulting density changes generate air flow patterns which are characteristic of the particular terrain involved.

# AGET Building, Athens, Greece

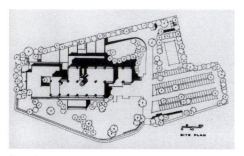

Site plan

Location: Sof. Venizelou 49–51, 141 23,
   Lykovrissi Attikis, Athens
Owner: Private
Total size: 6651 m²
Storeys: 4 plus basement
Construction year: 1975/1980
Degree of exposure: Free-standing
Module: Open space
Working hours: 06:00–16:00
Total energy consumption (1997): 371 kWh/m²
User system control: Central
Heating system: Central oil-fired boiler (3 units),
   air ducts, convectors
Cooling system: Refrigerant centrifugal coolers
   and cooling towers
Lighting system: Standard fluorescent tubes with
   electromagnetic ballasts. High frequency
   fluorescent tubes with electronic ballasts on
   the second and third floors.

The AGET building is the headquarters of Heraklis General Cement Company S.A. The building has a rectangular shape and consists of four floors and a basement. The building was constructed in 1975 and the upper floor was added in 1980. It is a free-standing building situated in a low traffic area in the northern suburbs of Athens. The long axis of the building runs southwest–northeast. The dense planting along the north side of the building creates a mild microclimate and protects the building from strong winds. A total of 350 people work in the building, which operates on a twelve-hour basis during weekdays. The interior space layout is open plan. All four floors are used as offices; part of the basement houses the heating and cooling plant while the rest is used for car parking.

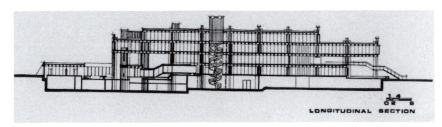

Longitudinal section

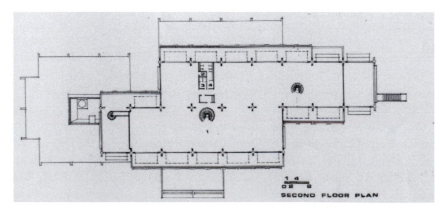

Typical floor plan

# BUILDING CHARACTERISTICS

## Architectural description

The main building structure is made of reinforced concrete. The external walls are not insulated. The basement and ground-floor floors are covered with marble. All intermediate storey floors are covered with carpet. Part of the ground floor is on stilts and the rest is above the basement. The roof is flat and insulated. All windows are single-glazed with fixed and horizontal sliding parts and metal frames. 22% of the window area is shaded using cool shadings, while 23% is shaded using curtains and Californian blinds. The southeast and northwest façades on the second floor have an additional external envelope formed by structural shading devices including overhangs and sidefins extending 0.5 m from the building façade. The working space is open plan and daylight penetration is insufficient, being restricted in the first 3 m from the windows. Internal office partitions reduce the daylight levels on the working planes further still to unacceptable values. As a result, artificial lighting is absolutely necessary during working hours.

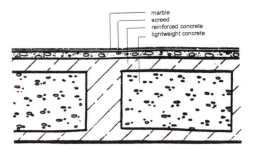

Floor detail

### Characteristics of roof and external walls

| Material | Conductivity (W/m °C) | Density (kg/m³) | Specific heat (J/kg °C) | Solar assortment | Thickness (m) | U value (W/m² °C) |
|---|---|---|---|---|---|---|
| Plaster | 1.39 | 2000 | 1000 | 0.6 | 0.025 | – |
| Concrete | 1.80 | 2400 | 800 | 0.6 | 0.300 | – |
| Plaster | 1.39 | 2000 | 1000 | 0.6 | 0.025 | – |
| TOTAL | – | – | – | – | 0.35 | 2.51 |

### Characteristics of floors (basement and ground-floor)

| Material | Conductivity (W/m °C) | Density (kg/m³) | Specific heat (J/kg °C) | Solar assortment | Thickness (m) | U value (W/m² °C) |
|---|---|---|---|---|---|---|
| Marble | 3.50 | 2800 | 1000 | 0.32 | 0.025 | – |
| Concrete | 1.80 | 2400 | 800 | 0.6 | 0.300 | – |
| Plaster | 1.39 | 2000 | 1000 | 0.6 | 0.025 | – |
| TOTAL | – | – | – | – | 0.35 | 2.63 |

Wall detail

### Characteristics of intermediate-storey floors

| Material | Conductivity (W/m °C) | Density (kg/m³) | Specific heat (J/kg °C) | Solar assortment | Thickness (m) | U value (W/m² °C) |
|---|---|---|---|---|---|---|
| Carpet | 0.06 | 198 | 1376 | 0.5 | 0.005 | – |
| Concrete | 1.80 | 2400 | 800 | 0.6 | 0.30 | – |
| Plaster | 1.39 | 2000 | 1000 | 0.6 | 0.025 | – |
| TOTAL | – | – | – | – | 0.330 | 2.19 |

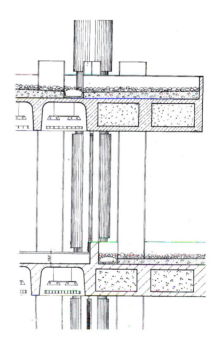

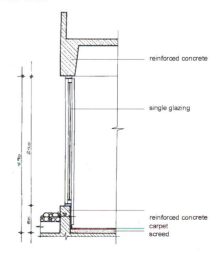

Vertical section

## System characteristics

### HEATING PLANT
System type: Central oil boiler
Units: 3
Nominal heating power (kW): 442/383/383
Heated floor area (m²): 6,403
Distribution system: Water based
Hours of operation (h/year): 1584
Set-point temperature: 24 °C
Maintenance state: Sufficient

### COOLING PLANT
System type: Refrigerant centrifugal
Units: 3
Nominal cooling power (kW): 493/493/316
Cooled floor area (m²): 6,403
Distribution system: Water based two pipe
    induction units, fan coil units
Hours of operation (h/year): 1020
Set-point temperature: 26 °C
Maintenance state: Sufficient

### VENTILATION PLANT
System type: Air-handling units
Units: 9
Supply air-flow rate (m³/s): 4.86/8.54/7.9/
    1.42/3.87/3.67/4.18/1.99/12.89
Return air-flow rate (m³/s): 4.86/8.54/7.9/
    1.42/3.87/3.67/4.18/1.99/12.89
Supply air fan (kW): 5.33/9.69/8.35/0.52/
    4.32/4.10/4.85/1.34/5.59
Return air fan (kW): 5.33/9.69/8.35/0.52/
    4.32/4.10/4.85/1.34/5.59

### LIGHTING
Fluorescent lamps: 323,059
Incandescent lamps: None
Hours of operation (h/day): 12
Maintenance state: Insufficient

### ELECTRICAL EQUIPMENT
Computers (units): 200
Hours of operation (h/day): 12
Printer (units): 30
Hours of operation (h/day): 12

# MECHANICAL AND ELECTRICAL EQUIPMENT

## Systems description

The building's **heating system** consists of three boiler units installed in the basement of the building with pumps leading to air ducts and is **water fed.** The system operates continuously for 11 hours per day, on weekdays from mid-October until the end of April, depending on the outdoor weather conditions. The indoor air temperature is centrally controlled with a set-point of 24 °C. The condition of the insulation of the heating system is fair. The system undergoes regular maintenance by external specialists once a year before the heating season and once a month by the building manager.

The building's **cooling system** consists of three **chillers** installed in the basement of the building and three cooling towers. The cool air is distributed in the working spaces by air ducts and fan coils. The system operates ten hours per day, on weekdays, from mid-May until the end of September. The indoor air temperature is centrally controlled and the set-point is 26 °C.

The **ventilation system** consists of nine air-handling units. The introduction of outdoor, fresh air is achieved through dampers that are manually operated according to the outdoor weather conditions.

**Electrical network and equipment:** the electrical network is first connected to a medium voltage power line, supplied by the Helenic Public Power Corporation. The applied tariffs are those for medium voltage power load which are subject to price differentiation, according to the obtained correction factor. A total of 14,991 fluorescent lamps are installed in the working areas of the building. As daylight penetration in the working spaces is poor, artificial lighting is used throughout the working hours. The lights are suspended on a Scheller-type ceiling on each floor. The lighting 'on/off' switches in all working areas are manually activated. Wall-mounted switches are placed at the entrance to each illuminated space. Installed electrical equipment comprises three main-frame computers, 200 PCs, and 40 printers and copiers. There is a restaurant and a cafeteria on the ground floor which use a variety of electrical equipment.

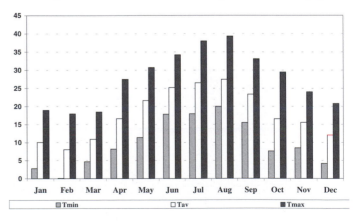

Monthly external temperatures °C

## BUILDING'S ENERGY PERFORMANCE

### General profile of energy use

The energy profile of the building illustrated in the following tables is based on information provided by the technical staff of the building during the energy audit, as well as on continuous measurements carried out in respect of total energy consumption and the energy consumption for cooling purposes. According to utility bills, approximately 1,044,207 kWh of oil is consumed for heating purposes in a year. This corresponds to a total annual energy consumption of 157 kWh/m$^2$ for heating. Continuous measurement by watt meters installed in the cooling system of the building showed the annual energy consumption for cooling to be 44 kWh/m$^2$. The corresponding value for lighting was 176 kWh/m$^2$. The energy consumed for lighting thus represents 30% of the total energy consumption of the building. The highest level of electrical energy consumption is observed during the summer months and is due to use of the cooling system. During the monitoring period the lighting system in the building was undergoing retrofitting. This has resulted in a significant decrease in the annual electrical energy consumption for lighting. Renovation work being carried out in the building also increased the electrical consumption indicated as 'other' in the tables.

Annual energy consumption breakdown by fuel type (1997)

| Energy | kWh/year | |
|---|---|---|
| Oil | 1,207,500 | for space heating |
| Electricity | 1,259,703 | for other uses |
| TOTAL | 2,467,203 | |
| Average energy consumption per month | 205,600 kWh | |
| Average energy consumption per m$^2$ | 371 kWh/year | |

Distribution of energy consumption (1997)

| Energy | kWh/year | kWh/m$^2$year |
|---|---|---|
| Space heating | 1,207,500 | 181 |
| Space cooling | 252,554 | 38 |
| Lighting | 582,957 | 88 |
| Other | 424,192 | 64 |
| TOTAL | 2,467,203 | 371 |

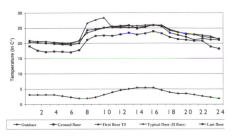

Air temperatures – Winter (19 December 1997)

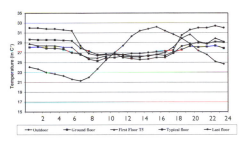

Air temperatures – Summer (21 July 1997)

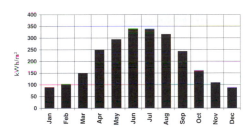

Global solar radiation – monthly average

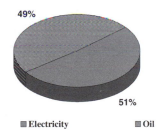

Annual energy consumption by fuel type

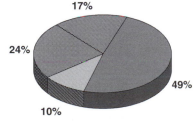

Distribution of energy consumption

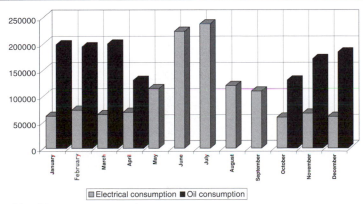

Monthly energy consumption

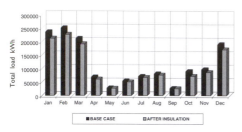

Monthly total energy consumption (kWh) – effect of Scenario 1.1, use of additional insulation

# ENERGY RETROFITTING SCENARIOS

## Scenario 1 – Building improvements

### 1.1 USE OF ADDITIONAL INSULATION

The external walls of the building are made of concrete 30 cm thick and are not insulated. As major interventions are restricted by the presence of architectural elements on the façades of the building, an additional 5-cm thick insulation layer is added on the **internal** side of the outer envelope. The thermal energy savings resulting from the application of this measure are estimated to be close to 10% for heating and 6% for cooling compared to the reference model.

Monthly total energy consumption (kWh) – effect of additional insulation

|  | Jan | Feb | Mar | Apr | May | Jun |
|---|---|---|---|---|---|---|
| Baseline | 235,601 | 250,473 | 211,370 | 67,940 | 27,793 | 53,650 |
| After additional insulation added | 211,672 | 225,989 | 191,157 | 60,611 | 26,871 | 50,345 |

|  | Jul | Aug | Sep | Oct | Nov | Dec |
|---|---|---|---|---|---|---|
| Baseline | 71,309 | 80,503 | 26,900 | 89,149 | 96,371 | 190,209 |
| After additional insulation added | 66,833 | 75,978 | 25,303 | 71,618 | 85,593 | 170,747 |

### 1.2 WEATHER STRIPPING OF WINDOWS AND DOORS

This measure will result in a reduction of the air infiltration rate from 1 ACH to 0.7 ACH. The thermal energy savings resulting from the application of this measure are estimated to be close to 13% for heating and 0.35% for cooling compared to the reference model.

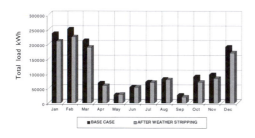

Monthly total energy consumption (kWh) – effect of Scenario 1.2, weather stripping of windows and doors

Monthly total energy consumption (kWh) – effect of weather stripping windows and doors

|  | Jan | Feb | Mar | Apr | May | Jun |
|---|---|---|---|---|---|---|
| Baseline | 235,601 | 250,473 | 211,370 | 67,940 | 27,793 | 53,650 |
| After weather stripping of windows and doors | 209,558 | 224,200 | 188,841 | 58,640 | 29,310 | 53,343 |

|  | Jul | Aug | Sep | Oct | Nov | Dec |
|---|---|---|---|---|---|---|
| Baseline | 71,309 | 80,503 | 26,900 | 89,149 | 96,371 | 190,209 |
| After weather stripping of windows and doors | 69,867 | 78,617 | 20,399 | 70,940 | 83,430 | 170,221 |

### 1.3 REPLACEMENT OF LEAKY WINDOW FRAMES

Currently a significant amount of air infiltration occurs through window frames that are leaky due to their poor condition. Replacement of those frames which are in poor condition reduces infiltration rates to 0.5 ACH and is estimated to result in energy savings close to 19% for heating and 4% for cooling.

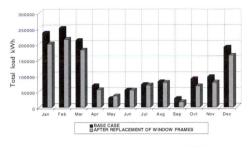

Monthly total energy consumption (kWh) – effect of Scenario 1.3, replacement of leaky window frames

Monthly total energy consumption (kWh) – effect of replacement of window frames

| | Jan | Feb | Mar | Apr | May | Jun |
|---|---|---|---|---|---|---|
| Baseline | 235,601 | 250,473 | 211,370 | 67,940 | 27,793 | 53,650 |
| After replacement of window frames | 201,054 | 215,569 | 181,017 | 54,606 | 35,27 | 53,274 |

| | Jul | Aug | Sep | Oct | Nov | Dec |
|---|---|---|---|---|---|---|
| Baseline | 71,309 | 80,503 | 26,900 | 89,149 | 96,371 | 190,209 |
| After replacement of window frames | 69,427 | 78,032 | 16,725 | 67,000 | 78,841 | 163,500 |

### 1.4 INSTALLATION OF DOUBLE GLAZING

Replacement of single-glazed windows with double-glazed units will reduce heat loss. The estimated annual energy savings resulting from this measure are 11% for heating and 8% for cooling.

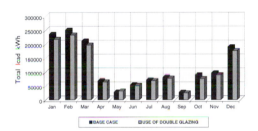

Monthly total energy consumption (kWh) – effect of Scenario 1.4, installation of double glazing

Monthly total energy consumption (kWh) – effect of double glazing

| | Jan | Feb | Mar | Apr | May | Jun |
|---|---|---|---|---|---|---|
| Baseline | 235,601 | 250,473 | 211,370 | 67,940 | 27,793 | 53,650 |
| After installation of double glazing | 217,544 | 232,535 | 196,596 | 63,827 | 31433 | 51,579 |

| | Jul | Aug | Sep | Oct | Nov | Dec |
|---|---|---|---|---|---|---|
| Baseline | 71,309 | 80,503 | 26,900 | 89,149 | 96,371 | 190,209 |
| After installation of double glazing | 68,290 | 77,074 | 24,676 | 75,370 | 89,200 | 176,358 |

### 1.5 INTEGRATION OF PASSIVE SOLAR AND DAYLIGHTING COMPONENTS

To improve natural lighting it is proposed to install three atria extending from the second to the third floor, and three skylights, one on the third floor and two on the second floor. This measure will result in a slight increase of the annual energy consumption for heating (0.113%) and a reduction of 4% for cooling compared to the reference model. The reduction of the electrical energy consumed for lighting is estimated to be close to 8%.

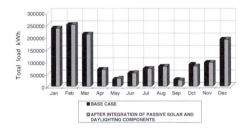

Monthly total energy consumption (kWh) – effect of Scenario 1.5, integration of passive solar and daylighting components

Monthly total energy consumption (kWh) – effect of installation of three atria and three skylights

| | Jan | Feb | Mar | Apr | May | Jun |
|---|---|---|---|---|---|---|
| Baseline | 235,601 | 250,473 | 211,370 | 67,940 | 27,793 | 53,650 |
| After installation of atria and skylights | 235,871 | 250,721 | 211,580 | 67,981 | 32,340 | 54,002 |

| | Jul | Aug | Sep | Oct | Nov | Dec |
|---|---|---|---|---|---|---|
| Baseline | 71,309 | 80,503 | 26,900 | 89,149 | 96,371 | 190,209 |
| After installation of atria and skylights | 71,659 | 80,914 | 25,543 | 81,769 | 96,500 | 190,512 |

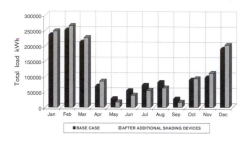

Monthly total energy consumption (kWh) – effect of Scenario 2.1, installation of additional shading devices for the first and second floors

# Scenario 2 – Use of passive cooling techniques

## 2.1 INSTALLATION OF ADDITIONAL SHADING DEVICES FOR THE FIRST AND SECOND FLOORS

In order to reduce internal temperature increase due to solar gain, additional shading devices are installed on the first and second floors. This results in an estimated 9% increase in the energy consumption for heating and a reduction of 29% in energy consumption cooling.

Monthly total energy consumption (kWh) – effect of additional shading devices on the first and second floors

|  | Jan | Feb | Mar | Apr | May | Jun |
|---|---|---|---|---|---|---|
| Baseline | 235,601 | 250,473 | 211,370 | 67,940 | 27,793 | 53,650 |
| After installation of additional shading devices | 248,095 | 264,881 | 226,055 | 84,132 | 17,056 | 38,906 |

|  | Jul | Aug | Sep | Oct | Nov | Dec |
|---|---|---|---|---|---|---|
| Baseline | 71,309 | 80,503 | 26,900 | 89,149 | 96,371 | 190,209 |
| After installation of additional shading devices | 54,642 | 63,049 | 16,417 | 93,289 | 110,803 | 203,033 |

## 2.2 USE OF NIGHT VENTILATION

The use of night ventilation is intended to reduce the cooling load of the building. An exchange rate of 5 ACH is proposed during the night-time (21:00–06:00) throughout the cooling period (mid-May until end September). The resulting cooling load reduction is estimated to be 1%.

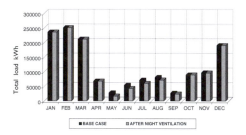

Monthly total energy consumption (kWh) – effect of Scenario 2.2, use of night ventilation

Monthly total energy consumption (kWh) – effect of use of night ventilation

|  | Jan | Feb | Mar | Apr | May | Jun |
|---|---|---|---|---|---|---|
| Baseline | 235,601 | 250,473 | 211,370 | 67,940 | 27,793 | 53,650 |
| With night ventilation | 235,601 | 250,473 | 211,370 | 67,940 | 16,741 | 42,427 |

|  | Jul | Aug | Sep | Oct | Nov | Dec |
|---|---|---|---|---|---|---|
| Baseline | 71,309 | 80,503 | 26,900 | 89,149 | 96,371 | 190,209 |
| With night ventilation | 60,512 | 71,646 | 23,953 | 89,149 | 96,370 | 190,209 |

## 2.3 INSTALLATION OF CEILING FANS

Installation of ceiling fans reportedly extends the comfort zone to temperatures up to 28 °C. Application of this measure is estimated to result in a reduction of the cooling load close to 31%.

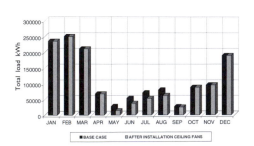

Monthly total energy consumption (kWh) – effect of Scenario 2.3, installation of ceiling fans

Monthly total energy consumption (kWh) – effect of ceiling fans

|  | Jan | Feb | Mar | Apr | May | Jun |
|---|---|---|---|---|---|---|
| Baseline | 235,601 | 250,473 | 211,370 | 67,940 | 27,793 | 53,650 |
| After installation of ceiling fans | 235,601 | 250,474 | 211,371 | 67,940 | 14,084 | 37,125 |

|  | Jul | Aug | Sep | Oct | Nov | Dec |
|---|---|---|---|---|---|---|
| Baseline | 71,309 | 80,503 | 26,900 | 89,149 | 96,371 | 190,209 |
| After installation of ceiling fans | 53,119 | 62,519 | 25,384 | 89,149 | 96,370 | 190,209 |

## 2.4 USE OF AN ECONOMIZER CYCLE

This measure involves installation of a sensor element which will control the return air dampers such that they close when the outdoor air temperature is greater than 26 °C. It is estimated that the resulting heating load reduction is close to 10%, and the cooling load is also reduced by nearly 4%.

Monthly total energy consumption (kWh) – effect of an economizer cycle

|                        | Jan     | Feb     | Mar     | Apr    | May    | Jun    |
|------------------------|---------|---------|---------|--------|--------|--------|
| Baseline               | 235,601 | 250,473 | 211,370 | 67,940 | 27,793 | 53,650 |
| With economizer control | 213,175 | 227,694 | 191,623 | 58,974 | 26,774 | 51,514 |
|                        | Jul     | Aug     | Sep     | Oct    | Nov    | Dec    |
| Baseline               | 71,309  | 80,503  | 26,900  | 89,149 | 96,371 | 190,209 |
| With economizer control | 68,337  | 77,523  | 26,020  | 71,918 | 84,836 | 172,820 |

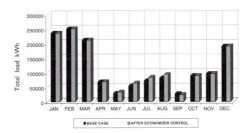

Monthly total energy consumption (kWh) – effect of Scenario 2.4, use of an economizer cycle

## 2.5 USE OF AN INDIRECT EVAPORATIVE COOLER

This measure involves the installation of a heat exchanger in the primary circuit of which the air is circulated and cooled while its humidity ratio remains constant. It is estimated that the resulting cooling load reduction is close to 9%.

Monthly total energy consumption (kWh) – effect of an indirect evaporative cooler

|                                          | Jan     | Feb     | Mar     | Apr    | May    | Jun    |
|------------------------------------------|---------|---------|---------|--------|--------|--------|
| Baseline                                 | 235,601 | 250,473 | 211,370 | 67,940 | 27,793 | 53,650 |
| After installation of indirect evaporative cooler | 235,602 | 250,474 | 211,371 | 67,940 | 32,635 | 63,148 |
|                                          | Jul     | Aug     | Sep     | Oct    | Nov    | Dec    |
| Baseline                                 | 71,309  | 80,503  | 26,900  | 89,149 | 96,371 | 190,209 |
| After installation of indirect evaporative cooler | 82,570  | 91,886  | 23,474  | 89,149 | 96,371 | 190,209 |

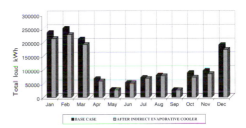

Monthly total energy consumption (kWh) – effect of Scenario 2.5, use of an indirect evaporative cooler

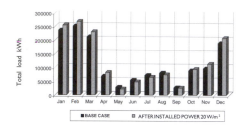

Monthly total energy consumption (kWh) – effect of Scenario 3.1, reduction of installed power to 20 W/m²

## Scenario 3 – Electric lighting improvements

### 3.1 REDUCTION OF INSTALLED POWER TO 20 W/M²

In order to reduce the energy consumed for lighting purposes, the existing lighting fixtures are replaced by new ones having lower electricity consumption while maintaining the same lighting levels in the working spaces. If the installed power for lighting is reduced from 50 W/m² to 20 W/m², a 45% reduction is expected in the energy consumption for lighting. The estimated energy saving for cooling is 15%. However, the reduction in the number of luminaires in the working spaces will result in an increase in energy consumption for heating of close to 7%.

Monthly total energy consumption (kWh) – effect of reducing installed power to 20 W/m²

|  | Jan | Feb | Mar | Apr | May | Jun |
|---|---|---|---|---|---|---|
| Baseline | 235,601 | 250,473 | 211,370 | 67,940 | 27,793 | 53,650 |
| After reducing installed power to 20 W/m² | 254,431 | 267,454 | 229,769 | 81,555 | 21,804 | 47,589 |

|  | Jul | Aug | Sep | Oct | Nov | Dec |
|---|---|---|---|---|---|---|
| Baseline | 71,309 | 80,503 | 26,900 | 89,149 | 96,371 | 190,209 |
| After reducing installed power to 20 W/m² | 64,802 | 73,976 | 25,412 | 94,212 | 113,380 | 208,481 |

### 3.2 REDUCTION OF INSTALLED POWER TO 15 W/M²

Further reduction of the installed power for lighting to 15 W/m² is expected to result in a 54% reduction in energy consumption for lighting. At the same time, the reduction in energy consumption for cooling is estimated to be close to 24%. The reduction of the number of luminaires in the working spaces will result in an increase in energy consumption for heating of close to 9%.

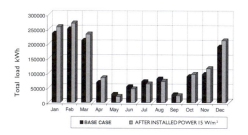

Monthly total energy consumption (kWh) – effect of Scenario 3.2, reduction of installed power to 15 W/m²

Monthly total energy consumption (kWh) – effect of reducing installed power to 15 W/m²

|  | Jan | Feb | Mar | Apr | May | Jun |
|---|---|---|---|---|---|---|
| Baseline | 235,601 | 250,473 | 211,370 | 67,940 | 27,793 | 53,650 |
| After reducing installed power to 15 W/m² | 257,608 | 270,238 | 232,854 | 83,961 | 20,772 | 46,472 |

|  | Jul | Aug | Sep | Oct | Nov | Dec |
|---|---|---|---|---|---|---|
| Baseline | 71,309 | 80,503 | 26,900 | 89,149 | 96,371 | 190,209 |
| After reducing installed power to 15 W/m² | 63,575 | 72,772 | 23,863 | 96,444 | 116,255 | 211,568 |

### 3.3 REDUCTION OF INSTALLED POWER TO 10 W/M²

Further reduction of the installed power for lighting to 10 W/m² is expected to result in a 67% reduction in energy consumption for lighting. At the same time, the reduction in energy consumption for cooling is estimated to be close to 26%. The reduction of the number of luminaires in the working spaces will result in an increase in energy consumption for heating of close to 11%.

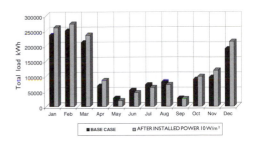

Monthly total energy consumption (kWh) – effect of reducing installed power to 10 W/m²

| | Jan | Feb | Mar | Apr | May | Jun |
|---|---|---|---|---|---|---|
| Baseline | 235,601 | 250,473 | 211,370 | 67,940 | 27,793 | 53,650 |
| After reducing installed power to 10 W/m² | 260,746 | 273,146 | 235,858 | 86,404 | 19,927 | 45,581 |
| | Jul | Aug | Sep | Oct | Nov | Dec |
| Baseline | 71,309 | 80,503 | 26,900 | 89,149 | 96,371 | 190,209 |
| After reducing installed power to 10 W/m² | 62,594 | 71,818 | 25,589 | 98,675 | 11,9212 | 214,661 |

Monthly total energy consumption (kWh) – effect of Scenario 3.3, reduction of installed power to 10 W/m²

### 3.4 USE OF TASK LIGHTING

This measure can be used to raise illumination levels locally, reducing the general illumination by only 10%. The measure is expected to result in a 65% reduction in the energy consumption for lighting and a reduction close to 26% for cooling. The reduction of the number of luminaires in the working spaces will result in an increase in energy consumption for heating of close to 11%.

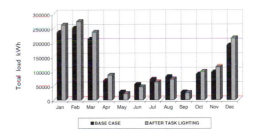

Monthly total energy consumption (kWh) – effect of using task lighting

| | Jan | Feb | Mar | Apr | May | Jun |
|---|---|---|---|---|---|---|
| Baseline | 235,601 | 250,473 | 211,370 | 67,940 | 27,793 | 53,650 |
| With task lighting | 260,638 | 273,035 | 235,772 | 86,324 | 21,977 | 45,619 |
| | Jul | Aug | Sep | Oct | Nov | Dec |
| Baseline | 71,309 | 80,503 | 26,900 | 89,149 | 96,371 | 190,209 |
| With task lighting | 62,634 | 71,833 | 25,340 | 98,589 | 114,469 | 214,572 |

Monthly total energy consumption (kWh) – effect of Scenario 3.4, use of task lighting

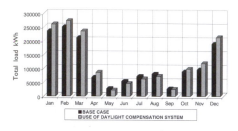

Monthly total energy consumption (kWh) –
effect of Scenario 3.5, use of a daylight
compensation system

### 3.5 USE OF A DAYLIGHT COMPENSATION SYSTEM

This measure involves control of the lighting levels achieved by daylight. The use of artificial lighting is restricted to the hours when the lighting levels achieved through daylight in the working spaces are insufficient. The most common lighting level control involves the use of daylight sensors, which are photocells measuring total illumination in a zone including daylight levels. The measure is expected to result in a 63% reduction in the energy consumption for lighting and a reduction of close to 26% for cooling. The reduction of the number of luminaires in the working spaces will result in an increase in energy consumption for heating close to 11%.

Monthly total energy consumption (kWh) – effect of using a daylight compensation system

|  | Jan | Feb | Mar | Apr | May | Jun |
|---|---|---|---|---|---|---|
| Baseline | 235,601 | 250,473 | 211,370 | 67,940 | 27,793 | 53,650 |
| With a daylight compensation system | 260,217 | 272,595 | 235,256 | 85,978 | 22,069 | 45,773 |

|  | Jul | Aug | Sep | Oct | Nov | Dec |
|---|---|---|---|---|---|---|
| Baseline | 71,309 | 80,503 | 26,900 | 89,149 | 96,371 | 190,209 |
| With a daylight compensation system | 62,788 | 71,995 | 25,152 | 98,163 | 118,654 | 214,097 |

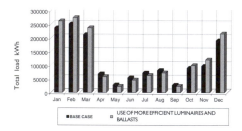

Monthly total energy consumption (kWh) –
effect of Scenario 3.6, installation of more
efficient luminaires and electronic ballasts

### 3.6 INSTALLATION OF MORE EFFICIENT LUMINAIRES AND ELECTRONIC BALLASTS

The replacement of existing luminaires with an equal number of new lamps equipped with electronic ballasts is expected to result in a 66% reduction of the energy consumption for lighting and a 26% reduction in the cooling load. The reduction of the number of luminaires in the working spaces will result in an increase in energy consumption for heating of close to 11%.

Monthly total energy consumption (kWh) – effect of installing more efficient luminaires and electronic ballasts

|  | Jan | Feb | Mar | Apr | May | Jun |
|---|---|---|---|---|---|---|
| Baseline | 235,601 | 250,473 | 211,370 | 67,940 | 27,793 | 53,650 |
| After installation of electronic ballasts | 261,210 | 273,446 | 236,371 | 57,716 | 22,275 | 45,447 |

|  | Jul | Aug | Sep | Oct | Nov | Dec |
|---|---|---|---|---|---|---|
| Baseline | 71,309 | 80,503 | 26,900 | 89,149 | 96,371 | 190,209 |
| After installation of electronic ballasts | 62,426 | 71,658 | 22,647 | 98,846 | 11,9601 | 215,038 |

### 3.7 USE OF REFLECTORS AND PRISMATIC PLASTIC FEATURES

This measure proposes the use of highly reflective, semi-rigid metal surfaces secured in the lighting fixtures. These reflectors will be placed on energy-efficient magnetic ballasts with input energy of 20.5 W/m². This measure is expected to result in a 66% reduction in energy consumption for lighting and a 25% reduction in the cooling load. The reduction of the number of luminaires in the working spaces will result in an increase in energy consumption for heating of close to 10%.

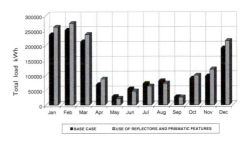

Monthly total energy consumption (kWh) – effect of Scenario 3.7, use of reflectors and prismatic plastic features

Monthly total energy consumption (kWh) – effect of installing more efficient reflectors

|  | Jan | Feb | Mar | Apr | May | Jun |
|---|---|---|---|---|---|---|
| Baseline | 235,601 | 250,473 | 211,370 | 67,940 | 27,793 | 53,650 |
| After installation of reflectors and prismatic plastic features | 261,129 | 273,420 | 236,356 | 86,529 | 22,275 | 45,952 |

|  | Jul | Aug | Sep | Oct | Nov | Dec |
|---|---|---|---|---|---|---|
| Baseline | 71,309 | 80,503 | 26,900 | 89,149 | 96,371 | 190,209 |
| After installation of reflectors and prismatic plastic features | 63,006 | 72,201 | 25,724 | 98,846 | 119,586 | 214,977 |

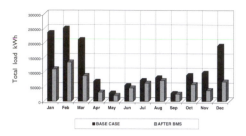

Monthly total energy consumption (kWh) – effect of Scenario 4.1, use of a BMS to control cooling and heating

# Scenario 4 – HVAC system improvements

### 4.1 USE OF A BMS TO CONTROL COOLING AND HEATING

This measure proposes the use of a building energy management system (BMS) to monitor and control the building services plant. Use of such a system will keep the set-point temperatures at 19 °C during the winter and 27 °C during the summer. Application of this measure with the above set-point temperatures is expected to result in a 64% reduction in the heating load and a 24% reduction in the cooling load.

Monthly total energy consumption (kWh) – effect of use of a BMS

|            | Jan     | Feb     | Mar     | Apr    | May    | Jun    |
|------------|---------|---------|---------|--------|--------|--------|
| Baseline   | 235,601 | 250,473 | 211,370 | 67,940 | 27,793 | 53,650 |
| Using a BMS| 110,186 | 134,084 | 87,869  | 31,001 | 20,413 | 45,303 |

|            | Jul    | Aug    | Sep    | Oct    | Nov    | Dec     |
|------------|--------|--------|--------|--------|--------|---------|
| Baseline   | 71,309 | 80,503 | 26,900 | 89,149 | 96,371 | 190,209 |
| Using a BMS| 62,184 | 71,500 | 24,561 | 57,796 | 37,323 | 66,992  |

### 4.2 HEAT RECOVERY FROM THE RETURN AIR

This measure uses the thermal energy of the return air, which otherwise would be wasted, to contribute in part to the heating/cooling load of the building. Application of this measure during the winter period is estimated to result in a 23% reduction in the heating load.

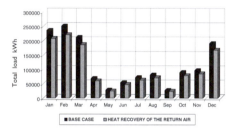

Monthly total energy consumption (kWh) – effect of Scenario 4.2, heat recovery from the return air

Monthly total energy consumption (kWh) – effect of use of heat recovery from the return air

|                                    | Jan     | Feb     | Mar     | Apr    | May    | Jun    |
|------------------------------------|---------|---------|---------|--------|--------|--------|
| Baseline                           | 235,601 | 250,473 | 211,370 | 67,940 | 27,793 | 53,650 |
| With heat recovery from the return air | 207,329 | 220,416 | 186,006 | 59,787 | 24,458 | 47,212 |

|                                    | Jul    | Aug    | Sep    | Oct    | Nov    | Dec     |
|------------------------------------|--------|--------|--------|--------|--------|---------|
| Baseline                           | 71,309 | 80,503 | 26,900 | 89,149 | 96,371 | 190,209 |
| With heat recovery from the return air | 62,752 | 70,842 | 23,672 | 78,451 | 84,806 | 167,384 |

### 4.3 RECOVERY OF THE WASTE HEAT FROM HIGH TEMPERATURE BOILER FLUE GASES

This measure uses heat recovery from the boiler flue gases exhausted at a temperature of 72 °C to contribute in part to the heating load of the building. Application of this measure during the winter period is estimated to result in a 40% reduction in the heating load.

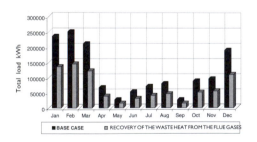

Monthly total energy consumption (kWh) – effect of Scenario 4.3, recovery of the waste heat from high temperature boiler flue gases

Monthly total energy consumption (kWh) – effect of heat recovery from boiler flue gases

|                                      | Jan     | Feb     | Mar     | Apr    | May    | Jun    |
|--------------------------------------|---------|---------|---------|--------|--------|--------|
| Baseline                             | 235,601 | 250,473 | 211,370 | 67,940 | 27,793 | 53,650 |
| After heat recovery from boiler flue gases | 136,649 | 145,274 | 122,595 | 39,405 | 16,120 | 31,117 |

|                                      | Jul    | Aug    | Sep    | Oct    | Nov    | Dec     |
|--------------------------------------|--------|--------|--------|--------|--------|---------|
| Baseline                             | 71,309 | 80,503 | 26,900 | 89,149 | 96,371 | 190,209 |
| After heat recovery from boiler flue gases | 41,359 | 46,692 | 15,602 | 51,706 | 55,895 | 110,321 |

### 4.4 INSTALLATION OF A MORE EFFICIENT BOILER

Replacement of the existing boiler that has an efficiency of 0.6 with a new one having an efficiency of 0.8 results in an energy saving for heating of close to 25%.

Monthly total energy consumption (kWh) – effect of installation of a more efficient boiler

|  | Jan | Feb | Mar | Apr | May | Jun |
|---|---|---|---|---|---|---|
| Baseline | 235,601 | 250,473 | 211,370 | 67,940 | 27,793 | 53,650 |
| After installation of more efficient boiler | 204,188 | 217,077 | 183,188 | 58,881 | 27,794 | 53,650 |

|  | Jul | Aug | Sep | Oct | Nov | Dec |
|---|---|---|---|---|---|---|
| Baseline | 71,309 | 80,503 | 26,900 | 89,149 | 96,371 | 190,209 |
| After installation of more efficient boiler | 71,309 | 80,503 | 26,900 | 77,262 | 83,521 | 164,646 |

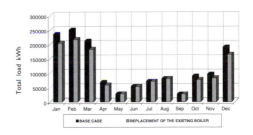

Monthly total energy consumption (kWh) – effect of Scenario 4.4, installation of a more efficient boiler

### 4.5 USE OF A FLUE GAS ANALYSER AND A COMPENSATION CONTROLLER FOR THE BURNER

This technology can increase the efficiency of the current heating system from 0.6 to 0.8. Application of this measure during the winter period is estimated to result in a 15% reduction in the heating load.

Monthly total energy consumption (kWh) – effect of use of a flue gas analyser

|  | Jan | Feb | Mar | Apr | May | Jun |
|---|---|---|---|---|---|---|
| Baseline | 235,601 | 250,473 | 211,370 | 67,940 | 27,793 | 53,650 |
| With use of a flue gas analyser and a compensation controller for the burner | 212,696 | 226,122 | 190,820 | 61,334 | 27,794 | 53,650 |

|  | Jul | Aug | Sep | Oct | Nov | Dec |
|---|---|---|---|---|---|---|
| Baseline | 71,309 | 80,503 | 26,900 | 89,149 | 96,371 | 190,209 |
| With use of a flue gas analyser and a compensation controller for the burner | 71,309 | 80,504 | 26,900 | 80,481 | 87,001 | 171,717 |

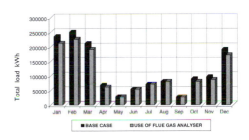

Monthly total energy consumption (kWh) – effect of Scenario 4.5, use of a flue gas analyser and a compensation controller for the burner

### 4.6 RECOVERY OF HEAT FROM THE CONDENSER

Installation of a shell and tube liquid-to-liquid heat exchanger in order to recover heat from the condenser brings an estimated reduction in the energy consumption for cooling of close to 10%.

Monthly total energy consumption (kWh) – effect of recovery of heat from the condenser

|  | Jan | Feb | Mar | Apr | May | Jun |
|---|---|---|---|---|---|---|
| Baseline | 235,601 | 250,473 | 211,370 | 67,940 | 27,793 | 53,650 |
| With recovery of heat from the condenser | 212,696 | 226,122 | 190,820 | 61,334 | 27,794 | 53,650 |

|  | Jul | Aug | Sep | Oct | Nov | Dec |
|---|---|---|---|---|---|---|
| Baseline | 71,309 | 80,503 | 26,900 | 89,149 | 96,371 | 190,209 |
| With recovery of heat from the condenser | 71,309 | 80,504 | 26,900 | 80,481 | 87,001 | 171,717 |

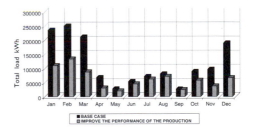

Monthly total energy consumption (kWh) – effect of Scenario 4.6, recovery of heat from the condenser

## Summaries

SCENARIO 1 – IMPROVEMENT OF THE BUILDING
ENVELOPE

### TOTAL VALUES

Estimated energy savings: 394,670 kWh
Required capital cost: 379,107 ECU
Cost per unit of energy: 0.13 ECU/kWh
Financial gain per year : 18,722 ECU
Payback period: 20.25 years

SCENARIO 2 – USE OF PASSIVE COOLING TECHNIQUES

### TOTAL VALUES

Estimated energy savings: 240,566 kWh
Required capital cost: 93,114 ECU
Cost per unit of energy: 0.13 ECU/kWh
Financial gain per year: 15,855 ECU
Payback period: 5.8 years

## EVALUATION

Each scenario was evaluated with regard to energy, capital costs, financial gains and payback period.

### Scenario 1 – Improvement of existing envelope

- Use of additional insulation
- Weather stripping of windows and doors
- Replacement of leaky window frames
- Installation of double glazing
- Integration of passive solar and daylighting components

Overall, retrofitting actions aiming to decrease heat losses, increase solar gains, and decrease infiltration rates, when applied together, will reduce the heating load up to 51 kWh/m$^2$ (29.6%), the cooling load up to 8 kWh/m$^2$ (18%), and the lighting load up to 10 kWh/m$^2$ (8%). Total energy gains may result in a decrease in the total energy used by the heating, cooling and lighting systems of up to 69 kWh/m$^2$, with a payback period of approximately 20 years at a cost over a ten-year period of nearly 0.08 ECU per saved kWh.

### Scenario 2 – Use of passive cooling techniques

- Installation of additional shading devices for the first and second floors
- Use of night ventilation
- Installation of ceiling fans
- Use of an economizer cycle
- Use of an indirect evaporative cooler

Combined application of all these measures contributes to a decrease in the cooling load of up to 19 kWh/m$^2$ (47%), while at the same time the heating load is reduced nearly 17 kWh/m$^2$ (10%). The combined application presents a cost of approximately 0.04 ECU per saved kWh over a ten-year period, with a payback period of 5.9 years.

This type of retrofitting programme almost satisfies the energy objectives set for this building at a very reasonable cost. Passive cooling retrofitting techniques may be considered as a first priority for buildings presenting a high cooling load that is not completely due to internal gains. The selection of the techniques to be considered in an individual case has to be made in conjunction with the characteristics of the building and the specific sources of cooling load.

## Scenario 3 – Electrical lighting improvements

- Reduction of installed power to 20 W/m$^2$
- Reduction of installed power to 15 W/m$^2$
- Reduction of installed power to 10 W/m$^2$
- Use of task lighting
- Use of a daylight compensation system
- Installation of more efficient luminaires and electronic ballasts
- Use of reflectors and prismatic plastic features

Global retrofitting actions aiming to decrease the lighting energy consumption of offices may consider a mixture of the above measures. For the AGET building, a global lighting retrofitting scenario has been modelled considering a reduction of the installed power up to 20 W/m$^2$, and use of electronic ballasts and daylight compensation systems in combination with task lighting and improved reflectors. The resulting combined energy gains are close to 67.5 kWh/m$^2$ (55.7%) for lighting, 6.9 kWh/m$^2$ (15.5%) for cooling, however the heating load increased up to 14.5 kWh/m$^2$ (8.5%). In total, the energy load is reduced by almost 60 kWh/m$^2$, at a cost of close to 0.14 ECU per saved kWh over a ten-year period, and a payback period close to 9.3 years.

The combination of all these techniques do not offer additional energy gains, and it significantly increases the cost of retrofitting. The same energy results may be achieved when just one of the studied measures is employed, i.e. decrease of the installed power.

## Scenario 4 – HVAC system improvements

- Use of a BMS to control cooling and heating
- Heat recovery from the return air
- Recovery of the waste heat from high temperature boiler flue gases
- Installation of a more efficient boiler
- Use of a flue gas analyser and a compensation controller for the burner
- Recovery of heat from the condenser

When a combination of the measures is considered as a global retrofitting action, the results are quite spectacular. When all the measures are combined, the heating energy consumption is reduced by 56 kWh/m$^2$ (33%), and the cooling load decreases by 13 kWh/m$^2$ (29.4%). The payback period is quite high at 42.2 years, while the cost is close to 0.1 ECU per saved kWh over a period of ten years.

## Package

Retrofitting of office buildings should involve actions in all the above categories, if necessary. Such a global combination has been considered for the AGET building. The energy gains for heating are close to 71 kWh/m$^2$ (41.5%), the gains for cooling are 21.1 kWh/m$^2$ (47.7%), and the lighting energy gains are

### SCENARIO 3 – ELECTRIC LIGHTING IMPROVEMENTS

**TOTAL VALUES**
Estimated energy savings: -51,611 kWh
Required capital cost: 565,335 ECU
Cost per unit of energy: 0.13 ECU/kWh
Financial gain per year: 60,883 ECU
Payback period: 9.3 years

### SCENARIO 4 – HVAC SYSTEM IMPROVEMENTS

**TOTAL VALUES**
Estimated energy savings: 460,608 kWh
Required capital cost: 1,296,945 ECU
Cost per unit of energy: 0.13 ECU/kWh
Financial gain per year: 22,826 ECU
Payback period: 42.2 years

### PACKAGE

**TOTAL VALUES**
Estimated energy savings: 614,552 kWh
Required capital cost: 1,072,340 ECU
Cost per unit of energy: 0.13 ECU/kWh
Financial gain per year: 91,783 ECU
Payback period: 15 years

67.4 kWh/m$^2$ (55.7%). The global energy gains are close to 160 kWh/m$^2$ — 55.7% of the total energy load. The payback period for this global scenario is high, 15 years and the cost close to 0.1 ECU per saved kWh over a ten-year period.

Thus, application of such a combination almost satisfies the initial energy targets. However, as previously shown and stated, the cost is high and a combination of some of the considered measures could offer almost the same energy results for a lower cost.

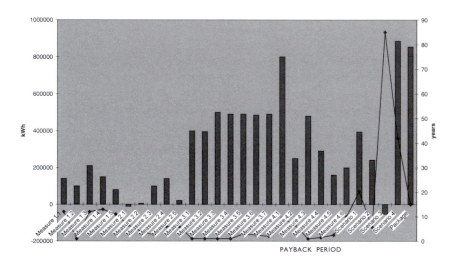

Estimated energy gains and payback periods

# Florence Bank 'Cassa di Risparmio di Firenze', Florence, Italy

The Florence Bank building was commissioned in 1976. It is privately owned and used by one of numerous agencies (well know as 'Centro estero') of the Cassa di Risparmio Bank. The building operates from 08:00 hours until 18:00 hours, Monday to Friday, with 85 people working there, mainly bank employees.

The building is located in the centre of Florence, on a road with heavy traffic. The area is very densely built up, with both residential and commercial buildings.

The building has seven floors and a basement level. There is office space on all floors from the first floor. Each level is an open space and has similar layout. On the ground floor are located the entrance hall, the porters lodge and a small bar. The underground level is used for archive rooms, a small parking area and technical spaces for heating and power systems. With the exception of the entrance hall, all levels have a 3-metre ceiling height. The building is developed longitudinally along a northeast axis, with the principal façade facing southwest. It is a free-standing, core-oriented block, with a heavy structure.

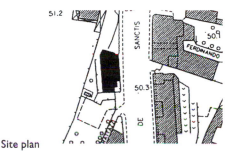

Site plan

Location: Via F. De Sanctis 47, Florence
Owner: Private
Total Size: 1872 m$^2$
Storeys: 7 plus basement
Construction year: 1977
Degree of exposure: Free-standing
Module: Open space
Working hours: 08:30–17:00
Total energy consumption (1996): 187 kWh/m$^2$
User systems control: Central
Heating system: Central gas boiler; electric boiler to heat water
Cooling system: Central all-water cooling system with water chillers and cooling towers
Lighting system: Fluorescent lamps with electromagnetic ballasts; incandescent lamps in same offices, stairway and conference room.

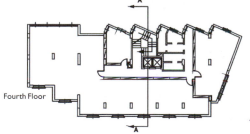

Front view

Fourth Floor

Typical floor plan

Vertical section

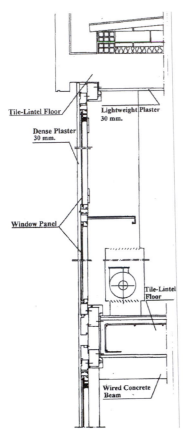

Vertical section

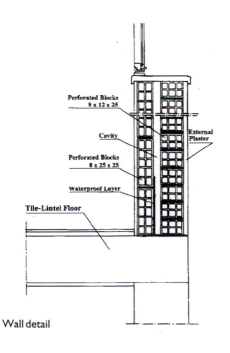

Wall detail

# BUILDING CHARACTERISTICS

## Architectural description

The building structure is characterized by a window module subdivided into two sections; the upper part, which opens completely, has a frame with single transparent glazing. The lower section is formed by a single-glazed panel of a dark colour. Fan-coils, the distribution system of the heating and cooling plant, are placed under each window module.

The quantity of natural lighting penetrating through these windows is sufficient for the daytime illumination of the workplaces during winter, while in summer it is insufficient because the excessive sun exposure forces the occupants to completely screen the windows, thereby making artificial lighting necessary during the whole working day.

The building is naturally ventilated and air exchanges take place by means of manual opening of the windows. However, the internal air quality is poor because the windows are often locked. Internal air circulation is only provided by the cooling system.

The ample glazed surfaces create the problem of overheating during the summer period due to the inefficient shading system, resulting in external thermal gains increase and a consequent increase in electrical energy consumption for the summer cooling of the building.

The building construction is of a conventional type, with structure in reinforced concrete and envelope walls in perforated bricks, with an air gap of 4 cm. The building envelope is formed by three layers: an external layer of plaster, the perforated bricks and an internal layer of plaster. The building, therefore, does not have thermal insulation – it was designed before the application of the Italian Building Regulations on energy consumption.

The roof of the building is flat and is not insulated, although the sixth and top floors are insulated with an insulation layer approximately 5 cm thick. The floors and ceilings are made from concrete slabs.

Characteristics of external walls

| Material | Conductivity (W/m² °C) | Density (kg/m³) | Specific heat (J/kg °C) | Solar assortment | Thickness (m) | U value (W/m² °C) |
|---|---|---|---|---|---|---|
| Dense plaster | 0.41 | 900 | 840 | 0.6 | 0.02 | – |
| Brick | 0.49 | 730 | 840 | 0.6 | 0.08 | – |
| Air space | 0.26 | 1 | 1 | 0.4 | 0.04 | – |
| Brick | 0.23 | 680 | 840 | 0.6 | 0.12 | – |
| Plaster | 0.9 | 1800 | 910 | 0.6 | 0.02 | – |
| TOTAL | – | – | – | – | 0.28 | 1.94 |

Characteristics of windows

| Material | Conductivity (W/m² °C) | Density (kg/m³) | Specific heat (J/kg °C) | Solar assortment | Thickness (m) | U value (W/m² °C) |
|---|---|---|---|---|---|---|
| Aluminium | 3.5 | 2700 | 880 | 0.20 | 0.05 | – |
| Clear glass | 1.80 | 2500 | 750 | 0.05 | 0.006 | – |
| Dark glass | 1.36 | 2500 | 750 | 0.07 | 0.007 | – |
| TOTAL | – | – | – | – | 0.063 | 6.11 |

# MECHANICAL AND ELECTRICAL EQUIPMENT

## Systems description

The building's **heating system** consists of one central gas boiler, installed in a common boiler room in the underground basement. The heating system operates continuously for 12 hours per day, Monday to Friday, from the beginning of November until mid-April. The hot-water heating system supplies fan coil units (FCUs) installed along the outer perimeter of each floor. The FCUs are equipped with individual room comfort controls: a manually operated thermostat for temperature control and a three-speed air-flow control allowing occupants to select low, medium or high circulation rates. The pipes of the heating system are well insulated with neoprene insulation material. Burner systems for hot water production are located on each floor.

The building's **cooling system** consists of two central cooling units, of equal cooling capacity, which operate continuously for 12 hours per day, Monday to Friday, in the summer season. No air handling units are installed in the building and ventilation occurs via the fan coil units or naturally (i.e. by opening the windows).

**Electrical network and equipment**: the electrical system is connected to the medium voltage power line, supplied by the Italian Public Power Corporation (ENEL). A total of 301 fluorescent lamps are installed in the working areas of the building and are typically used for general lighting throughout the day. A total of 20 incandescent lamps are installed in the corridors and the basement. The 'on/off' switch for all lights on each floor is manually controlled by a wall-mounted, 380V switch, situated in the corridor of each floor. The lighting system has operational flexibility in that it can be turned on or off either independently (automatically) or by the last worker leaving the building or the night security personnel.

## System characteristics

**HEATING PLANT**
System type: Central gas boiler
Units: 1
Nominal heating power (kW): 22.09
Heated floor area (m$^2$): 1872
Distribution system: Water fed convectors
Hours of operation (h/year): 5940
Set-point temperature: 22 °C
Maintenance state: Sufficient

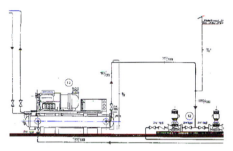

Cooling system

**COOLING PLANT**
System type: Refrigerant screws
Units: 4
Nominal cooling power (kW): 18.4
Cooled floor area (m$^2$): 1765.6
Distribution system: Two pipe fan coil units
Hours of operation (h/year): 1300
Set-point temperature: 22 °C
Maintenance state: Sufficient

**LIGHTING**
Fluorescent lamps: 301
Incandescent lamps: 20
Hours of operation (h/day): 12
Maintenance state: Medium

**ELECTRICAL EQUIPMENT**
Computers (units): 85
Hours of operation (h/day): 9
Printer (units): 51
Hours of operation (h/day): 5

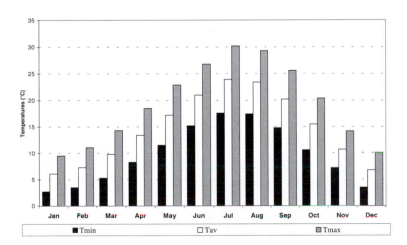

Monthly external temperatures

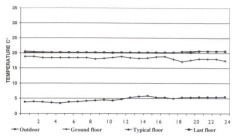

Air temperatures – Winter (4 December 1997)

Air temperatures – Summer (8 August 1997)

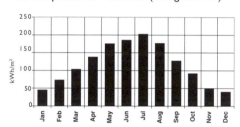

Global solar radiation – monthly average

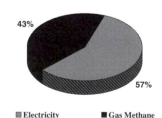

Annual energy consumption by fuel type

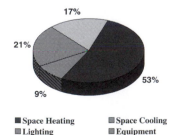

Distribution of energy consumption

# BUILDING'S ENERGY PERFORMANCE

## General profile of energy use

The building was built in the 1970s when the building code did not focus on energy consumption. The building has a concrete structure of minimal thickness, with no thermal isolation of the external walls; this construction does not allow maintenance of optimal levels of internal comfort without high levels of energy wastage. Also, the percentage of transparent surface components is higher than 50%, particular in the east and west walls, so there is very high thermal dispersion. Consequently, the building has significant problems of heat losses through the envelope and the energy demand for heating is very high compared to modern standards for office buildings.

During both winter and summer seasons, air changes are manually controlled via opening windows as there is no mechanical ventilation system installed in the building. It is easy to see that this leads to high waste of heat when the heating system is in operation, and in summer increased electricity consumption when the air-conditioning system is operating.

Climatic conditions in the summer period necessitate continuous use of the air-conditioning system, which not only uses electricity for the refrigerant cooling units, but also for the fan coil system of air distribution.

The existing lighting system is obsolete in terms of its electricity consumption. It is a traditional, manually controlled system (switched on in the morning, and off at night) with enormous energy consumption. The artificial illumination is used during the whole day without exploiting the daylighting potential.

Annual energy consumption breakdown by fuel type (1997)

| Energy | kWh/year | |
|---|---|---|
| Oil/fuel | 149,155 | for space heating |
| Electricity | 201,348 | for other uses |
| TOTAL | 350,503 | |
| Average energy consumption per month | 29,208 | kWh |
| Average energy consumption per m² | 187.2 | kWh/year |

Distribution of energy consumption (1997)

| Energy | kWh/year | kWh/m²year |
|---|---|---|
| Space heating | 149,155 | 79.6 |
| Space cooling | 44,060 | 23.5 |
| Lighting | 86,488 | 46.4 |
| Equipment | 70,800 | 37.7 |
| TOTAL | 350,503 | 187.2 |

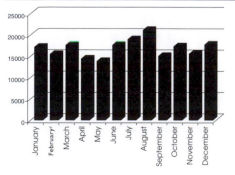

Monthly electricity consumption (in kWh)

# ENERGY RETROFITTING SCENARIOS

## Scenario 1 – Building improvements

### 1.1 – INSTALLATION OF THERMAL INSULATION

The roof's thermal performance is poor and analysis has shown that the top floors have higher heating and cooling loads than the intermediate levels. It is proposed to install 5-cm-thick insulation. This will reduce the U value of the roof from 0.47 W/m² °C to 0.3 W/m² °C and heat losses through the roof will reduce accordingly.

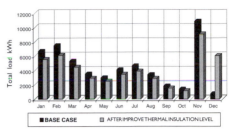

Monthly total energy consumption (kWh) – Effect of Scenario 1.1, installation of thermal insulation

Monthly total energy consumption (kWh) – effect of thermal insulation (top floor)

|  | Jan | Feb | Mar | Apr | May | Jun |
|---|---|---|---|---|---|---|
| Baseline | 6652 | 7467 | 5265 | 3499 | 2959 | 4075 |
| After installation of thermal insulation | 5522 | 6114 | 4422 | 2904 | 2486 | 3451 |
|  | Jul | Aug | Sep | Oct | Nov | Dec |
| Baseline | 4600 | 3394 | 1788 | 1379 | 10870 | 7179 |
| After installation of thermal insulation | 3865 | 2867 | 1511 | 1152 | 9087 | 6030 |

### 1.2 WEATHER STRIPPING OF WINDOWS AND DOORS

This retrofitting measure leads to the reduction of outside air infiltrating into the building through cracks and open gaps around windows and doors. It is well known that infiltration of external cold air replacing the warm air leaking out is responsible for a considerable portion of the heating load, particularly of well-insulated buildings. In this simulation, this measure results in a reduction of the air infiltration rate from an initial value of 1 ACH per zone to 0.7 ACH per zone.

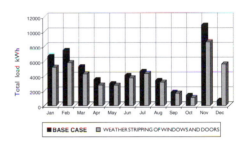

Monthly total energy consumption (kWh) – Effect of Scenario 1.2, weather stripping of windows and doors

Monthly total energy consumption (kWh) – effect of weather stripping windows and doors (one floor)

|  | Jan | Feb | Mar | Apr | May | Jun |
|---|---|---|---|---|---|---|
| Baseline | 6652 | 7467 | 5265 | 3499 | 2959 | 4075 |
| After weather stripping of windows and doors | 5189 | 5824 | 4275 | 2764 | 2751 | 3749 |
|  | Jul | Aug | Sep | Oct | Nov | Dec |
| Baseline | 4600 | 3394 | 1788 | 1379 | 10870 | 7179 |
| After weather stripping of windows and doors | 4319 | 3156 | 1661 | 1075 | 8587 | 5600 |

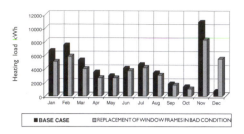

Monthly total energy consumption (kWh) – effect of Scenario 1.3, replacement of leaky window frames

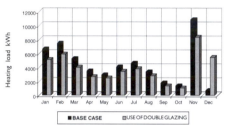

Monthly total energy consumption (kWh) – effect of Scenario 1.4, installation of double glazing

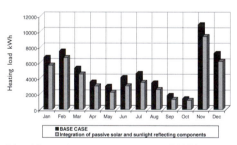

Monthly total energy consumption (kWh) – effect of Scenario 1.5, integration of passive solar and daylighting components

### 1.3 REPLACEMENT OF LEAKY WINDOW FRAMES

Replacement of old window frames which are in poor condition may significantly reduce infiltration rates. The reduction in energy demand for heating is approximately 5%, and for cooling 2%, greater than the previous measure, although in this case an infiltration rate value of 0.5 ACH was considered.

Monthly total energy consumption (kWh) – effect of replacement of window frames (one floor)

|                                   | Jan   | Feb   | Mar   | Apr   | May   | Jun   |
|-----------------------------------|-------|-------|-------|-------|-------|-------|
| Baseline                          | 6652  | 7467  | 5265  | 3499  | 2959  | 4075  |
| After replacement of window frames| 5056  | 5817  | 4001  | 2677  | 2664  | 3708  |

|                                   | Jul   | Aug   | Sep   | Oct   | Nov   | Dec   |
|-----------------------------------|-------|-------|-------|-------|-------|-------|
| Baseline                          | 4600  | 3394  | 1788  | 1379  | 10870 | 7179  |
| After replacement of window frames| 4150  | 3054  | 1609  | 1048  | 8262  | 5441  |

### 1.4 INSTALLATION OF DOUBLE GLAZING

Replacement of the single-glazed windows with double-glazed units will reduce heat loss. The reduction in energy demand for heating is approximately 47.7 %, and for cooling 16.3%

Monthly total energy consumption (kWh) – effect of double glazing (one floor)

|                                  | Jan   | Feb   | Mar   | Apr   | May   | Jun   |
|----------------------------------|-------|-------|-------|-------|-------|-------|
| Baseline                         | 6652  | 7467  | 5265  | 3499  | 2959  | 4075  |
| After installation of double glazing | 5123 | 5904 | 4028 | 2677 | 2486 | 3543 |

|                                  | Jul   | Aug   | Sep   | Oct   | Nov   | Dec   |
|----------------------------------|-------|-------|-------|-------|-------|-------|
| Baseline                         | 4600  | 3394  | 1788  | 1379  | 10870 | 7179  |
| After installation of double glazing | 3818 | 2817 | 1359 | 1055 | 8360 | 5456 |

### 1.5 INTEGRATION OF PASSIVE SOLAR AND SUNLIGHT REFLECTING COMPONENTS

As well as the addition of windows or the enlargement of the existing ones (measures that are costly and therefore difficult to implement on account of the long payback period), the installation of reflectors on the exterior of the windows was considered. Generally, reflectors can be horizontal or vertical and the reflected sunlight should be directed onto the ceiling. In this scenario, horizontal reflectors with reflectance value 0.37 were installed on each window.

The reduction in thermal energy demand is approximately 0.7 % and in particular 4.9% for cooling.

Monthly total energy consumption (kWh) – effect of integration of passive solar and sunlight reflecting components (one floor)

|                                                        | Jan   | Feb   | Mar   | Apr   | May   | Jun   |
|--------------------------------------------------------|-------|-------|-------|-------|-------|-------|
| Baseline                                               | 6652  | 7467  | 5265  | 3499  | 2959  | 4075  |
| After intergration of passive solar and daylighting components | 5655 | 6617 | 4528 | 3009 | 2190 | 3015 |

|                                                        | Jul   | Aug   | Sep   | Oct   | Nov   | Dec   |
|--------------------------------------------------------|-------|-------|-------|-------|-------|-------|
| Baseline                                               | 4600  | 3394  | 1788  | 1379  | 10870 | 7179  |
| After intergration of passive solar and daylighting components | 3450 | 2545 | 1300 | 1172 | 9350 | 6174 |

## 1.6 INSTALLATION OF A SOLAR WALL

The building's south-facing wall is completely void of windows, so a 'solar wall' covering the whole south-facing area is envisaged. The solar component is composed of TIM (transparent insulation material) panels with an air gap of circa 10 cm between them and the existing wall, where the air heated by the panels circulates. The TIM panels are formed by two glass panes between which is material which transmits the collected heat to the back wall while at the same time guaranteeing good insulation of the whole structure.

The solar wall collects sufficient heat to significantly reduce the heating load during the winter period. Furthermore, the installation of fixed horizontal sunshades across the whole façade to provide shade during summer avoids internal overheating in that period. The system is regulated by aeration grids.

The reduction in energy demand for heating is approximately 50%, and for cooling 8%, while the reduction in thermal demand is 38.7%.

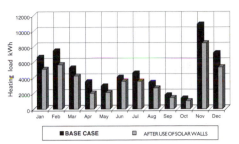

Monthly total energy consumption (kWh) – effect of Scenario 1.6, installation of a solar wall

Solar wall – section detail

Monthly total energy consumption (kWh) – effect of installation of a solar wall (one floor)

|  | Jan | Feb | Mar | Apr | May | Jun |
|---|---|---|---|---|---|---|
| Baseline | 6652 | 7467 | 5265 | 3499 | 2959 | 4075 |
| After installation of solar wall | 5103 | 5678 | 4231 | 2024 | 2125 | 3543 |

|  | Jul | Aug | Sep | Oct | Nov | Dec |
|---|---|---|---|---|---|---|
| Baseline | 4600 | 3394 | 1788 | 1379 | 10870 | 7179 |
| After installation of solar wall | 3543 | 2676 | 1436 | 1023 | 8463 | 5345 |

## 1.7 INSTALLATION OF 'INTELLIGENT WINDOWS'

'Intelligent windows' have two main sections. The upper section contains glazed panels which enclose an insulating roller shutter and a Venetian blind. The lower section is a compartment clad on the interior by a filter and on the exterior by a glass panel. Between these panels is an air exchanger consisting of an upper and a lower fan for air intake and exhaust, respectively. The air intake is regulated according to the internal temperature and to the difference between the indoor and the outdoor temperatures.

The reduction in thermal energy demand is approximately 32.5%.

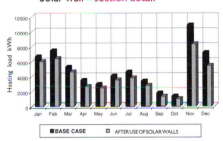

Monthly total energy consumption (kWh) – effect of Scenario 1.7, use of intelligent windows

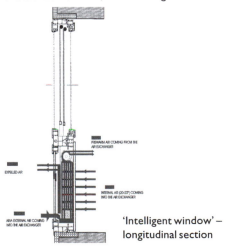

'Intelligent window' – longitudinal section

Monthly total energy consumption (kWh) – effect of installation of 'intelligent windows' (one floor)

|  | Jan | Feb | Mar | Apr | May | Jun |
|---|---|---|---|---|---|---|
| Baseline | 6652 | 7467 | 5265 | 3499 | 2959 | 4075 |
| After installation of intelligent windows | 6021 | 6411 | 4632 | 2677 | 2486 | 3543 |

|  | Jul | Aug | Sep | Oct | Nov | Dec |
|---|---|---|---|---|---|---|
| Baseline | 4600 | 3394 | 1788 | 1379 | 10870 | 7179 |
| After installation of intelligent windows | 3818 | 2817 | 1359 | 1055 | 8360 | 5456 |

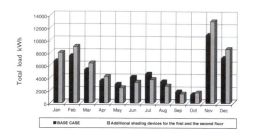

Monthly total energy consumption (kWh) –
effect of Scenario 2.1, installation of additional
shading devices for the first and second floors

# Scenario 2 – Use of passive cooling techniques

## 2.1 *INSTALLATION OF ADDITIONAL SHADING DEVICES FOR THE FIRST AND SECOND FLOORS*

Installing shading devices over the first and second floor windows reduces the cooling load by approximately 25% and increases the heating load by approximately 8%. When running the TRNSYS simulation program, this measure is modelled by changing the windows' reflectance value. In this simulation a reflectance value of 0.3 was assigned to each window.

Monthly total energy consumption (kWh) – effect of additional shading devices on the first and second floors (one floor)

|  | Jan | Feb | Mar | Apr | May | Jun |
|---|---|---|---|---|---|---|
| Baseline | 6652 | 7467 | 5265 | 3499 | 2959 | 4075 |
| After installation of additional shading devices | 7983 | 8959 | 6317 | 4199 | 2397 | 3301 |

|  | Jul | Aug | Sep | Oct | Nov | Dec |
|---|---|---|---|---|---|---|
| Baseline | 4600 | 3394 | 1788 | 1379 | 10870 | 7179 |
| After installation of additional shading devices | 3726 | 2715 | 1474 | 1655 | 13044 | 8615 |

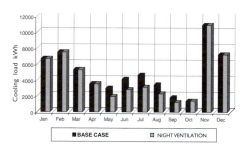

Monthly total energy consumption (kWh) –
effect of Scenario 2.2, use of night ventilation

## 2.2 *USE OF NIGHT VENTILATION*

It is well known that night ventilation is one of the more efficient passive cooling techniques. Based on this principle, a retrofitting action has been considered assuming an exchange rate of 5 ACH during night-time (20:00–07:00). A saving in total thermal energy consumption of approximately 1.40% is achieved, predominantly through reduction in cooling load (5.5%).

Monthly total energy consumption (kWh) – effect of use of night ventilation (one floor)

|  | Jan | Feb | Mar | Apr | May | Jun |
|---|---|---|---|---|---|---|
| Baseline | 6652 | 7467 | 5265 | 3499 | 2959 | 4075 |
| With night ventilation | 6652 | 7467 | 5265 | 3499 | 1909 | 2771 |

|  | Jul | Aug | Sep | Oct | Nov | Dec |
|---|---|---|---|---|---|---|
| Baseline | 4600 | 3394 | 1788 | 1379 | 10870 | 7179 |
| With night ventilation | 3085 | 2275 | 1198 | 1379 | 10870 | 7179 |

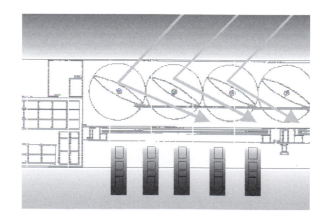

Shading devices –
Section view

## 2.3 INSTALLATION OF CEILING FANS

Recent research on the thermal comfort of inhabitants in buildings equipped with ceiling fans has shown that thermal comfort can be achieved at temperatures of up to 28 °C. When ceiling fans are installed in every zone, energy savings for cooling have been calculated to be almost 38% and the reduction in thermal energy demand is approximately 7.6%.

In this retrofitting scenario, using the TRNSYS simulation program, a set-point temperature of 28 °C has been considered, with ceiling fans installed in the 'major zones' of the building.

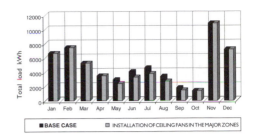

Monthly total energy consumption (kWh) – effect of Scenario 2.3, installation of ceiling fans

Monthly total energy consumption (kWh) – effect of ceiling fans (one floor)

|  | Jan | Feb | Mar | Apr | May | Jun |
|---|---|---|---|---|---|---|
| Baseline | 6652 | 7467 | 5265 | 3499 | 2959 | 4075 |
| After installation of ceiling fans | 6652 | 7467 | 5265 | 6499 | 2397 | 3301 |

|  | Jul | Aug | Sep | Oct | Nov | Dec |
|---|---|---|---|---|---|---|
| Baseline | 4600 | 3394 | 1788 | 1379 | 10870 | 7179 |
| After installation of ceiling fans | 3788 | 2745 | 1448 | 1379 | 10870 | 7179 |

## 2.4 USE OF INDIRECT EVAPORATIVE COOLING

When evaporation occurs in the primary circuit of a heat exchanger, while the air to be cooled circulates in the secondary circuit, the air temperature decreases but its humidity ratio remains constant. This is indirect evaporative cooling. Clearly, indirect evaporative cooling systems are better for cooling buildings as the moisture content of the indoor air remains constant.

Modelling this measure, the latest constant humidity cooler was considered, with a saturation efficiency given by the following expression: $e=1/(1+0,47*v^3)$, where v is the air velocity at the inlet of the cooler (if $v$ is unknown, a default value of 1 m/s is used). A temperature for the outlet of the cooler is given by the wet-bulb temperature calculated by the phychrometrics (type 33) module of the TRNSYS program, i.e. $T_{cooler} = T_{amb} - e*(T_{amb} - T_{wet})$. For this simulation, the above temperature was taken to be the ambient air temperature of the ventilation system.

The reduction in energy demand for cooling is approximately 6.2%, and for thermal energy demand is 1.6%

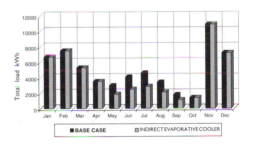

Monthly total energy consumption (kWh) – effect of Scenario 2.4, use of indirect evaporative cooling

Monthly total energy consumption (kWh) – effect of use of indirect evaporative cooling

|  | Jan | Feb | Mar | Apr | May | Jun |
|---|---|---|---|---|---|---|
| Baseline | 6652 | 7467 | 5265 | 3499 | 2959 | 4075 |
| With indirect evaporative cooling | 6652 | 7467 | 5265 | 3499 | 1835 | 2486 |

|  | Jul | Aug | Sep | Oct | Nov | Dec |
|---|---|---|---|---|---|---|
| Baseline | 4600 | 3394 | 1788 | 1379 | 10870 | 7179 |
| With indirect evaporative cooling | 1852 | 2128 | 1108 | 1379 | 10870 | 7179 |

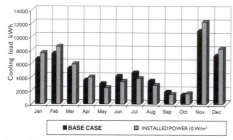

Monthly total energy consumption (kWh) – Effect of Scenario 3.1, reduction of installed power to 10 W/m²

# Scenario 3 – Electric lighting improvements

### 3.1 REDUCTION OF INSTALLED POWER TO 10 W/M²

Lighting is one of the most important consumers of electrical energy in buildings. It also contributes to the internal heat gains, increasing the energy required for cooling purposes. This retrofitting measure aims to reduce the indoor illumination levels. This is achieved by removing lamps, reducing the current installed lighting load of 14 W/m² to 10 W/m². This reduction in the number of lamps actually results in an *increase* (+9 %) in thermal energy consumption (due to the increased heating load of 16%).

Monthly total energy consumption (kWh) – effect of reducing installed power to 10 W/m² (one floor)

|                                          | Jan  | Feb  | Mar  | Apr  | May  | Jun  |
|------------------------------------------|------|------|------|------|------|------|
| Baseline                                 | 6652 | 7467 | 5265 | 3499 | 2959 | 4075 |
| After reducing installed power to 10 W/m²| 7551 | 8512 | 5912 | 3962 | 2392 | 3342 |

|                                          | Jul  | Aug  | Sep  | Oct  | Nov   | Dec  |
|------------------------------------------|------|------|------|------|-------|------|
| Baseline                                 | 4600 | 3394 | 1788 | 1379 | 10870 | 7179 |
| After reducing installed power to 10 W/m²| 3772 | 2783 | 1448 | 1562 | 12235 | 8224 |

### 3.2 USE OF DAYLIGHT COMPENSATION SYSTEM

Control of the lighting can be manual or automatic. Manual control would require the installation of additional switches for zones with multiple lighting fixtures which are not all required all the time. Automatic control could be based on time-scheduling procedures or on daylight or occupancy sensors. The most commonly used automatic lighting control system involves the use of daylight sensors. In this scenario, 4-lamp fixtures with a total consumption of 192 W each were considered. The reduction in electric energy demand is approximately 17%.

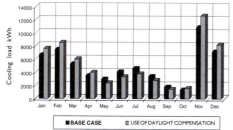

Monthly total energy consumption (kWh) – Effect of Scenario 3.2, use of a daylight compensation system

Monthly total energy consumption (kWh) – effect of using a daylight compensation system (one floor)

|                                     | Jan  | Feb  | Mar  | Apr  | May  | Jun  |
|-------------------------------------|------|------|------|------|------|------|
| Baseline                            | 6652 | 7467 | 5265 | 3499 | 2959 | 4075 |
| With a daylight compensation system | 7607 | 8538 | 6020 | 4001 | 2392 | 3342 |

|                                     | Jul  | Aug  | Sep  | Oct  | Nov   | Dec  |
|-------------------------------------|------|------|------|------|-------|------|
| Baseline                            | 4600 | 3394 | 1788 | 1379 | 10870 | 7179 |
| With a daylight compensation system | 2772 | 2783 | 1448 | 1577 | 1243  | 8208 |

### 3.3 USE OF ELECTRONIC BALLASTS AND A DAYLIGHT COMPENSATION SYSTEM

In this scenario the same configuration of fixtures per zone was used as described in the previous scenario. The only difference is the type of ballasts used: in this scenario, electronic ballasts were used achieving the highest energy savings of any lamp-ballast system, consuming only 112 W per fixture (two ballasts per fixture). This action results in an increase (+22.8 %) in thermal energy consumption (due to the increased heating load of 44.4%) and a reduction in electric energy consumption (18.6%)

Monthly total energy consumption (kWh) – effect of using a daylight compensation system with electronic ballasts (one floor)

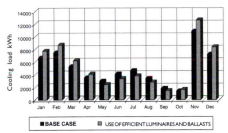

| | Jan | Feb | Mar | Apr | May | Jun |
|---|---|---|---|---|---|---|
| Baseline | 6652 | 7467 | 5265 | 3499 | 2959 | 4075 |
| With a daylight compensation system and electronic ballasts | 7730 | 8676 | 6118 | 4065 | 2392 | 3342 |

| | Jul | Aug | Sep | Oct | Nov | Dec |
|---|---|---|---|---|---|---|
| Baseline | 4600 | 3394 | 1788 | 1379 | 10870 | 7179 |
| With a daylight compensation system and electronic ballasts | 3772 | 2873 | 1448 | 1603 | 12632 | 8342 |

Monthly total energy consumption (kWh) – Effect of Scenario 3.3, use of electronic ballasts and a daylight compensation system

### 3.4 USE OF ENERGY-EFFICIENT BALLASTS AND REFLECTORS AND PRISMATIC PLASTIC FEATURES

Reflectors are highly reflective metal surfaces that are either semi-rigid and secured in a fixture, or an adhesive highly reflective film of aluminium or other material applied to the interior surface of a fixture. In this scenario, the first type of reflector was considered. These reflectors were placed on energy-efficient magnetic ballasts with input energy of 96 W.

The reduction in energy demand for lighting is approximately 28.5%, and for electric energy demand is 19%.

Monthly total energy consumption (kWh) – effect of installing energy-efficient ballasts and reflectors and prismatic plastic features (one floor)

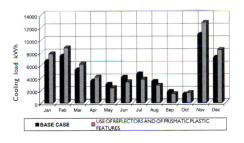

| | Jan | Feb | Mar | Apr | May | Jun |
|---|---|---|---|---|---|---|
| Baseline | 6652 | 7467 | 5265 | 3499 | 2959 | 4075 |
| After installation of reflectors and prismatic plastic features | 7810 | 8766 | 6181 | 4108 | 2392 | 3342 |

| | Jul | Aug | Sep | Oct | Nov | Dec |
|---|---|---|---|---|---|---|
| Baseline | 4600 | 3394 | 1788 | 1379 | 10870 | 7179 |
| After installation of reflectors and prismatic plastic features | 3772 | 2783 | 1448 | 1619 | 12762 | 8428 |

Monthly total energy consumption (kWh) – effect of Scenario 3.4, use of reflectors and prismatic plastic features

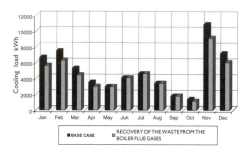

Monthly total energy consumption (kWh) –
effect of Scenario 4.1, recovery of the waste heat
from high temperature boiler flue gases

## Scenario 4 – HVAC system improvements

### 4.1 RECOVERY OF THE WASTE HEAT FROM HIGH-TEMPERATURE BOILER FLUE GASES

In this scenario the temperature of the flue gases is set at 72 °C, as this is the ideal temperature of the boiler flue gases.

The reduction in energy demand for heating is approximately 32.8%, and for thermal energy demand is 24%.

Monthly total energy consumption (kWh) – effect of heat recovery from boiler flue gases (one floor)

|  | Jan | Feb | Mar | Apr | May | Jun |
|---|---|---|---|---|---|---|
| Baseline | 6652 | 7467 | 5265 | 3499 | 2959 | 4075 |
| After heat recovery from boiler flue gases | 5522 | 6272 | 4422 | 2984 | 2959 | 4075 |

|  | Jul | Aug | Sep | Oct | Nov | Dec |
|---|---|---|---|---|---|---|
| Baseline | 4600 | 3394 | 1788 | 1379 | 10870 | 7179 |
| After heat recovery from boiler flue gases | 4600 | 3394 | 1788 | 1144 | 9132 | 6030 |

### 4.2 INSTALLATION OF A MORE EFFICIENT BOILER

Replacement of the existing boiler that has an efficiency of 0.6 with a new one having an efficiency of 0.8, results in an energy saving for heating of close to 3.5%, and for thermal energy demand is 2.5%.

Monthly total energy consumption (kWh) – Effect of installation of a more efficient boiler (one floor)

|  | Jan | Feb | Mar | Apr | May | Jun |
|---|---|---|---|---|---|---|
| Baseline | 6652 | 7467 | 5265 | 3499 | 2959 | 4075 |
| After installation of more efficient boiler | 5255 | 5899 | 4265 | 2799 | 2959 | 4075 |

|  | Jul | Aug | Sep | Oct | Nov | Dec |
|---|---|---|---|---|---|---|
| Baseline | 4600 | 3394 | 1788 | 1379 | 10870 | 7179 |
| After installation of more efficient boiler | 4600 | 3394 | 1788 | 1117 | 8588 | 5815 |

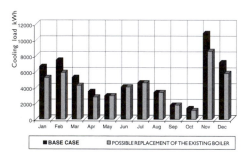

Monthly total energy consumption (kWh) –
effect of Scenario 4.2, installation of a more
efficient boiler

### 4.3 USE OF A FLUE GAS ANALYSER AND A COMPENSATION CONTROLLER FOR THE BURNER

For office buildings with large boilers, the installation of a device that continuously monitors the boiler and provides readings of many parameters such as fire rate, efficiency and flue temperature is a very efficient retrofitting measure. This instrumentation system can simplify the set-up and adjustment of the burner for maximum efficiency. In this simulation the system's baseline efficiency was 0.68 and after the installation of the analyser and the controller it increased to 0.80, resulting in a 4.5% saving in thermal energy consumption.

Monthly total energy consumption (kWh) – effect of use of a flue gas analyser (one floor)

| | Jan | Feb | Mar | Apr | May | Jun |
|---|---|---|---|---|---|---|
| Baseline | 6652 | 7467 | 5265 | 3499 | 2959 | 4075 |
| With use of a flue gas analyser and a compensation controller for the burner | 5834 | 6549 | 4617 | 3068 | 2959 | 4075 |

| | Jul | Aug | Sep | Oct | Nov | Dec |
|---|---|---|---|---|---|---|
| Baseline | 4600 | 3394 | 1788 | 1379 | 10870 | 7179 |
| With use of a flue gas analyser and a compensation controller for the burner | 4600 | 3394 | 1788 | 1210 | 9534 | 6296 |

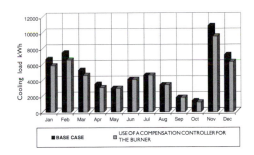

Monthly total energy consumption (kWh) – effect of Scenario 4.3, use of a flue gas analyser and a compensation controller for the burner

### 4.4 RECOVERY OF HEAT FROM THE CONDENSER

In this scenario, a shell and tube heat exchanger was installed to improve the performance of the cooling production or supply unit. This is a liquid-to-liquid heat exchanger, where the primary fluid circulates through the tubes while the secondary fluid circulates through the shell. A COP value of 2.1 was assigned to the condenser for this simulation.

The reduction in energy demand for cooling is approximately 8.5%, and for thermal energy demand is 2%.

Monthly total energy consumption (kWh) – effect of recovery of heat from the condenser (one floor)

| | Jan | Feb | Mar | Apr | May | Jun |
|---|---|---|---|---|---|---|
| Baseline | 6652 | 7467 | 5265 | 3499 | 2959 | 4075 |
| With recovery of heat from the condenser | 6652 | 7467 | 5265 | 3499 | 2465 | 3395 |

| | Jul | Aug | Sep | Oct | Nov | Dec |
|---|---|---|---|---|---|---|
| Baseline | 4600 | 3394 | 1788 | 1379 | 10870 | 7179 |
| With recovery of heat from the condenser | 3832 | 2827 | 1489 | 1379 | 10870 | 7179 |

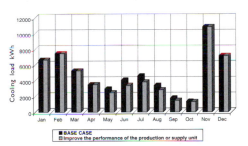

Monthly total energy consumption (kWh) – effect of Scenario 4.4, recovery of heat from the condenser

## Summaries

## EVALUATION

Each scenario was evaluated with regard to energy, capital costs, financial gains and payback period.

### Scenario 1 – Improvement of existing envelope

- Installation of thermal insulation
- Weather stripping of windows and doors
- Replacement of leaky window frames
- Installation of double glazing
- Integration of passive solar and sunlight reflecting components
- Installation of a solar wall
- Use of 'intelligent windows'

The results of measures aimed at improving the thermal characteristics of the building envelope show that high reductions in heating energy use can be achieved at acceptable investment and running costs.

In fact, when the measures are combined, the heating load is reduced by up to 51.7%, while the cooling load is reduced by up to 29.2%. In total, the thermal load may be reduced by up to 27.5%, at a cost of close to 200,000 ECU with a payback period of 17.8 years.

However, application of such a retrofitting scenario does not completely satisfy the objectives of this retrofitting exercise – to bring the total energy consumption down to the reference levels. For example, the decrease in the cooling load is low, because the cooling load is mainly due to the high lighting power and the consequent internal gains. It is also important to note that, in this southern, Mediterranean climate, the main priority is the decrease in energy consumption for cooling.

### Scenario 2 – Use of passive cooling techniques

- Installation of additional shading devices for the first and second floors
- Use of night ventilation
- Installation of ceiling fans
- Use of indirect evaporative cooling

One of the most significant end uses of energy in this Italian case study is cooling. Thus, in order to minimise the high cooling load and to reduce the use of air-conditioning, the application of passive cooling retrofitting measures may be considered a first priority.

In the simulated scenario all the above cooling strategies were applied together. This mixed strategy was feasible with respect of the economic evaluation of techniques and components and also from the point of view of internal comfort levels. The mixed application of passive cooling measures decreases the total cooling load up to 42.3% and the total thermal load up to 13%, at a cost close to 24,380 ECU with a payback period of 6.4 years.

In conclusion, this selection of measures satisfies a central objective of such a retrofitting project, that is, to produce a building that operates with low energy consumption. In fact, the simulation has shown that the use of passive cooling techniques, at a very reasonable cost, can have an important role to play in reducing dependency on mechanical systems in an office building. Moreover, passive measures can be successfully applied to buildings located in warmer climates which originally required the complexity and associated high-energy use of an air-conditioning system.

## Scenario 3 – Electrical lighting improvements

- Reduction of installed power to 10 $W/m^2$
- Use of daylight compensation system
- Use of electronic ballasts and a daylight compensation system
- Use of reflectors and prismatic plastic features

Retrofitting measures were chosen taking into account the Florence Bank building's high specific consumption for lighting, mainly due to its unnecessarily high installed lighting loads with poor control, and the low efficiency of the artificial lighting system. Priority has been given to actions aiming to reduce the installed power and improve the lighting efficiency, avoiding the high heat gains from old lighting systems. In fact, good lighting design not only results in lower energy consumption but also, as recent research has shown, increased worker productivity and reduced absenteeism.

For the Florence Bank building, a global lighting retrofitting scenario has been studied. The energy savings for lighting are circa 47% and for cooling 14%, while the increase in the heating load was up to 8.5%. In total, the thermal energy load is reduced by almost 31%, at a cost of 46,245 ECU with a payback period of 7.5 years.

The studied retrofitting scenario achieved the initial target of reducing the high lighting consumption. Many techniques are available but the results show that the reduction of lighting loads is often combined with a significant increase in other end uses. Obviously, any retrofitting measures dealing with a building's high lighting requirements should be combined with other appropriate techniques in order to balance the total energy consumption.

## Scenario 4 – HVAC system improvements

- Recovery of the waste heat from high temperature boiler flue gases
- Installation of a more efficient boiler
- Use of a flue gas analyser and a compensation controller for the burner
- Recovery of heat from the condenser

The efficiency of the HVAC and the control system are the overall regulators of the energy consumption in this case study. Consequently, these three main types of retrofitting measures have been considered. When applied together in the global retrofitting strategy, these measures enhance the energy performance of the building: the heating energy consumption is reduced by 40.7%, and the cooling load by 42.5%, while the decrease in the thermal load was up to 41%. The cost is close to 50,900 ECU, with a payback period of 6.8 years.

These results indicate that such a retrofitting combination offers considerable potential for energy savings, but is not really feasible because it requires a high investment and incurs high running costs.

## Package

The strategic approach used in the simulated package has been based upon an understanding of how to resolve the main critical factors of energy efficiency. In order to achieve the retrofitting objectives a mixed strategy is preferred. In fact, the analyses show that any single scenario can only satisfy, to any significant degree, the initial energy targets for that single end use.

Therefore, to improve the overall energy efficiency of this building a package has been simulated which incorporates all the measures of each of the above scenarios. When such a combination of technologies is considered, the energy savings for heating are close to 56.7%, for cooling 17.8%, and for lighting 51.1%. The thermal energy savings are close to 44.9% of the total energy load while the electric energy savings are close to 47.1%. The cost of this global scenario is approximately 210.3 ECU/m$^2$, with a payback period of 9.2 years.

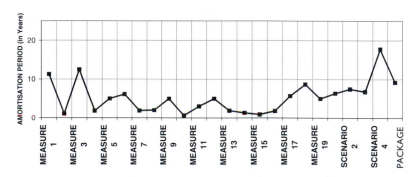

Estimated payback period

# References/Further reading

ADEME and AICVF, (1993), *Bureaux*, Programme, Concevoir, Gerer. Pyc edition.

Arthur E, Cote PE (eds), (1991), *Fire Protection Handbook*, 17th ed., Quincy, MA, NFPA.

Baker N, Franchiotti A, Steemers K. (eds), (1993), *Daylighting in Architecture – A European Reference Book*, London, James & James Ltd.

Bluyssen P, de Oliveira Fernandes E, Fanger PO, *et al,* (1995), *European Audit Project to Optimise Indoor Air Quality and Energy Consumption in Office Buildings*, Delft, final report edited by TNO, 1995. Information on this project can also be found in the proceedings of the *Healthy Buildings '96* conference, 1995, Milano.

Buckley M, Burton S, Bordass B, (1994), *Passive Refurbishment of Offices: UK Potential and Practice,* Proceedings of the European Conference on Energy Performance and Indoor Climate in Buildings.

Campbell J, (1988), Use of passive solar energy in offices, in O'Sullivan P, *Passive Solar Energy in Buildings*, published on behalf of The Watt Committee on Energy.

CIBSE, (1994), *Code for Interior Lighting*", London, The Chartered Institution of Building Services Engineers.

Cremer, (1961), *Die Wissenschaflischn Grundlagen der Raumakustik*, Leipzig, Hirzel Verlag.

Debat National Energie et Environment, (1994), *L'energie dans le Residentiel et le Tertiaire et l' Environment*".

Department of the Environment and the Welsh Office, (1991), *The Building Regulations 1991. Document B. Fire safety*, 1992 edition.

Dimoudi A, Santamouris M, Guarracino G, Energy characteristics of buildings; Greece – France, in Santamouris M and Asimakopoulos DN (eds), *Energy Conservation in Buildings*, SAVE Program, European Commission.

EN 832, *Thermal Performance of Buildings – Calculation of Energy Use for Heating – Residential Buildings*.

EN/ISO 13179, *Thermal Performance of Buildings – Internal temperature in summer in a room without cooling. General criteria and validation method*, ISO.

EN/ISO 7730, (1993), *Ambiances thermiques modérées. Détermination des indices PMV et PPD et spécifications des conditions de confort thermique* (*Moderate thermal environment – Determination of the PMV and PPD indices and specification of the conditions of thermal comfort*), Bruxelles, CEN, and Geneva, ISO.

Esbensens Consultants, ECD Energy & Environment (eds), (1998), *Information Dossier Number One. Fire Safety in Atria*, European Commission.

Fanger PO, Melikov AK, Hansawa H, Ring J, (1988) Air turbulence and the sensation of draught, *Energy and Buildings*, **12**, 21–39.

Fanger PO, (1982), *Thermal Comfort*, Florida, USA, RE Krieger.

Fernandez EO and Bluysen P (eds), (1994), *Final Report of the European IAQ Survey Program* (draft), European Commission, DG12.

Good Practice Guide 35, (1993), *Energy Efficient Options for Refurbished Offices*, EEO/BRESCU, January, 1993.

Hansell GO, *et al,* (1994), *Design Approaches for Smoke Control in Atrium Buildings*, Fire Research Station, BRE.

Jagemar L, (1995), *Learning from Experiences with Energy Efficient HVAC Systems in Office Buildings*, CADDET Analyses Series No. 15, Sittard, The Netherlands, Centre for the Analysis and Dissemination of Demonstrated Energy Technologies & CADDET Analysis Support Unit.

Kattler P, (1993), *Electrical Lighting Sources*, Stenlose, Denmark, Lysteknisk Selskap.

Maystre LY, Pictet J, Simos J, (1994), *Méthodes Multicritères Electre* Lausanne, PPUR.

prENV 1752, (1996), *Ventilation for Buildings – Design Criteria for the Indoor Environment*, 1996 draft submitted by TC 156 to CEN for formal vote.

Private communication from Bill Bordass and ECD Architects and Energy Consultants, 1995.

Roulet CA, Flourentzos F, Santamouris M, *et al*, (1991), *ORME – Office Building Rating Methodology for Europe. OFFICE project report*, University of Athens.

Ruck NC (ed), (1990), *Guide on Daylighting of Building Interiors* (draft). CIE Technical Committee TC-4.2 Daylighting.

Suter P, Frischknecht R, *et al*, (1996), *Oekoinventare für Energiesysteme*, Zurich.

Guildford College
## Learning Resource Centre

Please return on or before the last date shown.
No further issues or renewals if any items are overdue.
"7 Day" loans are **NOT** renewable.

696

Class: 333.7916 BUR

Title: ENERGY EFFICIENT OFFICE...

Author: BURTON, Simon